Apocalyptic Tribes, Smugglers & Freaks

RICHARD S. EHRLICH

Copyright © 2021 Richard S. Ehrlich

World rights reserved. No part of this book may be reproduced or transmitted in any form or by any means, electronic or mechanical, including photocopying, recording or by information storage and retrieval system, without the written permission of the author, except for small quotes used during reviews of this book.

ISBN:

Cover & design by Richard S. Ehrlich

Feral young people.

Escaping America, Europe and elsewhere.

Basking in Asia's slums and paradises.

Proudly shredding themselves through hedonism, poverty, hashish, opium, revelations, jails, death, insanity, and love.

This nonfiction book documents and enshrines raw quotes from people who journeyed on those dilapidated, utopian routes -- starting in the 1960s to today.

Nothing censored, except the names of the living, because of their illegalities and innocence.

Most travelled east, carried onward by the Earth's rotation.

Through Turkey to Iran, into Afghanistan.

Then Pakistan into India, and to Nepal.

Often wondering if they would reach Kathmandu.

In 1972, 1975 and 1978 on, I travelled overland by public transportation across Asia.

I am a Bangkok-based journalist from San Francisco, California, reporting news from Asia since 1978 and winner of Columbia University's Foreign Correspondent's Award.

RICHARD S. EHRLICH

"In the beginning there was unity in the tribe.

The hash *chillums* were king."

~ The *Bom Shankars* Clan

Special thanks to Dweezie, The V, Mars, Squid, Circus
& Tom Vater for eyes & inspiration,
& Kanchana Chanawong for sanctuary.

1 • **TURKEY**

2 • **IRAN'S PERSIAN GATES**

3 • **AFGHANISTAN**

4 • **PAKISTAN**

5 • **INDIA**

6 • **GOA, THE CHILLUM COAST**

7 • **KATHMANDU & NEPAL**

8 • **LOST**

9 • **SOUTHEAST ASIA**

10 • **MEDIEVAL WORLDS COLLIDE**

1 • TURKEY

Under the Galata Bridge:
I shot opium tincture from a pharmacy, along with opium scored in [Istanbul's] Taxim Park, and smoked Blond hash from under the Galata Bridge, before leaving overland to have our son in Calangute beach, Goa [a west coast state in India].

This was actual liquid opium in a bottle, like cough medicine. Not paregoric.

You had to cook the alcohol out before you shot it.

Being in a half-European city and half-Eastern Muslim city, started to prepare me for the trip to the East.

Solemn and Respectful:
Nur Hotel, bottles of tincture of O, shared giant needles, bad hash, too much *halvah* and tangerines, moments when we thought we would die.

Police, bad, bad characters.

The Turks following us everywhere, pushing us to the limits of our patience.

Deals -- trying to come up with ways to break in the [Istanbul] Post Office to retrieve a Christmas present full of hash butter brittle, cheap California pot, and rolling papers.

Oh yeah, and a finger of some *deelish* Shitrali [hashish from Chitral, Pakistan].

We were friends with Perihan, The Hippie Queen.

When she overdosed, the papers were full of photos of her.

Some even in her underwear.

It was so sad. Her family disowned her.

The papers would pay for the funeral, if they could take photos of her friends.

The stories were all lies.

We were extremely solemn and respectful. They said we drank, smoked and danced on the grave. Even referred to me as a Catholic priest because of the long black cloak I was given by a friend in Luxembourg.

We spent six weeks in Istanbul, in December 1969 and January 1970.

Part of a total overland trip to India that started in Luxembourg.

Naked and Barefoot:
During my first trip overland in 1978, in Izmir [a Turkish port on the Aegean Sea], me and my friend arrived very late one night, after a long bus journey.

The bus terminal was quite a way outside the city, so we made the decision to get a few hours sleep in a nearby park.

We thought we were O.K. to sleep with our heads on our backpacks, as security.

Woke up with my pack knifed open. Clothes, shoes and camera gone. And this is why I have no pictures from my first travel.

Fortunately I had my money, passport, and [bus] ticket from Istanbul, inside the sleeping bag.

I just had to walk into Izmir the next morning, naked and barefoot, for new clothes, with the sleeping bag wrapped around my waist.

It was very embarrassing for a 19-year-old, who had never left England before this journey. Traveling really is a learning curve.

It's an education like no other.

Blue Prayer:
I stayed in the Gulhane Hotel [in Istanbul], in the tent on the roof, in 1968.

Got given a capsule of Blue Cheer acid.

Came up in the Blue Mosque at prayer time.

Red Beauties:
I went to India in 1968, with a girlfriend.

We both had red hair, and we left France before the events of May [the Paris insurrection].

Istanbul, at the Gulhane Hotel in May, was my first awakenings to other places within.

Spiritually awakened.

What a magical place it was.

We were on the road.

We belonged together, and survived.

Sadly not all of us.

Too many died at their first shot of real heroin.

Or went crazy with acid.

Or the road was simply too much.

It took me until January 1969, to reach India.

Nine months.

A real birthing.

So many stories, beauties, and insanities.

All one.

A big *Bom Shankar* [Praise to the Hindu God Shankar, also known as Shiva].

The journey that was, and still is.

Love to all of us.

Many Camels:
I was 18, and in Istanbul's bazaar, a man asked my boyfriend how many camels he wanted in exchange for me.

My boyfriend responded:

"How many times do you want my fist in your face?"

Onlookers had to separate them, and we hurried out of the bazaar.

Clothes Rip:
Tralala wanted to sew pins and tacks into her clothing. Ouch! Fight them off.

We couldn't rip our clothes off until we got to Goa, way

down Colva beach.

My Legs:
I didn't have my legs uncovered, from Istanbul to Bangkok.

Cookie Summer [displays a photograph of himself, standing among three Turkish men]:
I'm chilling in Erdemli, Turkey. June 1966.
On my way back to England from Afghanistan -- my second trip out there -- I was busted with 50 grams of Kandahar hash.
One cookie.
This photo was taken outside the jail.
Ahmet, myself in the middle, and Halil, returning from the courthouse about half a mile down the coastal road from the jail.
I was very lucky. Instead of the two years handed down by the judge, I qualified at the end of the summer for inclusion in a general amnesty, and only ended up serving three months.

Just East:
Just east of Silifke, where I camped on the beach, we headed for Cappadocia, so we must've passed by your jail in 1971.

Cookie Summer:
I was stopped at the beach at Silifke.
Taken to Erdemli by Rural Guard.

Early Picture:
That's scary, man.
You got lucky with early release.
And you got to keep the picture.
I had my mug shot [jail identification photograph] from Nevada in 1967, but mom threw it out.

Raising Tougher:
My schoolmate [redacted] -- from Swanley Comprehensive

School [on London's outskirts] -- was arrested in Turkey at 14 years old for 22 kilos of hash.

Set up by the C.I.A., to get Turkey to get tougher on drugs.

He was caught, dressed as a girl, on the [Turkish] border, while trying to reach Beirut.

He did time -- two to three years, at least -- and was released on a royal pardon.

He knew Billy Hayes from the film *Midnight Express*, a harrowing story.

Blue Prayer:
Anyone remember Yener's little cafe and the books where people left messages and travelers' tips?

Wondering Yes:
Yes, I remember Yener's and the guest books.

I think the owner's name was Sitki, and I have been wondering what happened to him. Very nice guy.

After Then:
Yener's then became an Indian restaurant.

Sitki Yener had had to retire from the business after 26 years -- his son didn't want to take over -- and he later died in Ankara [Turkey's capital].

Blue Prayer:
I often wonder what happened to those books.
I was there in 1972, and left messages in the books.
Great food. Very funny man.
Ended up in there tripping [on L.S.D.].

It was a Sunday night, and someone managed to tune his radio into a Western station, and picked up The Beatles playing *I Am The Walrus*.

I fell off my stool giggling, while Sitki danced around with a rose between his teeth, which he gave to me saying:

"For the crazy boy."

I was 18.

I went back to the tent on the roof of the Gulhane, which was very strange.

The acid was very strong.

When I went to the toilet, I discovered I had crabs.

I already had body lice, and head lice, from the straw mats the hotel provided.

I woke up the next day, covered in D.D.T. powder.

The hotel had decided to fumigate the mats, and didn't bother to wake me up before they did it!

Way Overland:

I was there in March [1968] and again in October, stayed in the tent both times, didn't catch crabs or lice.

The first visit, I learned you could go overland to India.

The second, I was on my way.

Blue Prayer:

I hitched from the U.K. in March, so was there by end of March.

I got stuck there for nearly a month, because I did the scam -- importing a car on my passport into Turkey -- and the gang wouldn't give me my passport back.

By the time I got it back, I only had about £10 left.

So I hitched home via Athens's [Greece] boat to Bari, Italy.

Ended up getting repatriated from Florence.

Found Thriving:

The Pudding Shop, Istanbul's message center in the 1960s and 1970s, is still alive and thriving.

No hippies to be found on our last visit.

The Pudding:

It's more of a trendy place now.

But the pudding, very tasty.

Going It:
In 1972, I saw a notice:
"V.W. van going to India."
And that was it.
With five other freaks.

Early Picture:
The worst was on a train in Turkey.
The conductor mixed hash and black tobacco, rolled it in newspaper, and tied it with a thread he pulled from his uniform.
Horrible, but getting high outside the last car, while rolling across Asia for the first time, was pretty cool.

Especially Still:
I had a bad experience I never forget.
A child, two years old, travelled with us, and died during the way, in Turkey.
It was not my child, but still horrible and sad, especially for the mother.
She decided to bury the child in Erzurum [a city] in Turkey.

Nostrils Frozen:
I do remember the freezing cold of eastern Turkey, and feeling the hairs of my nostrils frozen.
And the frozen animal blood in the gullies, by the side of roads.

Ran Away:
After spending many months crossing Asia in 1975 and 1976, I got stabbed twice on a Turkish island near Istanbul.
Two stabs, in two seconds, on Buyukada.
I was enjoying the scenery, walking by myself, and someone came up behind me and stabbed me in the back.
When I turned, they stabbed me in the front.
My adrenalin kicked in and I ran away. I was operated on in Istanbul, and my trip was over.

The back stab went into my lung -- which collapsed -- and the front stab didn't hurt immediately, but I needed morphine when I got to the hospital.

Both healed fully, and I was ready for more travel when I got back to the U.S.

I didn't even see his face.

When I was in the hospital, the Istanbul Homicide Squad brought two suspects, and one looked guilty as hell, but I told them I didn't see his face.

I wanted to get out of Istanbul as quickly as possible, and caught a plane to London the day I got out. The next day, I was in Toronto at my brother's.

I had lost 65 pounds and looked like a skeleton.

My brother didn't recognize me.

Split People:

Hubby had to fight off bandits on a train one night, going thru Turkey.

The train had stopped, and a bunch of men came through windows, and tried to rape a girl down the aisle.

November, 1973.

Him and another guy with a gun managed to have them take off, not without one of them sustaining a gunshot in the arm.

Made It Thinking:

I was in Athens in 1976, and I had long hair and a backpack.

No hotel would give me a room, because they didn't want the hassle when people O.D.'d [overdosed] with heroin on the premises.

I finally got a bed in a hostel, where there were at least a couple of deaths a week.

I believe it was even worse in Turkey.

Here's thinking of all those on the trail to Kabul, who never made it there.

Or back.

2 • IRAN'S PERSIAN GATES

Secret Nervous:
In Iran, a family who hosted us were nervous to talk about the Shah when we out in public, and aware there were secret police everywhere.

Outrageously Invited:
In the Shah's time, Iran was awash with opium and, if you knew where to look, there were dens everywhere.

Prohibition had been in force for some years, with harsh penalties, including execution for dealing.

But upon its implementation in the late 1950s, all existing adult male addicts were issued prescriptions for life.

Hence the relative ease with which it could be found, in a country where it was particularly hard to find a decent smoke anywhere west of Meshad [city in northeast Iran].

The first time we discovered this, was parked up on a beach, near Babolsar on the Caspian coast, a hot spot for Iranian middle class tourists.

Throughout the day, we noted a string of high-end vehicles pulling up to a humble little shack on the beachfront.

We wondered if maybe it was the local whorehouse.

But it turned out to be the local den, to which we were invited -- possibly because of their interest in Mona, the pretty little American girl who was not averse to using her feminine wiles to get outrageously smashed for free.

The Iranians all got out their government approved stashes [of opium] -- looking like crayons -- the wrapping around each stick being the government stamp of approval, perhaps a tax stamp.

And the boss of the place set to work, preparing the raw

opium for smoking.

Unlike the Indians, they didn't prepare *chandoo* [refined opium].

They simply put a [raw opium] blob on a knitting needle type thing, and ran it through a flame until it bubbled, spinning the needle against their finger to burst the resulting bubbles and condense it down, before inserting it into the pipe, which was like a small vase with a little hole in its side -- with the mouthpiece inserted where the flowers would go.

The den master would plunge his knitting needle, with its sticky load, into the small hole in the side, withdrawing the needle to leave a little donut of opium around the lip of the hole.

A coal from the fire, held with brazier tongs, was used to heat the opium, until it melted and dripped into the body of the pipe.

As always, there was some tension when it became clear to our hosts that Mona was not in fact a slut, and could handle her opium to the point that she could not be *roofied* [knocked-out, as if by taking Rohyphenol].

It came time to say our polite goodbye and thank you.

It was one of those glimpses into another side of Iranian culture.

Black Proof:

In Iran during the Shah, people older then 60 could buy black medicine [opium] in a pharmacy, with I.D. as a proof of age.

Was organic, clean, and used as medicine.

No one died.

It was good for old and sick.

The Shah's family were very tolerant toward opium.

Almost every house had a *taraki* room, or den, where they smoked for recreation purpose or other.

All the Shah's children were [redacted].

I don't judge.

Now is a horror story.

The Heart:
I have a problem with the Shah nostalgia.

I've seen too many Persian dissidents kidnapped and tortured by SAVAK [the Shah's secret police], right in the heart of Vienna [Austria], let alone in the country [Iran] itself.

It doesn't make the current regime look any better -- same oppression, same elites that profit -- only from a different corner of society.

Time Controlled:
I spent a long day hearing from Brion [British artist Brion Gysin] on his visit to Iran, during the time of the Shah.

Brion visited Alamut [the ruins of a mountain fortress linked to a legendary cult of hashish-eating Ismaili Muslim assassins].

He told me the [redacted] of the Shah controlled the opium trade.

I would think the Gysin archives at Emory [University] might have more.

That Sect:
Is that the same Ismailis that the Aga Khan is the head of?
Or are they a different sect?

Time Controlled:
Yes they are the same -- Aga Khan and the Ismailis.

They don't use "hashishins" or "assassins" -- which they find offensive -- a label that their enemies popularized to despise them.

I don't think Burroughs [American author William Burroughs] and Gysin were aware of Aga Khan being an Ismaili.

Their Sabbah [*Last Words of Hassan Sabbah*, a fictitious leader of hashish assassins] is a cut-up product.

I haven't come across any Arabic or Persian phrase

equivalent of, "Nothing is true, everything is permitted" -- attributed to Sabbah, or any other Islamic figure or sect -- though the phrase appears in Nietzsche and Dostoevsky.

Cookie Summer:
In November 1965, I went to The National Stadium, for a Girl Scout rally hosted by Empress Farah Diba, patron and titular of the organization in Iran.

The group of women that I escorted were rich housewives from the suburbs in the north of Tehran.

We were seated two rows above, and about 30 feet over, from the empress.

There were at least 10,000 women there, and they were all dressed in the very latest fashion from London and Paris.

Way Overland:
How come you were an escort?

Cookie Summer:
I was at the border at Barzargan, on the Turkish side, looking for a ride into Persia [Iran].

There was a Persian family with a V.W. camper, with German plates.

When I asked if they were going to Tehran, I was brusquely told there was no room by the 50-ish father, Jalal.

I'm a scruffy hippie, with longish hair -- carrying all my worldly belongings rolled up in a sleeping bag -- having been on the road hitch hiking from Istanbul.

So the rebuff is not unexpected.

Half an hour later, he calls me over to the crossing point from the Persian side.

He has a deal for me.

The Persians are charging him 5,000 dollars to import the vehicle, which he doesn't have, nor does he want to pay.

He's found an amiable official who'll put the car in my passport.

I'll ride with them to Tehran, where he'll put me up in his house while he finagles a way to get the car back in his name without having to pay all the duties, because he's got connections.

So the car goes in my passport.

And we drive off to Tehran, and his large apartment on Avenue Hafaz.

He's a fat, lazy, overweight prick who likes to get up late, and spends an inordinate amount of time in bed drinking tea, eating cakes, and making phone calls.

They are an upper middle class family, and the missus has social connections, so she takes me under her wing.

Gets me a haircut, buys me some suitable clothes, and voila!

She has a presentable young American to drive her around to visit her friends, go shopping, and do all the things a 35-year-old Tehran woman does in her spare time.

Since she has servants, there's plenty of that. And a husband, who'd rather stay in bed scheming ways to scam the system, and make deals using his connections.

I drove her every Thursday to a big fancy house, up the mountain in Tajrish, where she and eight or nine friends would drink coffee and talk.

Lots of talk.

And these young, very stylish, and well turned out bored housewives, would flirt mercilessly with me, the 17-year-old blond, blue-eyed American.

This went on for several weeks.

Jalal would trot me around in the afternoons, visiting his connections in various ministries, paying bribes, and trying to get his car transferred out of my passport.

On Thursdays, I'd drive the missus to her social functions.

And that's how I ended up in the stadium a stone's throw from the Empress Farah Diba, sitting there through a very boring and long Girl Scout event, with the missus and all her friends.

After a month of fruitless visits, I went to the American

Consulate and got myself a new passport, and left Jalal with his car problem.

And hitched to Kabul.

Way Overland:
You were lucky with the passport.

When I was 17 and had mine stolen in Trieste, Italy, the British consul got me a train ticket back to London, and said I couldn't get another passport without parents' consent.

Not sure I could of handled the flirting housewives , totally out of my league.

In October 1968, I got a ride hitching along the Black Sea with a convoy of Mercedes saloons [cars], on German export plates, heading for Tehran.

When we got to a big hotel before the Turkey-Iran border, the head of the convoy -- Iranian guy -- took me to another car he had parked there, and wanted me to drive it across.

But when I asked him which was the clutch, and which was the brake pedal, he changed his mind.

Later in India, I met the American driver of the car who had picked me up.

He said they were in Tehran for weeks, to get cars removed from passports, and it had turned into a nightmare.

Cookie Summer:
There is a continuing story to my new passport.

I got to the [Iran-Afghanistan] border at Taybad, and I was refused exit, because I had no stamps in the passport.

Heart Unprepared:
When I was staying at the Amir Kabir [a hotel in Tehran], there was a Western guy there who had brought a B.M.W. in on his passport, for some Iranians he'd met at the Turkish border.

They had then pissed off, and left him with a passport that claimed he owned an expensive car.

Never found out how that ended.

Begged Lucrative:
We drove a car from Frankfurt to Tehran for a Persian who paid 200 dollars.

That was all the money in the world we had, and we stayed two years in Asia -- all the way from Germany to Japan and back.

We begged in Calcutta on the street, when we were dead broke.

We also begged in Japan, which was extremely lucrative.

Nice Marks:
When I started my first 1997 trip overland, [smuggling] Iranians' cars -- from Munich to Tehran -- I was [rewarded with] food, and about 300 to 400 marks [West Germany's currency].

Nice when you have very little money, and you are just an 18-year-old boy.

Someone Something:
O.K., time to tell the tale of how Mohammed Ali [an American boxer also known as Cassius Clay] saved me.

And it was just his picture!

Stephen and I were on one of those charter buses than ran from Delhi to Istanbul in the fall of 1971, returning West from months in Kathmandu.

When we arrived in Tehran, we went into sticker shock at the hotel prices.

We were used to sleeping on the roof of the last place you drank a cup of *chai* [tea] -- wrapped in the blanket everyone carried -- for the price of the tea.

We remembered that on the way east, the Hog Farm buses [carrying members of a California-based commune, founded by Wavy Gravy] had pulled into a campground in Tehran.

So we hopped in a cab.

After driving around for a couple of hours, the cabbie tried to drop us off in the middle of an unknown place, and demanded most of our remaining dollars.

We refused to pay him, since he had not delivered us as promised.

We argued.

A large angry crowd with sticks appeared instantly ready to crush us.

We were startled and frightened.

But then, Stephen pulls a picture of Mohamed Ali out of his wallet!

Who carries a picture of Ali in his wallet?

He said later that he thought it might come in handy.

The crowd passed the photo around for a while, excitedly talking, but we could not understand.

They hugged us and put us back in the cab.

The driver took us to the top of a hill in a wealthy neighborhood, up to a large gate, and had a few words with the guard.

We slept that night in a tiny magical marble walled garden, with a fountain and a bed they made for us, with a marble hot shower room in the corner.

In the morning, they brought a traditional breakfast of flat bread, cheese, grapes, and olives on a beautiful tray.

I stepped out -- to thank our mystery hosts -- though a larger garden, into a stone room, that when I entered was three stories tall.

On one wall, was painted a full portrait of the Shah, standing the whole 30 feet.

We had spent the night in the palace!

They had a driver return us to the bus.

One of those times when it's easy to believe that life is but a dream.

My Legs:

Tehran was the worst for sexual harassment, followed closely by the rest of Iran.

I couldn't leave my hotel without a guy with me, and I would still get grabbed.

I didn't care about their comments.

I couldn't understand most of them anyway.

Cookie Summer:

Two German friends -- that I met at the Gulhane Hotel in Istanbul in September -- were busted by the Iranians on the [Iran-Afghanistan] border in November 1965.

Osman and Detlef, one short and one tall, were already on the bus on the Afghan side ready to depart, when we spotted each other.

I was heading east [from Iran into Afghanistan], and was waiting for a ride to Herat [the first city in Afghanistan near the frontier crossing].

We had a quick gab. They passed me a nice cookie out the window.

They ended up at [Iran's] Torbat-i-Jar Prison, and I believe spent about a year there, before being tossed out of Iran back to Germany.

Young We:
How young we were then.

Red Entering:
Traveling west [into Iran], upon entering Iranian Customs and Passport Control from Afghanistan, we looked up to see on a huge wall above us, a very large piece of red cloth, tacked up.

There was a message on it in English. It read:
IF THEY DIDN'T FIND IT, WE WILL

Someone Something:
Oh, I remember that sign.

Going west, I tried to smoke the rest of my hash in no man's land.

Threw the remainder out the window, with my *chillum* [a

hand-held vertical cone pipe, for smoking hashish mixed with tobacco] wrapped in a red cloth -- hoping someone would find it.

Got way too high, and worried there was something I forgot in my bags.

Abiding Hallowed:

My abiding memory of the Iranian Customs Hall, on that [Iran-Afghanistan] border, was the display cabinets, showing where they found smuggled stuff.

Hollowed-out books.

Tubular ruck sacks -- remember them? -- etcetera.

Quite frightening.

On the Border:

The Museum of Failed Scams on the Iran border.

That was sobering.

Curious Eyes:

I remember that hall.

They would leave you in there for a while, so you could see all the busts they made, and make you paranoid.

It was curious that there were always pictures of the person being busted surrounded by the police, and very often the person being busted was smiling.

I crossed that border six times.

And one of those times, the Customs official looked me in the eyes, put one hand on my chest, and another hand on my back, and said:

"You have hashish?"

If I did, I probably would have had a heart attack.

Heart Unprepared:

The male Iranian officer tried something similar. He shoved his hand up the denim vest I was wearing, presumably to feel my heart rate.

But being utterly unprepared, I squeaked like a girl.
And he quickly withdrew his hand.

Pulse Crossed:
Yes, I remember a male officer taking the pulse of the driver, whilst searching the vehicle, when we crossed in 1975.

Hard Boot:
I crossed [into Iran] from Islam Qala [an Afghan border town] in 1971, after a night spent smoking opium with a friend -- while two or three Afghans were pressing one kilo of Mazar [cannabis from Mazar-i-Sharif, Afghanistan] pollen, the right way.
Tola by *tola* [10 grams each time].
And not pressed by machine.
They complained: "Hard work."
But we laughed, smoking opium pipes, while they worked hard the palms of their hands.
At the dreaded Iranian border, there were two lines:
One for Afghan pilgrims, and one for foreigners.
My mate looked like Frank Zappa.
We both wore long Afghan *chapans* [coats].
And he had half a kilo [of cannabis] in each boot.
There was this very strong smell of opium.
We only realized later, it came from our *chapans*.

3 • AFGHANISTAN

Much Friendlier:
The [Afghan border] guards were much friendlier, offering to sell you hash as you exited the border area and headed to Herat.

Eastward Pure:
Herat, on the eastward drive.
Ah! I've finally landed in pure, unadulterated Asia!

Early Picture:
Another amazing place, I had never heard of, until I climbed down off a truck.

All Immobile:
A friend and I hitched a lift in 1968 all the way from Istanbul to Amritsar [a city in India's Punjab state], and stayed a few days in Herat.
In the actual [Afghan border] Customs Office -- or was it the Police Station? -- we were sold a few ounces of beautiful beige hash, which kept us immobile for several days, along with a bout of dysentery.

Mister Border:
At the border [after leaving Iran and entering Afghanistan]:
"You want to buy hashish, mister?" directly after the [Afghan] immigration stamp hit the passport.

Nobody Alley:
I bought my piece of Afghan hash my first day in Herat, in 1963 -- 25 cents for a round, flat chunk about the size of a deck of cards.

I put it away in my pack, and carried it through Asia for another 18 months, all the way home to Canada.

Nobody ever checked.

It was much appreciated among my friends.

Opium I found in Singapore, in a small den down a back alley.

Very pleasant.

Always Journeys:
Opium is always good for tedious journeys.

Clothes Rip:
You remember Tralala?

O.D.'d on hash candy in Herat.

We had to load her on the bus.

She became my wife, and mother of my child.

Poindexter said we were going to spend the night [in Iran] at the camp ground in Meshad.

So Tralala and I went to the market, in town.

When we returned, the bus was gone.

Our passports were in our backpacks on the bus.

We rolled up in a Persian carpet to sleep that night.

After a while, the Canadian guy [riding] in the bus, got worried. Went through our packs, found our passports, came back across the border to get us.

We hadn't eaten in days. And when we got there [Herat], you guys had a big tin of hash candy made.

We ate until we were full.

I was pissed, and was going to smack Poindexter, but the hash mellowed me out.

Way out!

Far out!

We had to stop the bus at night to take her [Tralala] off, and change her pants, because she was passed out on the hash candy Poindexter had, lost control of her bowels, and stunk up the bus.

Everybody woke up, and started squawking.

Tralala and I were childhood sweethearts, together since she was 16, until she died at 27.

We hung out with Red Dog.

Got invited to a hash den in old Kabul by an Afghan guy, who said he was going to wrestle in the Olympics that summer.

The proprietor of the den was a dwarf.

He was the same height as the *hubble bubble* [*hookah* pipe].

He had to stand up and tilt it, to flame it.

After we all got stoned, all of a sudden the big wrestler was on top of Tralala.

Red Dog and I looked at each other and said, "Oh man."

You remember how skinny Red Dog was? And this Afghan wrestler was beefy. Took us awhile to pull him off.

Tralala scratching and biting.

Dog and I, kicking and pulling.

We pulled him off and all ran out, into the darkness.

No electricity up there.

Ran towards the first light down the hill, and got a cab.

Candy Kilometers [reads]:

Diary entry -- Friday, July 20, 1972:

"Trucked through the night, until I put the handbrake on -- in front of the Khyber Restaurant, Kabul -- one thousand kilometers later, and three hits of speed [methedrine].

Camels rose in early sun.

Such insanity, Milton puking on the floor.

And Tralala -- stoned out on hash candy -- shit in her pants.

So insane.

A good highway to truck on, in Afghanistan.

My friend Jughead -- who was with my ex-girlfriend Shelly when we got there [Bamiyan, Afghanistan] -- dropped acid and made their way up to the [gigantic] Buddha's head, and sat there smoking *chillums*.

Clothes Rip:

Tralala and I also climbed up to the Buddha's head, and looked out across the Bamiyan Valley, enclosed in the high mountains of the Hindu Kush, in the central highlands.

Initial This:
A friend of mine said he did that. About 1975.
As he was lighting up, soldiers approached him.
His initial concerns were unfounded, as they sat down to share.

Abdul Abdul:
That was Afghanistan.

Slave Words:
In Farsi, the words "Hindu Kush" mean "Hindu Death" -- because so many millions of Hindu captives were marched over the Hindu Kush to slave markets in Sundarkhad.
Their corpses littered the mountain masses.

Persian Indian:
The early Buddha statues were made by Afghan Greeks who we [Persian Indian's ancient Persian ancestors] had converted.
That's why they look like that.
But the funny incident I can relate was when my elder sister, Bubbles, visited Uzbekistan.
In her guest's courtyard, she found *tulsi*, sacred basil of Hindus -- growing, which is very typical of Hindu homes' courtyards in India.
She asked about it.
And the Uzbek replied:
"It is a *khoda* [sacred] plant.
She was amazed.
I later explained to her that before the Arab conquest, Central Asia had been Buddhist for centuries, and such things were Indic cultural artifacts, that came down from an earlier age.

Indian traders from the Indus Valley Civilization were trading with Ancient Mesopotamia, as far back as 2600 B.C.

The Mesopotamians brought fabrics, produce, spices, jewelry and most importantly -- chicken from India.

Chicken was India's gift to the world.

The ancient Akkadians [in Mesopotamia] called it, The Royal Bird of *Meluhha* [India].

Archaeological finds show the Indians were eating their famous Tandoori Chicken 6,000 years ago.

The earliest-ever written record about an Indian, is in a 4,500-year-old cuneiform tablet, which was a court record from ancient Mesopotamia.

It records that a *Meluhhan* had got into a brawl at a drinking house, and broken the teeth of a local, and had been fined eight silver pieces.

Not a great start for our old civilization's record.

Cuneiform Everywhere:

The funniest cuneiform correspondence I've seen, was between Hitites and Assyrians.

The Assyrians say:

"We have spotted that a certain amount of olive oil is missing. Next time seal the jars and then send it."

Corruption and fraud was there all the time, everywhere.

Persian Indian:

Hittites and Mitanni, were our cousins.

Worshipped the same, or similar, gods and spoke related languages.

No wonder they resorted to sharp practices.

Clothes Rip:

I went to the pharmacy in Bamiyan for lice.

Tried to explain -- itchy hair, bugs.

He pulled out morphine.

"No." I explained again.

He pulled out pharmaceutical cocaine.
I said, "No."
And he said,
"All the other hippies want these."
Finally, he gave me what I wanted.
Yep, D.D.T.
Dusted our heads and bags.
No more lice.

Beard's Shadow:
Once I met a young lady, she was a guest in my same hotel [in Kandahar, a city in southern Afghanistan].
To my surprise she was Italian. I barely met any Italian people [traveling across Asia] up until then.
We talked a lot and drink *chai* [tea] in a very happy and relaxed atmosphere, until she told me she was traveling with her husband, and he was in jail at the time.
She was very calm in saying that.
I asked her how could she be so serene.
She said the men were having a good time in jail, playing chess with the guards, eating with them too.
The cell door was always opened at night.
He was allowed to go to his wife, and spend the night out of jail.
In the morning, he went back to jail and spent the day there, in good company, waiting to be judged for smuggling.
In 1971 and 1972, the king was there [ruling Afghanistan].
Afghan people were friendly and open.
That dope was so good.
Old beards sitting by the dusty main road inviting the hippie for *chai*, and sit with them in the shadow for some time, in silence.
Respect for women was absolute.
A young German girl could go alone outside.
All that period, I heard of no crime against foreigners.
Four years later entering Herat, I felt something different.

No songs in the air.

People going their way, like in a hurry.

Same on the way to Kandahar. And when we got to Kabul, we understand that everything was changing fast.

Three years later, they closed the border, and we know what happened [Afghanistan's 1976 Marxist revolution].

Since then, Afghan people are suffering years of war.

Shopkeeper's Daughter:

Lots of *burqas* when I first went there in 1974 and 1975.

A shopkeeper's daughter lent my friend and I one, and we went for a walk wearing it, down Chicken Street [a popular street for restaurants and shops, nicknamed by travelers].

It was a weird feeling, but I think people on the street knew we weren't Afghan.

On the Border:

A scammer friend from New York flew out [to Kabul]. He had never been out of the U.S.A., and wasn't a freak by a long shot.

I tried to warn him it was medieval.

I picked him up, and took him to our hotel off Chicken Street.

Shortly after we got there, some freak started a fire.

Someone else was robbed, when everyone ran out, not knowing the extent of the fire.

And a woman was grabbed by the breasts, in the mess.

My friend turned to me and said:

"Man when you said it would be medieval here, I didn't expect this!

"Fire, rape and pillage all in the first hour! I'm gonna love this place!"

Never a dull moment in Kabul those days.

Candy Kilometers:

That is the truth.

We were heading to Afghanistan to get our hands and *chillums* on Afghani hash, basically 20 *bucks* [U.S. dollars] a kilo.

Now, how can we get this to America, where it was then going for around 1,000 dollars a pound?

Where there was a will, there was a way.

On my second trip to Afghanistan in the summer of 1972, I drove my V.W. bus with my girlfriend Pluto and her daughter Chacha.

We got to that border, Taybad [a frontier city in northeast Iran], and they had a quite bright light there.

The border was closed, as it was night, so I drove maybe a quarter mile away, for us to sleep.

Damn, all of a sudden a while later, we were asleep and someone pounded on the side of my vehicle, at the same time yelling:

"Afghan bandits! Afghan bandits."

Well, it was the security for the border who had done that, and we dutifully drove over to the border, chagrined.

Sugar Shack:
Tell me when did she leave you, and shack up with Taffy? India?
I was with them in 1973.
Never a mention of you.

Candy Kilometers:
Au contraire.
She took Chacha from Pakistan, and went to visit.
I was in Pakistan, and an interesting business deal came my way.
I was supposed to meet them in Kathmandu two weeks after they left, but now I couldn't go to Nepal.
I sent two telegrams that I wouldn't be there, then successfully crossed the Wagah Border [from Pakistan into India], and went into Delhi.
I went to Connaught Place, to check my mail [at Poste

Restante's free public mail boxes].

I got out of my car and it seemed like thousands of people were all in my way.

And then, as if in a dream, they all parted.

And the most beautiful woman -- who I had just met once before, and with Pluto, in Kabul -- walked up to me, and gave me a huge hug.

And said they had been waiting for me.

Turned out, she and around five other people were all traveling in one V.W. van, owned by a friend of mine named Lettuce.

He had told me to come to Delhi by December 14, his birthday.

I had truly forgotten all about his birthday, but with this new, young, gorgeous woman, we started our vans heading toward Agra.

At a railroad crossing, she came up to my van, and asked if it would be O.K. for her to ride with me, as it was crowded in Lettuce's van.

We spent the next four years together in Asia.

Around the New Year 1973, she and I were driving down the road in Goa when Pluto pulled up next to us in a V.W. bug.

She could quickly see what was going on, and said:

"Let's talk down at the beach."

And there, she told me she had gotten a lot of money together, *yada yada yada*, and it would all be mine, except she came with it.

Love triumphed, and I said goodbye to her then.

Of course she wouldn't say one word about me, as I had dumped her -- and this was not the first time.

Now tell me about Taffy, and his vehicles, and dogs, and horses.

Is he still alive?

How well did you and Pluto get along?

Sugar Shack:

Ha ha ha.

No she hated me, because me and Taffy were old buddies for a long time.

My story, Pluto in Kabul and Pakistan -- it's huge -- and why I got there with Taffy, while she was waiting for him to return.

I would so love to make a movie of the notorious Taffy and his women.

Taffy was murdered.

Not sure when.

My brother would not tell me more, because he knows it would be too upsetting for me.

Outrageously Invited:

My father's business partner and mentor, back in the early 1970s, was a German guy called Ludwig, who had been trading Afghan carpets -- along with other Eastern artifacts -- since the late 1960s.

He spoke fluent Farsi, and had many good contacts.

It was his idea to take most of the seats out of old busses, and fit them out more like a big camper van.

This meant less room for passengers, but the trade in goods was always more important.

After the 1973 coup [overthrowing the king], one of the new rules brought in by the Marxist-leaning new regime was the banning -- for export -- of any carpet older than 20 years.

Each carpet required a certificate from the museum stating it to be no older than that.

This of course meant that many long-established carpet merchants were faced with penury.

Their fortunes were held in antique carpets they could no longer trade to their Western clients.

Desperate to unload them, they offered to provide as many as he could transport for them, with payment on return.

Thus on one trip back in that period, we had 42 Baluchi and Kuchi rugs -- some as old as 80 years -- laid on the floor of the bus, underneath a new one on top.

The only illegal bit was crossing from Afghanistan into Iran, but the Chief of Customs on the Afghan side was a friend, and the Iranians only interested in drugs, so that was not really a problem.

Back in Germany, I was present when he sold one, to one of his well-heeled German clients.

Jokingly I said:

"At that price, I bet that is not going on the floor. On the wall maybe?"

To which he replied, with no trace of humor:

"No. It will go into my bank vault."

Much Friendlier:

Wandering around the cloth market alone in Kabul -- and completely covered, except for my head -- I noticed a guy following me.

And so I went into one the shops, and talked to the merchant, and had tea with him.

Seeing it was getting late, I knew it was time to get back to my hotel, and saw the same guy hanging outside staring at me.

So I told the store owner.

He asked which man.

And I told him:

"The guy in the pink turban."

He immediately got up and started yelling at the guy, and a crowd Afghan men chased the guy out of the area.

And then the merchant ordered one of his boys to escort me back to my hotel, and said that this guy had dishonored Afghans by not treating a guest properly.

Cute Beaches:

I think I communicated with the Afghan men through our mutual love of hashish and getting high together.

Smiles and gestures were exchanged, instead of communicating verbally.

On the Border:
In the days before bottled water, we drank tea, and hoped it had been boiled properly.
In Afghanistan, I bought a three-meter cotton turban.
I carried a pocket knife, and cut slices, to use as toilet paper.
In a few weeks, it was barely a headband.

Begged Lucrative:
On the trail in the 1960s, we stayed at the Maiwand Hotel in Kabul, where for 50 cents a night, you got a bed in a room with eight other beds.
The toilet was a hole in the floor in the bathroom.
Where the shit fell down to the alley behind, it had reached a height to the second floor already.
This was Christmas 1964, and in the middle of the room was a wood-burning stove, with a stove pipe running across the room and reaching the wall, where it exited through a hole in the wall.
It was here that I experienced my first earthquake, which caused the stovepipe to fall down into the room, covering all inhabitants in soot.
The Afghans all hit the floor shouting, "*Allah o Akbar*!"
We were the only Westerners in the room, and I was the only woman.

Very Nowadays:
The best *charas* [hashish made from live cannabis leaves] from Afghanistan nowadays is from Panjshir [a northeast valley].
Used to be Mazar-i-Sharif [a city in northern Afghanistan].
Andarab [a district in Baghlan, a northern province] and Badakhshan [a northeast province] also have very good *charas*.

Smooth Yes:
Yes, I've had hash from Nuristan province [in Afghanistan's northeast].

It's really smooth from Tirah Valley.

Eggs Spaghetti:
Also Mazari Eggs or Jalalabad's wonderful Spaghetti [hash from Mazar-i-Sharif, and thick strings of hashish from Jalalabad city, near the Khyber Pass].

Loved:
I loved Black [a regional hashish] back in the day.
Had a little a few weeks ago, but don't really see it in Scotland now.
Not since the Russians left [Afghanistan in 1989].

Solid Ideas:
I really struggle to find anything solid here in South Wales.
Only Green [another regional hashish], that I have never liked.
Any helpful ideas?

Move Move:
Move to Afghanistan?

Nobody Alley:
I remember when the Afghan men used to spend all morning pressing a smoking piece [of hashish] in their hands.
In a few hours, it would be black, shiny, and softly pliable, and looked like a fish shape.
They would smoke in the afternoon and evening, and toss away what was left before bedtime.
They were all devotees of a mythical hashish smoker called Baba Hoobas [Baba Ku].
If you could make a flame jump from the *chillum* while lighting it, you were boss.

Chants Creator: [points to a book titled *Hashish!* by Robert Connell Clarke]:

I have no clue as to who he is, or about the legend.

I thought it to be interesting, and probably people who travelled those parts can shed more light on this.

[begins reading]:

"A *baba* is a religious teacher.

"Baba Ku is considered by Afghan smokers to be the man, sent to earth by the Creator, to populate the entire world with cannabis and to introduce hashish-making technology and smoking techniques to the Afghan people.

"Another legend -- the character Baba Ku as a herbal healer -- from Samarkand or Bukhara, in Russian Turkestan -- who traveled south into Afghanistan.

"Afghans tell the tale of Baba Ku walking through the countryside and healing plague victims with 'little sticky balls' administered like a modern-day pill.

"Twentieth-century folklorists suspect these sticky balls to be hand-rubbed hashish.

"Legends about Baba Ku may account for the spread of knowledge of hashish throughout Afghanistan.

"Baba Ku is portrayed with a huge water pipe, the jar of which held approximately 40 liters of water, cooled by a mountain stream.

"The fresh flowing water circulated up through the bottom of the jar to cool the smoke.

"Baba Ku purportedly smoked up to three kilograms of hashish per day in this water pipe.

"Before his death, Baba Ku gave cannabis seeds and other medicinal plants -- along with an allotment of gold -- to ten Afghan families who were charged with carrying on the cultivation of healing herbs.

"Baba Ku is said to be buried in a tomb near Balkh in northern Afghanistan.

"However, other incarnations of Baba Ku may have predated the famous healer.

"His spirit surely lives on, in the reverent chants of modern hashish *babas*."

Oh Never:
I could tell you a lot, because that was my way of life back then.

The prayers mean a hash smoker never dies.

Impressive Earth:
Very impressive.

Cute Beaches:
We used to have big Legends of Hashish dinners in Amsterdam, and smoking sessions using a *bubbly bubbly*.

One year, Baba Ku was the legend we celebrated, so everyone there learned a bit about him.

My husband collects old books on hashish and cannabis.

His collection is so old and extensive, that I haven't read even half of his books.

His library is in such disarray, that I don't dare set foot in his cannabis treasure room.

But all I have to do is mention a subject, and he knows exactly the book and author, and then proceeds to tell me all about it [laughs].

He likes historical accounts, and I prefer reading autobiographies of smugglers of our times, so I've read a lot of the current ones.

I just finished *Brotherhood Hashish* that recently came out.

There's also a movie which is said to be pretty accurate. It's called *Orange Sunshine*.

You might like both, if you're into these kinds of stories.

Strange Mountains:
How wonderful.

When I lived there, I heard so much about a "Baba Who Bas".

All the big hash hunters spoke of him being back in the mountains, and having the very best stash on earth.

I guess lack of language, and not knowing the past tense, led me to think he was a contemporary, and we might meet him over an amazing *chillum* one day.

Now I learn his story is like Santa Claus!

Such is the fate of an illiterate immigrant, in a strange new place [laughs].

Oh Never:
I've been to the grave of Baba Ku in Balkh [a city and province in northern Afghanistan] in 1973.

When you research the history of Bactria [the Hindu Kush region], you realize Zoroaster [an ancient Persian prophet, also known as Zarathustra] lived around the same time in the same place.

Baba Ku was also a healer, and a wise man, making me think the two might be one and the same person.

The steppe of that part of the world has been inhabited for at least 10,000 years.

There is a lot of history there.

Some say there is another giant Buddha buried in the area.

Let's hope they get a true peace, and people can travel there again.

Fascinating part of the world.

Ran Away:
I visited [the 13th century poet] Rumi's Balkh in 1976.
Very old town.

Low Ceiling:
This is from the Afghanistan Analysts Network's *The Myth of "Afghan Black," The Cultural History of Hashish Consumption in Afghanistan*:

"Baba Ku, a figure who lived in the first half of the 20th century and whose historical persona borders on the mythical, still inspires a form of mystical devotion.

"He is buried in the ancient town of Balkh of the namesake

province, and is still remembered across northern Afghanistan as a generous and chivalrous man, who would always provide lavish hospitality of food and *charas* to anyone in need.

"Even today, when local *charsies* [devout *charas* smokers] light their cigarettes or *chillum* filled with *charas*, they first praise Baba Ku:

"Baba Ku / Your grave is a flower garden / be it summer or winter.

"When *charas* is being smoked collectively, and the cigarette or *chillum* passes from one person to another, smokers repeat this invocation:

"Pass on / pass on to the brave youngsters. / Death to those who hate.

"After Baba Ku's death, his fellow *charsies* built what is known as the *chillumkhana* -- *chillum* house -- or *saqikhana* next to his grave.

"This is a small building consisting of a main hall, very dark, and with a low ceiling, furnished with stone-made benches lining the inner walls.

"There are several *chillums* available in the room, and a caretaker in charge of filling and lighting them.

The rules of the *chillumkhana* are clear.

Whoever gets inside, has to smoke, and failing to do so would be disrespectful.

Visitors are welcome to contribute with offers of money or *charas* – provided they have a good batch, for in the *chillumkhana* only top-quality Shirak-e-Mazar [Milk of Mazar hashish] is used.

"If they do not wish, or cannot afford to contribute, this is no problem. They get to smoke for free.

But most importantly they have to smoke and pay a tribute to Baba Ku.

"At any rate, inside the *chillumkhana* the air is saturated with the fumes of burning hemp.

"All the windows and doors are kept shut, and there is no fresh air circulating, augmenting the effects on the smokers.

"This way of smoking is called *shishaband* or *darwazaband* --

closed window or door."

Flying Whatever:
Whatever happened to the three-*tola* Flying Saucers [30-gram discs of hashish]?
The whole thing would be ripped up and put in a hooker.
Such fond memories.

Abdul Abdul:
Put in a hooker?
Never tried it like that.

Flying Whatever:
I can assure you that it works.

Abdul Abdul:
I've smoked in *hookahs* before, but just playing here.

Secret Nervous:
So cheap after Istanbul.
In Afghanistan, the bus journey between Herat and Kabul cost £1. A pot of tea 2-1/2 pence.
My friend saw a guy selling popcorn and gave him a 2p coin -- she then had to take her jacket off to carry it all.
A palm-sized block of hash cost 10 pence.
We didn't smoke, but were with a couple of Danish guys who'd never smoked, and I prepared it for them in a *bubble bubble* pipe.
When we came back to the hotel after a meal, they were totally out of it.

Cute Beaches:
The Afghan water pipe is called a *chillum*.
But I associate *chillum* with the little pipes that you wrap a *safi* [a hand-sized scrap of cotton cloth] around, which are used in India.

Zero 101:

My last five dollars were stolen in Kabul, 1973, in a dorm room, from under my pillow where I skillfully thought no one would think to look.

It's a long way from Kabul to Torino [Turin, Italy] on zero dollars.

And I would do that trip again, in a heartbeat.

If only I had tattooed the names of the group I hitched with, from Kabul.

I now look back and call this move, *Throwing Oneself Onto The Bosom Of The Universe, Hippie Move 101.*

Wondering Yes:

Since the bus from Meshad to the Afghan border left only once a week in 1967, we were a crowd of travelers going together.

It turned out that the bus only went to the last village before the border. So from there, we had to get a minivan.

It was already dark when we arrived at Islam Qala, at the Afghan Customs Control.

There were no more buses to Herat that evening, so we were shown a big room with Afghan rugs on the floor, and told we could sleep there.

It happened to be on the 31st of December, New Year's Eve, and we were quite hungry after the day's traveling.

We told one of the Customs guys this, and asked if it was possible to get some food to celebrate New Year.

He nodded and disappeared.

About half an hour later, he reappeared with a big pot of rice and some sort of stew.

And when we had eaten, he came back and very politely asked if we wanted something to smoke after dinner?

Of course we said yes, and he produced a fair size piece of black Afghan *charas* for our New Year's party at the Afghan Customs.

The next day, we took the bus to Herat.

I really liked that town, and stayed there about two weeks -- one reason being that many of us got the first hit of Afghan belly.

But Herat at that time was wild.

The main street was a dirt road, where the horse-drawn taxi carts -- with their horses all decorated with red tassels -- used to have races from one end to the other, raising a big cloud of dust behind them.

Many Afghan men seemed to spend a lot of time squatting at the street corners.

And the few cars around had no license plates.

There were some nomads who had come in from the desert, and raised their black tents near the great [Musalla] Minarets and the Mausoleum from the [medieval] time of the Timurids.

Their women had beautiful red dresses, lots of jewelry, lots of braids in their hair, and no *burqa*.

All other women I saw in Herat were covered in this [*burqa*] garment, that has mesh in front of the eyes.

Much Friendlier:

Wild West Afghanistan in Herat, the fall of 1970.

The men would gallop into town, firing their rifles in the air.

The policeman on his raised platform -- at the main crossroads -- grandly waved his arms to direct the traffic, which consisted of a few horse carts, an occasional tourist car, and horse riders.

All ignored his directions, except for the tourist who stopped and wondered why he was stopping.

Having done his duty for the afternoon, the policeman would hop down, and join his buddy on a shaded bench by the road, and have a smoke.

The view out the back of our hotel [in Herat] was this old fortress [Bala Hissar], where many of the local dogs lazed about in the sun.

Lucky Magic:
The most magic [opium] den I visited was in Herat 1971.
But my body rejected the stuff.
So I didn't become a junkie ever since. Lucky me.
Om Shanti [harmony and peace].

Fortress Hovel:
In Herat 1972, the hovel hotel where the bus from the Iranian border delivered us, was a long hallway.
Small rooms, down a dim hall.
Freaks staying there would stumble out of their rooms, down the hall, and poke their heads out the front door, to find a ragged Afghan boy who had a wooden tray offering small circles of black opium, and small circles of very dark green hashish, for sale.
The freaks would say:
"I want five of those, and 10 of those," or whatever number, pay the kid, and disappear.
Our room had a small window looking out back, on a dry dirt yard.
Nearby, off to the left, was Bala Hissar fortress on a little hill.
Total silence, except for the sound of an Afghan sweeping the dirt yard, with a broom made of dried sticks.
That scratching rhythm sounded like he was sweeping dirt off ancient graves.

Nobody Alley:
Cheap shit holes [hotels] were our favorite places.

It Cared:
Nobody back in those days cared about the room.
It was the Afghani *shit* [hashish] that got us stoned.

Luxury Road:
After a life on the road, it [a room] was luxury, as long as one had good hashish.

Very Stark:
That [Bala Hissar] fort has a very stark resemblance with the Bala Hissar in Peshawar, Pakistan.

Style All:
There's one in Kabul as well.
They all are built on the same style.

Young Night:
In 1971 or 1972, the border between Iran and Afghanistan was closed at night, so we spent the night in no man's land in our tents, visited by young Afghans selling hash.
Very surreal night indeed.

Enjoy Early:
There was no border like the Afghan border in the early days.
So relaxed.
One almost wanted to stay overnight to enjoy it, after Turkey and Iran.

Vibe First:
Was like that on my first trip.
I miss that vibe.

Honey Hand:
In 1975 I was a member of a dance company that had been invited to perform at the Shiraz International Theater Festival [in Iran], after which we planned to travel on to India and Nepal.
Our choreography was based on spinning [whirling dervishes].
So naturally, we were encouraged to look up some [Muslim mystic] Sufis on our way through Afghanistan.
We found them in Herat, and were invited to visit Gazar Gah, a shrine outside Herat that houses the tomb of the Sufi

mystic and saint Khwajah Abdullah Ansari.

In the morning before meeting our newfound friends, I wandered around the old quarter of Herat and, seeing a beautiful garden being tended by a gardener, I asked permission to come inside and take a look around.

He waved me in.

As I approached, a pack of street dogs lolling about on an embankment rose as one and attacked.

Fortunately, the gardener drove them off, but not before a couple did some serious damage.

I staggered out onto the street where people just laughed at the sight of a disheveled Westerner.

Finally a little boy approached, and took me by the hand, and led me to a rather funky pharmacy, where the proprietor told me to wait, while he looked for a doctor.

A while later, a doctor arrived, examined the bites, and left to find something to treat them with.

He returned carrying a metal tray with what looked like catgut and a needle, and said he'd stitch me up.

I wasn't having any of that, and begged him to just throw some iodine on the wounds and bandage me up.

I could tell that he was offended.

But he did as I asked, and I found my way back to the hotel, where we were to meet our Sufi friends.

When I explained my encounter with the dogs to the Sufis, they laughed hilariously and said that the dogs had been waiting a lifetime for me -- which didn't seem very funny at the time, but made perfect sense two months later when I began to learn about karma in a Tibetan Buddhist monastery in Nepal.

Anyway, they took us out to Gazar Gah, a beautiful open-air shrine, where groups of pilgrims were milling about the tomb of Ansari.

It was enclosed by a lattice-work structure, out of which an ancient tree was growing.

Ansari was revered for his healing power.

Pilgrims would arrive, hammer and nails in hand, to pound

nails into the tree and pray for his blessings to cure their illness, or bring an end to their suffering.

A very old man approached me, with a long white beard, and carrying a white Persian cat.

He saw that I was bandaged and limping and explained, in French, that if I prayed to Ansari, he would heal me.

The old man gave me a hammer and nail, and led me up to the tree.

I had no way of knowing whether the dogs were rabid, but I figured that I could use all the help I could get.

So I stepped up, hammered the nail into the tree, and genuinely asked for healing.

Moments later, I felt a sensation like warm honey enter the crown of my head and suffuse my whole body.

And somehow, I had a strong sense that I would be fine after that.

The next morning as we were getting ready to leave Herat, I went to change the bandages, and saw that the wounds were completely closed with no infection.

Even though I felt the power of Ansari's healing, when we reached Kabul, I went to the American Embassy hospital to start the rabies shots.

I wasn't taking any chances.

Even though I was an American citizen, the officials at the hospital told me they wouldn't admit or treat me.

I was dressed in classic hippie garb.

By the mid-1970s, they had hardened against the liberated young travelers who were passing through Afghanistan on the hippie trail.

I threw a fit, and finally got them to give me a shot, but then they told me that either I had to go back to Tehran or on to Delhi -- but they absolutely refused to do anything more to help me.

Long story short, I got the shots in a twisted odyssey across India and Nepal, and have lived to tell the tale.

To this day, I am grateful to have experienced his healing

power.

So Invaded:
In 1979, I was ready to go to Afghanistan.
Then the Russians invaded.
So of course it affected us.

Fortress Hovel:
In 1980, immediately after the Soviet invasion, the poorest Afghan refugees fled overland into Pakistan.
The wealthier refugees flew from Kabul direct to New Delhi, India.
The most gorgeous Afghan woman I ever met in New Delhi, was tall, stunning, cheerful, university-educated, and young.
She knew only two phrases in English:
"I like it!" she would exclaim, laughing.
Later, totally out of context, she would suddenly blurt:
"Johnny Walker!"
Alas, she was already engaged to be married and leaving Delhi on a refugee visa to the West.

Nobody Alley:
I am Canadian, and was traveling with a buddy from Florida.
We never felt threatened.
Afghanistan was still a monarchy [until the 1973 coup], and everyone quite friendly.
My first real introduction to hashish was at a roadside camp of four Afghans, with camels, just outside of Kandahar.
They were set up for the night with a campfire, carpets on the ground, and a very large *hookah*.
Place a chunk [of hashish] in the bowl -- along with some coarse tobacco, and an ember from the fire on top -- draw deeply.
Then go cough like a fiend, over in the corner.
There were quite a few Americans around Kandahar, as they were building the road [northeast] to Kabul, while the Russians

were building the western part to Herat.

A few hours prior to our hash interlude, we had been invited into an American compound along the highway.

It was as though a subdivision in Texas had been transplanted there.

Single family bungalows with driveways and gardens.

The family treated us to a meat and potatoes American dinner, which was much appreciated after the real lack of any food but melons between there and Herat.

It was quite a day there in Kandahar, and as we hiked off down the road in the dark after the smoke-up, it was all in slow motion.

At the Khyber [Pass], the bus just stopped and everyone got off and walked over [the border into Pakistan].

We met a family in Peshawar [in northwest Pakistan] who invited us to stay with them for a few days.

Finally the World:
When I was traveling the hippie trail through Afghanistan in 1972, there were two brothers walking around the world.

They were attacked by bandits on the road, and one was killed.

I think the other brother finished the journey finally.

Dark Talk:
It was probably talk about this story that had me almost crapping my pants, when we entered the Khyber Pass after dark.

Sleeping Horses:
In 1970, two buddies of mine had their van jacked up, while sleeping on the Khyber Pass.

And when they woke up, all their tires were gone.

They bought horses, and rode to Kabul.

Survival Uprisings:

The ones who were more involved with the locals, and stayed longer times, were very influenced by the politics.

The king being dethroned in Afghanistan, and subsequent uprisings, created a lot of insecurity in Kabul, for example.

The [1971] war between [West] Pakistan and India -- over East Pakistan [which became Bangladesh] -- had many of us stranded. Me in Kabul.

Then the [1979] Russian invasion, ended the possibility to stay in Afghanistan.

The Vietnam War was previous, and mostly affected me in Europe, with manifestations against the war.

Sweden was a haven for the [American] military defectors, who dealt in acid, for survival.

East Consciousness:
Of course, all the moving to the East started from political consciousness.

Strolling Headless:
I was in Herat, first time in October 1974, and I am still remembering how that [main] street was something special to me.

I was strolling with a friend, and locals were calling us from one shop.

We went in, and immediately they start to show us plenty of Black Afghan for sale.

We didn't buy at the moment, and were ready to leave. So to make sure we will come back, they gave us a very big sample.

Then from another shop, other locals also called us. We stepped in and the same thing happened!

And again, as soon as we stepped out.

And again, and again.

Within a short time, we went back to our hotel with so much stuff -- maybe one kilo -- that it was impossible to buy anymore.

Long ride through the Salang Pass to Mazar.

Beautiful Blue Mosque -- and a hash den -- in Mazar-i-Sharif.

We also bought pollen from a farmer near Balkh, but it was a bugger to press by hand.

I saw *buzkashi* [men on horseback competing to hold onto a headless, disemboweled goat, and score points by depositing it in a goal's circle] somewhere, but think it was nearer Kabul.

Tales of the [British colonial] Raj and all that.

Style All:
That is the kind of Afghanistan many of us wish for.
Medieval, and frozen in time.
The beauty of the place lies much in its harshness.

Ran Away:
At a final wrestling match in Mazari-i Sharif, the local favorite lost, and the crowd rioted, knocking down the clay stadium.

I jumped over the wall and ran, while several cops entered melee, took off their belts, and started whipping guys.

They got overwhelmed, and ran too.

Fucking Afghans. I love them.

Fortress Hovel:
In Mazar-i-Sharif, if someone asks to borrow your pen, you hand it to them and exclaim:

"I remember. You forget!"

Then you always refuse to accept it back, while repeating that phrase, with a sort of superior mocking tone.

This goes on forever.

If, one day, you absent-mindedly accept the pen without thinking, then the other person exclaims fiendishly:

"Ah ha! I remember and now you forget!"

Now that person always says that to you, whenever you try to loan or give the pen back to that person.

This also goes on forever, back and forth over the years, or until you are killed in the war or whatever.

Women Amazing:
Amazing country, and shitty culture that is enslaving women.

Well Yeah:
Yeah, you are right with that.
Well said.

Women Amazing:
I feel it's my duty, as a woman, to keep pointing that out -- as it's all I can do.

And it seems to me, that the [Western] men visiting there were so stoned, that they didn't even think twice how that tea -- that was always given to visitors -- magically appeared, while their host never left to make it.

And what was behind that curtain?

And where did the delicious food come from?

Applaud Time:
You are spot on, and I applaud your tenacious attitude on this.

I was appalled by the lot of women then, and it certainly doesn't seem to have improved with time.

Sleeping Horses:
I remember [Afghan] men throwing acid in the faces of girls, because they went to school.

Just read, *A Thousand Splendid Suns*, and you realize what monsters men in Afghanistan are.

On the Border:
As I had it explained to me, by an Afghan woman, we in the West commodify a woman's flesh, and use it to sell products and display it as a vulgar status symbol.

A *burqa* is worn, because a woman is cherished and protected, not displayed and objectified.

This is not my belief, but we were happy to finally be able to

get it from that perspective.
My girlfriend was horrified, but smiled and didn't debate it.

Sleeping Horses:
I think behind closed doors, women were brutalized.
And when there is adultery, it's the woman who is stoned to death, in public.
Not the man.

Holy Exponential:
Afghanistan got much worse in the treatment of women, with the exponential growth of radical Islam during the communist regime, and the so-called *jihad* [holy war] bankrolled by the U.S. and Saudis.

Women Amazing:
I haven't even mentioned the woman's oppression written in their law.
A woman owns nothing.
Cannot vote.
Has no passport.
Can be divorced by text message.
Cannot read or write.
Can be legally beaten by any male in her family, even her son.
Raped by the husband.
Beaten up by the so-called religious police.
They are effectively sold to any man by the dowry paid.
And worth a lot less than a good horse.
No male doctor is allowed to examine them at all, or help when they are giving birth.
When they get sick, and need hospitalization, most of the time they are not taken there because it's expensive and they are worth nothing, and it's useless as they can't be examined anyways .
They are thrown away, and replaced as easy as a mobile phone.

Yes war and the Taliban has made things worse, but the principles of their oppression have firmly been in place for as long as the country existed.

And the U.N. or W.H.O. [the United Nations and World Health Organization] has never even dared to mention it.

The whole world is ignoring their plight.

They are not even offered refugee status in principle, because in reality, they could never leave, or flee.

They are not allowed to go anywhere without a male escort, have no money, and no passport.

I am sick to the bone of the glorification of that place [Afghanistan], the endless pictures of [Afghan] men -- only men -- very stupid and cruel men, who don't understand that their best asset would be a woman, who's uneducated mothers could teach them nothing but how to beat their wives.

Night Confession:
Confession time here.

I was once having a sexual relationship with an Afghan man, when I stayed in his hotel in Kabul.

His wife, every night after he had gone, would come and tuck me in.

Fortress Hovel:
Even more decadent was what finally happened to Najibullah, Afghanistan's president, at the end of his Soviet-backed regime.

When the U.S.-backed *mujahideen* seized Kabul, they hung Najibullah from a street lamp post, with two cigarettes stuck in his nostrils.

Sleeping Horses:
With cigarettes in his nostrils?
Nice effect.

Fortress Hovel:

Cigarettes dangling from the nostrils seems to be some sort of Afghan vaudeville.

Cool Fire:
You can go into the shops [in Kabul] with great intentions of buying some cool clothes, then the shopkeepers bring out the hash, and you wake up a day later to discover that you bought 1,000 Camel fags [cigarettes], a second-hand pinstripe three-piece suit, and a packet of fire lighters.

Strange Mountains:
Shari Nau [an upper class Kabul neighborhood] was a great step up, out of that dank, muddy, cold bazaar area.
As three Goa girls -- who couldn't keep their clothes on -- we caused quite a stir, but we had borrowed a huge Afghan dog called Gork who lived with us, and terrified even the bravest Afghan [men] -- when it got loose in the narrow alleyways.

Eventually Dark:
I was bitten by a dog in Kabul in 1977.
I had stitches in my knee and 14 anti-rabies injections, one a day, in a clinic -- I can't remember where.
It was a walk, then a bus ride, then another walk, to get there.
There were lots of Afghans getting the injections with me.
Every morning, the men all stood in line and were injected first, while we women waited in a dark windowless room.
Then we were injected later.
It was a difficult two weeks feeling ill, not knowing if it was from the injections or from being ill.
But I was eventually fine.
Also, I was very grateful for being able to have the injections.

Women Amazing:
Oh my god, what an ordeal.
It was the same [for me] in India. The government injections were lots of them, in the stomach.

From what I heard, my husband Mister Amazing will always feel a bit guilty, because a famous drunkard called [redacted] hit him up for some rupees, years ago, telling him he needed the money to have an injection [against rabies].

But Mister Amazing was not in the mood, and thought the story was bullshit.

Later, [redacted] and his girlfriend both died of rabies.

Fun Change [displays a photograph of hashish]:
If you smoked hash in Afghanistan, did it change your life, or was it just fun?

Solemn and Respectful:
Did have to be Afghanistan?
And damn, I can smell this [photograph].

Experiences First:
That's the reason I went there in the first place.
And yes, travel to these places did change my life. It opened my eyes to a different world.
I believe it was the experiences I had, more than the hash that changed me.

Multiple Memorable:
No life changer -- I had already been smoking for a while.
What was memorable was, getting to have the top quality product -- in quantity.
We used to put grams of premium hash into the big *bubbly bubbly*, multiple times a day.
And the quality of the high you got, was so beyond anything you could get back home.

Marvelous Blood:
I remember more the *tongas* [horse-pulled carriage taxis] in Herat, the getting rocks thrown at me in Kandahar, the shitting blood in Kabul, the marvelous Hindu Kush, and finally the

warmth of Peshawar [Pakistan] after the cold of Afghanistan.

Though Afghan hash was nice, I don't see how it was life-changingly different from the Moroccan, Lebanese, Kashmiri, or any of the others I sampled on the road.

Chocolate Looks:
Wow, that [photograph] looks like chocolate cake.
The physical trip was a life changer, not the drugs.

Beard's Shadow:
The first time I smoked hash in my life, was in Herat.
I was 22, and I was really amazed about the effect.
After a few days, I decided it was another of God's gifts, given to the people for relaxing, enjoying, and sharing with others -- often met for the first time.
It made me consider reality from a different point of view.
To dig inside myself.
My brain activity was happily excited, and never felt bad smoking.
Afghan people were gentle and friendly.
They made half of the fun I had.
Sure it changed my way of living on the trail.
But the real fun was the trail itself.
This is true for both young men and women, traveling 50 years ago on the trail.
The extraordinary empathy of Afghan people, or Indian people, towards us foreigners helped us going through the difficulties of the trail.
I never felt threatened in Afghanistan, when many people had a gun.
A lady could go by night, alone, through the main street in Herat, knowing that if somebody hassled her, she would have had 10 Afghan men ready to protect her.
That was the place then.
In the middle of incredible crowds in India, I never felt fear, as in a modern subway in Europe.

The locals helped the foreigners almost everywhere in Asia. That was the time.

Cool Fire:
I first had it [hashish] in Edinburgh, early 1970s. When I got to Afghanistan, I was like a kid in a sweet shop.
But it screwed the stomach up a bit, because I also took to eating it.
I don't miss it now.

Universe Alive:
Well, I heard music, and saw the world as alive for the first time, but nothing like L.S.D. when I saw the universe and its workings.

Shock Body:
I had quite a trip on Afghani Black when in Herat in 1974.
I felt lucky to make it back to my body the next morning.
It was profound and frightening.
The morning after, was a state of shock and disorientation.

Gooey Time:
During the 1970s, the best Afghan hash was hand-pressed and -- if you had connections -- they kept the very best for themselves.
Kind of gooey.
A friend was very picky about the quality he exported, and would give it back to them until they gave him the best.
He felt it was *karmic* [good *karma*] to only sell the best.
I was the tester, because I hardly smoked anymore.
That hash was famous, especially when you got the really, really good stuff. Nothing like it anywhere.
My only complaint in those parts of the world?
Nearly everyone was stoned all the time.
I even stopped partaking.

Pleasure Asia:
It was just part of the traveling life.
Everyone smoked and shared.
Afghani hash was available in most parts of Asia.
Who even wants to analyze pleasure?

Wind Swept:
The biggest change for me was that after two years of not smoking tobacco, I started smoking again.
Afghanistan made me do it.
This was in 1973. Nobody in that wind-swept war-swept nation smokes marijuana or hashish plain.
It is always mixed with tobacco.
There were lots of opportunities to smoke hashish everyday, and I was on an adventure, so hell yes I hit the pipe when it came my way with tobacco and hash.
I also hit the *bubbly bubbly* when it carried the same load.
And the *joints* [cannabis cigarettes] too.
And the occasional *chillum*.
There was hash pizza, and that had no tobacco.
Or cheese.
Or tomato sauce.
I was sick also, and realized I might die in Afghanistan without ever getting to India.
So one morning, I got on a bus out of Kabul, and caught another one in Jalalabad, on down through the Khyber Pass, and into Pakistan.

Heart and Soul:
I'm a child of hippies, and also have the heart and soul of a hippie.
My father, whose nickname was James -- whom my mother left when I was 18 months old -- went on the hippie trail, hitch-hiking from Mulhouse, France, to Afghanistan in the early 1970s.
Before my birth.

He was repatriated, because he was too high on opiates.
He O.D.'d [and died] in 1985.
I did not know him at all.
Did any of you know a James, from France?
Who got repatriated via the French embassy?
Very tall. Brown hair and moustache.
Got stories to tell about him?
Maybe, maybe, have a picture?
Thank you so much for opening the way for us, the following generations.
Be assured, we do our best not to fail the spirit.
Except for the opiates.

Under the Galata Bridge:
He looks really familiar.
I was in Kabul at this time.
And, as my wife back then was French, I knew most of the French junkies, and shared the needle and the spoon with many.
I was in Kabul in 1970 with a pregnant Angelique, on our way to Goa to have our son.
I did six weeks jail in Kabul.
Afghan police, with Interpol advisors, went to all hotels and arrested everyone with quantities of hash.
Locked us up in two fire truck garages, across from the jail.
Busted some English guys with a double-decker bus, and drove us to the Persian [Iranian] border, and deported us.
I stayed at the Nooristani Hotel in later years, and hung out a lot at Siggi's [a restaurant on Chicken Street], which was the place to hang in the 1970s.
I was one of the lucky ones, as I got clean in 1982, and into recovery.
Your father's story is very familiar.
I still, to this day, have friends who relapse, O.D., and die.
There, but for the grace of God, go I.

Initial This:

I had an opiate period.
Hard to put it down.
Glad you broke out of the grip.

Heart and Soul:
Somehow my dad's experience kept me away from it, although it was all available, all around me.

My heart sings to know one more has been able to come back from it.

Well done.

Water Time:
I was there at that time, but all that I remember was a very sad incident.

A tall French guy -- not your father, for sure -- he stole a traveler's check off an American tourist, and they punished him by pouring hot water on him.

I hope one day you get what you want, information about your father.

May he rest in peace.

Women Amazing:
Very sorry about your dad. What a waste.

Indeed almost nobody could handle the opiates, especially heroin.

Even those that are very proud that they managed for a few years to function normally while on it -- and very proud to hide it -- they never stopped hankering after it, when they stopped.

They were forever changed, and not for the better.

Admitted Crazy:
I met two French guys in Kabul. They had a house in the Swat valley [of northern Pakistan].

They were heroin users.

They financed themselves by buying pollen in Mazar-i-Sharif, and then head to Goa, to sell it there.

Then buy morphine in Benares, and take it to Kabul, to sell.
And then from the proceeds, go to Mazar to get the pollen.

Cool Fire:
One of my biggest regrets was buying, and helping to buy, a large quantity of morphine for three Brit *heavies*, not *heads* [criminals, not stoners], probably from the same pharmacy in Benares, back in the 1970s.

I got a pang of conscience, and dumped mine on the train, on the way back to Calcutta.

Hash was O.K., but I had to draw the line on that stuff.

Love Face:
My last night in Herat, before Iran in 1973, I was given a small piece [of hashish] by an Afghan -- who I had asked if he could let me have some -- as we had run out.

My Farsi was just good enough to ask if someone was a smoker, and the word for "stoned."

He gave me what I thought was a rather small piece, but I didn't complain, as I never did in Afghanistan.

Put the four of us completely out.

When we crossed the border in the morning, we saw them also crossing.

The guy said, "Do you want some hashish?" with a big smile on his face, presumably aware of how we had been the night before.

Such good times. Unforgettable.

I was eventually forced at knifepoint to leave Kabul, by the brothers of the princess I had fallen in love with.

I had the pleasure of staying with her and the family.

The king was just about to be deposed, and the tension was intense.

I never got back to Afghanistan.

I was at the border, about to enter, when the Russians invaded.

I ended up staying in the tribal territories [in Pakistan], in a fort, for a few weeks instead.

Under the Galata Bridge:
We stayed at the Nooristani Hotel [in Kabul], but Siggi's was my hang out, in 1971.

I bought my white Afghan hound from some Spanish guy living there.

He had the dog roped to his bed, in the big room full of beds.

When he mistreated the dog, I grabbed his hand in mid-flight, and told him if he touched this dog again, I would beat him!

I told him he didn't love this dog, and that he should sell him to me.

He said O.K. for 1,000 Afghanis.

I ran back to the hotel, and asked Angelique if I could buy him, as we only had a little over 1,000 Afghanis left.

She told me:

"Go buy your dog. With all the money we had, that having 1,000 Afghanis or nothing was almost the same."

I ran back, and bought this puppy, changed his name from Linda to Spooky -- as he was pure white with big black eyes.

We later smuggled him out of the country with a bunch of hash, and took him to Goa.

He lived with us there.

And at the Rex [Hotel] Bombay, and the Crown [Hotel] in Delhi.

Was a wonderful dog.

Firewood Street:
In October 1973 and January 1975, everything was frozen solid.

And the shop [in Kabul] that had that beautiful handmade ice cream in summer, was now selling hot, sweetened milk with a raw egg mixed into it.

We were smoking Mazar, but I do remember having to go

out in the street on firewood safari, for the stove and the water boiler in the room.

My Legs:
Afghanistan was wonderful in 1970.
I don't think it would be as wonderful now.
I believe the Inca had a concept -- *pacha* -- that was both temporal and spatial.
One of the wonders of travel is sometimes you get to see things, or a way of life, that no longer exist.

Candy Kilometers:
I co-drove a Leyland bus from Amsterdam to Kabul in July of 1972, and one of the young guys got amoebic dysentery soon after arrival there.
And it got worse and worse.
I called his father in Kansas City, who was a defense contractor.
The phone connection was terrible so I finally screamed loudly:
"Your son is dying!"
Within an hour, an embassy employee came and arranged a doctor, who hooked him up to I.V.s, [intravenous drip feeds].
In one arm, he quickly had a saline I.V. bag in [injected]. And in the other, a sugar I.V. bag.
A few days later, I got him to the airport, and put him on a plane out of Kabul.
And he regained his health.
He was quite lucky. I am sure many others weren't.
A lot of bad things happened to your health out there.
I was 29 then, and most of the people on the bus were in their very early 20s.

Vagabonds Now:
I remember her full name, just now:
Marsha Smith.

So now I have to tell you guys this story, because she told me that she had been on a Hog Farm bus.

She told me she had gotten kicked off that bus in someplace like Afghanistan, or in that part of the world.

Marsha Smith.

Short, dark hair, talkative, vivacious, extremely extroverted.

I believed her when she said she had been on a Hog Farm bus, because she was a close friend of Paul Foster [a Hog Farm founder], and he would know.

And she knew we were close friends with Paul Foster.

For a few months somewhere in 1967, Marsha lived with us, as part of our extended family in Santa Monica.

Now this is where the story gets a little tricky for me to tell.

It is kind of personal.

My birthday is in November, so I was a few weeks away from turning 15. We had been full-blown hippies for a few years, at that point.

That all started for me just before I turned 12.

We had just moved to Venice, California, and my mother gave me a healthy dose of very pure L.S.D.

I don't remember a whole lot about that first trip, except that we lived a few blocks from the beach, and we spent some of it wandering in the fog, listening to the waves.

By Thanksgiving of 1968, I had been right in the middle of the free love movement for a few years, but I had still not gotten laid.

Apparently my mother was aware of this, because she decided to do something about it.

This is where Marsha Smith comes back into the story.

Yes, my mother arranged for me to lose my virginity to Marsha Smith.

I will spare you the details. Suffice it to say that her plan worked just fine.

Fast forward to the fall of 1973.

I had had a terrible, horrible, no good, very bad year, starting in the fall of 1972.

I had been suffering from a thought disorder.

I was quite literally crazy for about one whole year.

In and out of psychiatric hospitals, hearing voices, doing what the voices told me to do. This was not drug related.

It is also a separate story, that I'm sure I will tell someday.

For the purposes of this story about Marsha Smith, all you need to know is that by the fall of 1973, I had come completely out of it.

I was turning 20 that fall. I had a job.

I had my own apartment in Sacramento [the capital of California], my home town.

I'm extremely fortunate to be in the very rare category of people -- who met all of the diagnostic criteria for schizophrenia at some point -- and then never, ever, had any symptoms of that disease again for the rest of their life.

So who shows up on my doorstep?

Marsha Smith.

Marsha was around 13 years older then me, but naturally I moved her right in because, you know, sex.

She convinced me to go with her to Mexico, so we could live off of her Social Security disability check.

But first we had to travel to Oregon, so she could retrieve some of her stuff that was being held for her by Paul Foster.

I quit my job and we hit the road, hitch-hiking vagabonds, doing our best to be free spirits.

When we got to Paul Foster's house, he pulled me aside and he gave me a very long, intense lecture about who Marsha Smith really was.

And what would happen to me if I continued to hitch my wagon to hers.

I was very taken aback by this.

He was very, very serious, in a way I've never seen him be before.

I think he told me stories of her behavior that got her kicked off the bus, but my memory is a bit hazy on what he actually said.

From the way our conversation went down, I could tell that he had completely arranged it with his wife -- or partner at the time -- to keep Marsha occupied, so that he could have a long, private conversation with me.

I was convinced by what he said.

I told Marsha that I was going north to visit one of my uncles in Washington state, that she could not come with me, and that she would have to go on to Mexico without me.

The last I heard about Marsha Smith was a few decades later.

My mother told me she had heard that Marsha was living in San Francisco.

That Marsha had elected to undergo a gender reassignment surgery.

She was now a he.

Amazing Hog:
I remember Marsha very, very well.

She hung out periodically at the Sunland-Tujunga Hog Farm [on the outskirts of Los Angeles, California].

Yes, you are right about the Hog Farm bus -- the Road Hog -- and Marsha getting off in Afghanistan.

Then she ended up going to India, and riding a Harley [Harley Davidson motorcycle] all around the continent.

She was quite mad, but not in a horrible way.

Just nuts though.

And riding a Harley Davidson, yet again she turned up at the Hog Farm.

Fun to have around, on occasion, at dinners on the Farm.

She was also busted with all of us Hog Farm Haight [San Francisco] people, and Merry [Prankster] ones, and the bands.

Everyone who was part of the [police] clean-up of the Haight.

The south San Francisco jail was full of us freaks, and the [Grateful] Dead.

And a couple other bands were also in the sweep of the Haight by the cops.

It was a phenomenon.
Amazing, two days later, our mutual lawyer got us all out.

Vagabonds Now:
Wow. You are the first I have met, since all that went down, who knew Marsha.

She was crazy, but man did we have some good times.

I am so grateful she went through my life like a tornado, for a time.

Garden Seasons:
They [Hog Farm travelers] came in our hippie garden for many pot lucks [informal group dinners], for a few seasons, in Goa.

4 • PAKISTAN

The Khyber Pass:
When I came over the Khyber Pass into Peshawar [a city in northwest Pakistan], there were two French guys that were junkies.
Really down on their luck.
I often wondered if they ever made it home.
That was so sad.
I'm sure the locals looked at them as hippies, but in reality, it gave all of us on the road -- hippies or travelers -- a bad name.

Rented Clutch:
I remember a clutch of morphine freaks in Peshawar in 1968.
They used to hang out with the cops.
I think the girls were being rented out.
It was an ugly scene for them.

Sleeping Forest:
There were a lot who never made it home.
I remember some Germans living in the forest near Aabpara Market in Islamabad [the capital of Pakistan], in 1985.
Hopeless junkies, begging for food in the market.
Sleeping under plastic sheets.
Many other examples unfortunately, back in those days.

Big Breath:
I remember getting bottles of 20 -- of the big half-grains of morphine -- for 20 rupees in Peshawar.
About two dollars.
Could take your breath away.

Genetic Bazaars:
Being a native of Peshawar myself, I have many pictures of the bazaars and people occupying these streets -- of a later era though.

Peshawar, being the border town and at the gateway of empires, has always been on the forefront of many wars, invasions, and cultural and genetic mixings.

Not only the Soviet invasion [of Afghanistan] in recent history, but many before that, and several after that, including the dreadful Taliban.

The region remains extremely volatile, and the effects and aftermath will still remain to be seen and felt for a long, long time.

Wondered Big:
Remember police looking at the bottom of cars, using a mirror on a pole?

Genetic Bazaars:
That hasn't been changed a bit to this day.

It's still a very common practice, and came into existence after car bombings became a daily and weekly affair in the 1980s and 1990s.

In the very start of 1990s, our own car was devastated in a parking in the Cantonment area, when a nearby car had a bomb and it blew out everything in the surroundings.

Luckily, no human casualties occurred in that accident.

Abdul Abdul:
In Turkham, the first town where you cleared Pakistan immigration in the Khyber Pass [leaving Afghanistan], right outside the Customs House -- where there were signs telling you to only change money at official banks -- sat your [illegal] money changers if you hadn't bought your money in Kabul.

And drug sellers.

Also a sign saying it was illegal -- and dangerous -- to

photograph tribal women.
Fun town.
A bit further was Landi Kotal, where the fun really began.

Fortress Hovel:
In January 1988 in Darra, outside of Peshawar, they took me to a cemetery and gave me an AK-47 assault rifle to test fire.
The Muslim cemetery's bleak scattered headstones covered a tiny hill.
A young boy scampered through the jagged tombstones, collecting whatever old bullets he could find near the target, which was a rusty tin can balanced on top of a small pile of rocks.
When I aimed, an old man said softly to me:
"Do not shoot the boy."

Wondered Big:
I remember [in Pakistan] how drear it was traveling during Ramadan.

Fascinating Much:
Eating opium made it so much bearable and fascinating.

Wondered Big:
First thing we looked for in Peshawar, actually.

Wind Swept:
I caught a train in Peshawar or Rawalpindi, riding in basically a boxcar with two small windows, several loose benches, and 30 Pakistanis.
I was the only Western guy, and that was a great curiosity.
At first everybody wanted to be my friend. One young guy spoke a bit of English.
Then he, in a good spirit, offered me a cigarette.
"No thank you. I don't smoke."
He was offended. Maybe he didn't understand why I didn't

accept.

He pulled back like I was a leper.

He said something to the attentive crowd. A second man, perhaps thinking I'd prefer a different brand, offered me one of his.

I said, "No. No." and held my palm up.

Then he was personally offended.

The crowd suddenly vibed hostile.

A third guy -- already angry at my insolence -- held out an opened pack with a few slender white cigarettes extended.

And the truth was, I was in a state of tobacco withdrawal [while trying to quit smoking].

My life may have been hanging by a thread. If I didn't start smoking with this crew, what difference would it make if I was dead?

Those were my thoughts as I gratefully accepted his offer and smoked *ciggie* after nasty *ciggie*, all the way to Lahore [in eastern Pakistan near India]

In Lahore, I bought my own pack, better to offer to others, and made my way east into India.

I smoked for the next two or three years -- although I never bought a carton.

Vibe First:

A squalid little place, 75 paisa [three-fourths of a rupee] a night, tiny Chinese padlocks on the doors, no beds, just straw mats.

The Musliman Hotel. 1967. Quetta [a city in southern Pakistan].

I arrived on the water train from Zahedan [in southeastern Iran's Baluchistan province], dropped off my pack, and went out to score a meal.

Upon my return, the lock was gone and anything of any value -- admittedly not much -- had been taken.

What I missed most was my down jacket, and my harmonica.

I learned to keep everything important in my shoulder bag.

I was only 16.

Swallowed Nowhere:
I always remember [in Baluchistan], how they [train robbers] arrived on both sides of the slow-running train, some on horses, some on [motor] bikes.

The ones sitting on the back, jumped inside the train.

They scared all the passengers by holding their *kalach* [Kalashnikov AK-47 assault rifles] and old guns.

The train had to stop in middle of nowhere.

And in two hours time, they fucking cleaned out the whole train.

Many passengers were Iranians, carrying all their goods.

It was November 1978.

Hard times already in Iran.

They [passengers] tried to escape from the train, but got busted by the *dacoits* [thieves] outside, and forced to surrender their goods.

They [*dacoits*] fired a few shots in the air, to make it more frightening, but most of them were laughing as the looting went on.

I had swallowed some opium when we left Nokundi station [in Baluchistan], to make the journey easier, and was quite high when the whole story happened.

Surely, because of it, I didn't even feel any fear at that time.

I always thought that both the *dacoits* and Pakistani police acted in collusion on the whole affair.

Fresh Staying:
I remember staying at the Shabnom [Hotel] in Chitral [a province in northern Pakistan].

Every morning, the hashish man would bring us fresh hash to our room.

Best Early:
They stopped producing Chitral [hashish from Chitral] in

general, way back in early 2000s.

Chitral is the center of the Hindu Kush [the Himalayas across Afghanistan and northern Pakistan].

It produced some of the best hash in the world.

Wondered Big:

I was there [in Peshawar] several times in the 1970s, and I remember the restaurants with big, old, bearded Pathans [an ethnic tribe also known as Pashtun], with ammo belts, propping their rifles up against the wall.

The only Western food seemed to be Chicken a la Kiev.

I often wondered about that.

Zero 101:

All the women I travelled with in Iran, Afghanistan, and Pakistan were harassed daily.

It was a nightmare for many.

I still remember them showing me the bruises they suffered, just from walking in the bazaars.

Holy Exponential:

I lived that nightmare everyday growing up in Tehran.

Applaud Time:

As a woman who also travelled in Pakistan alone, I understand.

I was looking like a tent, and still was stared at so much .

Nice people, but very hard as a single gal.

Totally Challenging:

I agree. I travelled overland as a single woman, and found it quite challenging.

I was groped on local buses, chased down the street by a gang of men, and had to lock myself in the bathroom of the hotel one night, amongst other incidents.

I dressed appropriately, and was always respectful, but could never totally relax -- and it certainly impacted upon my experience.

Body Target:
I was not so fortunate.
With pale skin, and red hair, I was the target of Pakistani men, who ran their hands all over my body.

Under the Galata Bridge:
Afghanistan wasn't a problem, but when we crossed into Pakistan it was crazy.
I got into so many fights because of Pakistan men grabbing a pregnant Angelique, and I would just punch them in the face.
They would see her with me, and the next day out with a [different] male friend.
They thought all Western women were whores.
I remember getting in a fight with a guy in a restaurant in Peshawar, and he pulled out a gun.
Thank God, a bunch of men jumped on him, and we were able to get away.

Sold Survival:
I was there too in Peshawar, late 1973.
At that hippie hotel.
I forget the name.
Anyone remember?
On main drag, lots of us hippies and druggies stayed there.
The proprietor was older, bearded, pot-bellied Baba.
Nice fellow.
My horror story -- my partner had lost his passport and we got stuck there for months.
Dirt poor.
I'm sorry to offend anyone, but for me as a female, Peshawar was -- with some exceptions in amazing excursions -- utterly awful.
Pakistan was the pits for me, on an otherwise glorious hippie

sojourn lasting nearly two years, and ending up living with writing and musician expats in Kathmandu [capital of Nepal], and having mind-blowing experiences around at Swayambhu [also known as The Monkey Temple, on Kathmandu's outskirts].

In Pakistan, I was never unaccompanied.

And I was stoned once, pelted, with rocks, by a mob of angry men.

And more than once, I had to fight off sexual assault and violent groping.

And once in Islamabad, I was sexually attacked in broad daylight -- on a big, populated street -- by a very well-clad dude, and a vicious knockdown fight ensued.

We were both badly pummeled, and then pulled apart.

I felt victorious having bashed back pretty good.

It was liberating, to be honest.

This was long before having any training, and then spending the next three-plus decades as a professional and pioneer in self-defense -- on a continuum, not just bashing-back of course -- and also for non-stranger violence.

And trauma recovery.

Heavily patriarchal cultures of all stripes historically love to oppress and violate women.

Keep them in their place.

Of course that is changing, and today I am connected to feminist groups all over that region, including Pakistan, where women and girls are rising up.

As best they can -- for example, in Afghanistan -- and taking their bodies back.

I don't mean to suggest all men are pigs.

Not at all.

But for me, parts of that extraordinary, life-changing, amazing trip was deeply marred by double-standards, and a particular pervasive fear not experienced by my [male] mate.

It was a rude awakening.

And shit like that also happened a few times in Israel, where my Kibbutz Father invited me for tea one day, then mauled and tried to forcibly rape me.

I fought him off too, and escaped intact.

These trips were often fraught or laced with certain dangers and adrenaline-filled wildness.

But I was jealous and envious of my then-partner's freedoms, mobility, and beautiful male-male bonding and brotherhood he experienced, so much of the time.

A beautiful witnessing.

He expanded and filled space with others, the man in the street, smoking, making music while in Peshawar and other locales.

In contrast, I often contracted and felt terribly restrained, so often deflecting ogling men, and roaming grabby hands, causing me to shrink and hunker down inside myself.

Just to feel safe.

Many times I wished to be invisible.

And I was always properly dressed in full-length attire.

Wondered Big:
I experienced getting molested a whole lot too.
Turkey, not so bad.
East Turkey, Erzurum, terrible.
Pakistan, bad.
Afghanistan, fine, fine, fine.
Loved Afghanistan.
Forgot Iran. That was bad.
Northern Iran was okay.
Isn't this all strange?

Disturbed Love:
It is not easy to be woman in India and in Pakistan.

Like when a group of drunken Indians tried to rape me in Diu [a town near Goa].

Or to be disturbed on buses, especially when I was younger.

So after a few years going to India, I started to get tired of the classic questions, like, "Are you married?" or being touched in the buses or bazaars, and all that.

It was this, that made me go further east.

Don't get me wrong, I love India.

But the problem of violence against women is huge.

Secret Nervous:

I've just been reading about the new metro train in Lahore, built by the Chinese.

I stayed with American missionaries in Empress Road, near the station, for two months in 1969.

I made a lot of friends with the young people, who lived in small houses called, The Lines.

I can imagine all their area would have been demolished to build this.

Born Alive:

I studied in a missionary school, and our papers were sent to England for correction.

I am familiar with the area, well enough.

Empress Road is still alive.

Lahore is Lahore.

If you have not seen Lahore, you are not born.

Strange Mountains:

I was walking down the street in Lahore.

A leper, or a man with suppurating sores, was lying on the sidewalk.

A local man, seeing his filthy and desperate condition, dashed into a pharmacy and came out with supplies.

He re-bandaged and cleaned up the man, right there on the street.

For a very long time I had to wonder about myself, and how I don't help people in that direct way.

Very few people do.

I still wonder why?

Born Alive:
We used to hang around next to Lahore Museum and National College of Arts, on the mall next to Kim's Gun.

All [Pakistani] artists smoked *joints* in those days, so we shared with hippies, who were passing by.

City intellectuals came towards the evening, to have hot discussions.

Things were cheap, so we shared.

I was a college student in 1971.

Early Picture:
On my first day in Lahore in 1969, they burned down the train station.

For some political reason.

Strange Mountains:
One dawn in the early 1970s, in a park in Lahore, I watched men gently training a beautifully *hennaed* white horse [decorated with *henna* dye], in the art of dancing, to the beat of the drum.

The ladies of Lahore in those days wore the prettiest *hijab*, with little face veils, shiny black satin, and quite stylish compared to the usual bags.

I remember Lahore as beautiful city.

Born Alive:
Lahore changed drastically after the C.I.A.-backed coup in 1977 [when General Muhammad Zia-ul Haq seized power].

All liberals went down the drain for good.

Secret Nervous:
We lived opposite Kinnaird High School for Girls, and got quite friendly with the head, who started to try and teach us Urdu, starting: "*che-la, te-la.*"

We were also offered jobs to teach English.

But we had set out to tour the world, and were getting itchy feet after a couple of months -- although we never got further than Nepal, where we lived for a year.

Beyond Amalgamation:
Hindi is a mixture of many languages, like Urdu.
One major difference in Hindi and Urdu is that Hindi is an amalgamation of native subcontinent languages, and its dialects.
Urdu has gathered words beyond the subcontinent regions like Persian, Arabic, Portuguese, Azerbaijan.

Persian Indian:
"Hindi" itself is a Persian word.
"Hindu" is also a Persian word.
"Hindi comes from the Persian name for India -- "Hind".

My Legs [reads]:
This is from a letter home, December 1970.
"I am in Rawalpindi, Pakistan. In a hotel that costs 25 cents a night.
"The hotel, which reeks of hashish -- it is semi-legal here -- is in the bazaar district.
"Beggars, shoe-shine men, cigarette shops, fruit stands, and *hookah* shops line the streets.
"Incredible scene."

Born Alive:
I started following music [in Lahore] after Woodstock, as hippies brought this music to Asia.
A friend of mine opened the first black-light [lit by ultraviolet light] basement in Lahore, by the name of *Blowup*.
Lahore, in those days, was full of hippies.
Near the museum and university, young students became very, very actively involved with this new wave of thinking, followed by music.

Beetroot Voice:

In 1967, just south of Cox's Bazaar [a Bay of Bengal port in then-East Pakistan, which became Bangladesh], we met a young English missionary, who was pretty nervous, saying Naxalites [Marxist rebels] and C.I.A. were everywhere.

He even lowered his voice in our hut, which was half-an-hour from anyone.

There was one English guy, stationed in town, working with a German firm.

One day, a minibus full of Russian scientists arrived -- fed us beetroot and eggs -- but wouldn't let us anywhere near their van.

As far as I know, everyone was looking for uranium, which the sand was meant to be very rich in.

Fortress Hovel:
In Pakistan, someone gave me a piece of paper that said:
"While being stoned by four persons who are required to testify the crime, the convict can also be shot dead, at which point the stoning would stop."

Late Talk:
In the early 1980s I received some money from home. I was staying in Paharganj [a neighborhood in New Delhi popular with travelers], and was quite broke.

It was not a big amount, so I wanted to make it stretch.

So along with a Danish friend of mine called Peter, we decided to go to Peshawar and bring back a kilo of fine Afghan pollen hash, to sell in Delhi.

Smuggling hash into India was the best we could come up with!

So off we went to Peshawar, and bought the hash, and very unprofessionally just rolled it up in a blanket, with a straw mat around.

We had a couple of very narrow escapes, but miraculously got it back into India.

I don't remember if we made any money at all, but we had an

exciting trip.

Under the Galata Bridge:
I used to smuggle hash from Mazar-i-Sharif or, one time, Kathmandu to Goa, just to sell *tolas* for the season.
Pakistani *shit* was usually garbage.
But Peshawar was famous for selling morphine from their pharmacies.
A bottle of 32-milligram German Merck tablets -- known as Peshawar Tablets, to those who indulged.
Then again, that was the early 1970s.
Things may have changed by the 1980s.

Candy Kilometers:
I was at Tom's place in Peshawar. Tom [also known as Tom the Bomb] and Texas Jack had taken off, and I was in the process of closing the place up.
A knock on the door revealed a young, well dressed Paki who asked for Tom, and was sad he wasn't there.
I asked if I could be of any help, and he said he had 15 kilos of Afghan pollen.
I said, I was interested.
I got on in back of him, on his Lambretta.
We go a few miles inside the tribal area to his compound, and he swings open the gates.
The big dogs would have ripped the life out of me, if he had said the right word.
We go into this room, and it's murky, but I can see hundreds of *keys* [kilos] of commercial stacked in there.
But he shows me this beautiful large bag of pollen, and I agree to buy it, if he presses it that night.
He takes me back to Tom's, and shows up the next day with it.
In Tom's lab are gallons of [plastic] resin and fiberglass, something I am quite familiar with, being a surfer from Newport Beach [in southern California].

I build it [the pollen] into my VW van, and go across into India and to Goa.

It was easy there to relieve myself of it.

Under the Galata Bridge:

I'm an old surfer who learned to surf at the Newport River mouth in 1962.

Small world.

Although I'm also familiar with resin and cloth, I had suitcase-makers in Calcutta and Bombay, so I never made my own cases.

Tom the Bomb, and Jack, were my buddies also.

May they rest in paradise.

I bought it [hashish] in Mazar for 10 dollars -- less then 100 rupees a *key* in 1970 -- and sold in Goa for 10 rupees a *tola* which was 100 times my cost.

Split People:

My husband met a Vietnam veteran in 1973 in Iran, on the trail, named Fritz Sparingi -- not sure of spelling.

He travelled with him until Pakistan, and they split up at Lahore, because Fritz was headed to India to Nepal.

Not sure what happened to him.

My husband always wondered.

He also met two Canadians -- one from Vancouver and one from British Columbia -- in a prison in Herat.

They had stopped him, accompanied by a guard, asking my husband to use his passport to cash traveler's checks for them.

They had been taken prisoner for transporting illicit products across the border from Pakistan to Afghanistan.

He often wondered about them too.

Anyone know something about these people?

5 • INDIA

Fortress Hovel:
India, where at the age of 20, I was turbaned by the ricey hands of Kulu tribesmen [Kulu Valley in India's northwest Himachal Pradesh state].

Village Colors:
After spending a month traveling overland, and a month in amazing Afghanistan, it really was a breath of fresh air going through the [Pakistan] border into India.
Finally seeing women in public and dressed in beautiful colorful saris.
Colors!
I did get pick-pocketed on the first bus, from the border to Amritsar [a city in India's northwest Punjab state, near the frontier].
They only got my small stash, meant for such occasions.
When we arrived at the bus depot [in Amritsar], and had no clue where to head, a nice older Sikh guy gave us a ride, and invited us to stay at his house.
It turned out he owned the whole village, and land, and village brick factory, for miles around.
He sent out the boy in the morning, to get us whatever we wanted.
He apologized for not finding any *ganja* or hashish, only opium!

Shimmering Joy:
My very first sight of India at the Ferozepore land border, 1969, consisted of one young boy standing on the road under the blazing sunlight, flanked by tall water grass, all brown-

skinned, barefooted, only wearing a white shirt and his shimmering oiled black hair falling straight down to his hips.

Sheer joy.

I felt I had arrived in Mowgli's jungle, expecting Shere Khan to burst upon the scene at any time [British author Rudyard Kipling's fictional Bengal tiger leaping at a character in *The Jungle Book*]

I realized later on that he was a Sikh child, drying himself up under the sun, after his morning bath.

Romance:
The romance of India.

On the Border:
Does anyone remember the [Indian] clairvoyant Customs agent at the India-Pakistan border?

Outfoxed Well:
I remember her well.

She used to place her hand on your heart, and then ask about hashish or rupees.

At least she was bent. She took her cut and let you go.

Much better than going to jail.

She could be outfoxed, but most just allowed for her tax.

This was just before the [India-Pakistan-Bangladesh] war in 1971.

She definitely had a retirement plan.

Shimmering Joy:
The Dragon Lady, on the Kasur-Ferozepore border.
South of Wagah.

The border moved to Wagah after the destruction of a bridge on the first border post, in the 1971-1972 Pakistan and India war.

She was not seen again at Wagah, I think.

Expert as a psychologist in finding hidden *charas* and black market Indian rupees bought in Kabul.

On the Border:
I remember this Canadian guy we met, he had long, bright, red hair and freckles.

We hadn't seen him since Balkh, but ran into him at the Pakistan-Indian border.

He wore a black short-haired wig, and a comical idea of what he thought was straight-looking shirt and jacket.

We tried to avoid him.

To the left of the main entrance [to enter India, through a Passport and Customs Control room], was a small area with toilet paper strewn about, and lots of small piles of human shit.

We watched him carrying a package, the size of a shoebox, as he waded through the mine field [of excrement], and deposit it next to the back door of the Custom House, tiptoe back again, and go through Customs.

Once we got through -- and it took over an hour -- we saw him emerge without his disguise, and he had been really torn apart and even body-searched.

He looked around, picked up his package, and went happily on his way.

We got right through.

There was a woman clairvoyant there.

She just looked in your eyes and asked.

And she thought she knew.

We couldn't help but wonder how she got that armload of gold bangles, on her salary.

Candy Kilometers:
All along the hippie trail, you heard about her, so I approached the border with a little trepidation -- and 15 kilos of *primo* Afghan fiberglassed and built into my Coleman cooler.

I get in line in back of a lot of pedestrians, but only a couple minutes later, a man comes and takes me to a table.

I sit down, and show him my passport and Carnet passage [a

Customs permit to take a car across an international border].
He then says,
"Let's go have a look at your vehicle."
As we walk to my VW van, two other men come along with us.
I unlock the big side doors.
The original guy says,
"Excuse me" -- and pauses -- and then says,
"Do you have any..." -- long pause here -- "guns?"
I start to laugh, and he then says,
"Well, do you have any gold?"
And I am so relaxed as I say no, when he asks if I have any hashish, I just shake my head no, as I said no, and he said,
"Enjoy India."
I got in my car and drove into India, being cool not to get so excited -- as I heard they watched you for the first 10 miles.
Got rid of it quite easily in Goa.

Early Picture:
The lady at the border wasn't clairvoyant.
She would take your wrist, and ask questions and -- if she felt your pulse beat hard -- busted!
You could please her with women's sanitary napkins.

On the Border:
Just smoke a fat one, and they won't even find your pulse.
We got to know each other.
She walked over to our van, tapped exactly where it was and said,
"Not even here?" -- and smiled knowingly.

Boots Fortunate:
My friend and I were forewarned about her.
And we were full of trepidation, as we were carrying fine goods [hashish] from Mazar-i-Sharif.
Luckily for us, we arrived at the border [into India], just

before it closed for the night, and she had gone home.

We were incredibly fortunate to get through without getting busted.

We had to give our passports and details, to a guard inside the hut.

As he wrote, he was feeling your body as you stood beside him.

I thought I would be smart, and stood with his desk between us.

However, when he had finished writing, he tapped his partner -- who was searching the baggage -- on the shoulder and they swapped places.

He came outside with me and after searching my guitar -- which I initially concealed goods in, but thought better of it -- then my bags.

Finally he started to body-search me. I had a kilo sewn into my Y-fronts [underwear].

He put in hand right on it, and looked me in the eye.

I looked back like a rabbit caught in a snake's gaze, and felt my heart beating so loud I was sure he could hear it.

To my amazement, he smiled and, with a nod of his head, signaled me to go.

I can only think that he felt pity for a naive young kid on the biggest adventure of his life.

I was interrogated at the Iran border [after crossing westward from Afghanistan] by a snake-eyed little Hitler who looked at me menacingly and asked:

"How long have you been on heroin?"

Stupidly, I laughed, which didn't go down well.

In the ensuing search, he ripped the heels off my only boots, which wiped the stoned grin off my face.

Night Confession:

It was good in Afghanistan, I admit, but I preferred Malana hash [from Malana, a Himalayan village in Parvati Valley in Himachal Pradesh state].

Persian Indian:
Afghan hash and Kerala grass [from Kerala, a southwest coastal state].
It was the best in the 1980s.
Now it's Malana Cream from the hills. Cream Rolls.

Door Out:
Before smoking with the real *charsies*, it was fun.
But I found out, it's really a holy sacrament, and the key to the door.

Red Entering:
Besides Manali resin [hashish from Manali, a Himalayan village in Kulu Valley], which affected me like peyote, Afghani hash possessed the most pungent and seductive aroma.
Lebanese Red had its own delicious, and familiar attraction, but hands down Afghani was the best.

Near Good:
Once I stayed in Vashisht [a village with hot mineral springs for public bathing] in 1979. It is a few kilometers from Manali.
On the way, a local and a chief of Vashisht invited.
They were smoking *chillum*.
We smoked.
It was good stuff.
We just stayed there.
Could not go.
Just watching mountain.
It took time, then we moved.

Clouds:
Wrapped in Manali clouds.

Admitted Crazy:
I was arrested in Manali with two *tolas* [of hashish].

Police refused *baksheesh* [a bribe or tip].

It took 10 days to get a chemical examiner's report on it, even though I admitted the offence.

The guards would rub *charas* for us every day, and give it us.

There was a Nepalese apple picker, in for alleged murder.

He apparently was cheated out of his earnings, and took revenge.

A major gold smuggler was also there as well.

Only two cells, with 10 guys in each.

We were told if a woman was to be jailed, we would be all in one cell.

Crazy times.

Village Foreigner:

When Indira Gandhi got assassinated [in 1984 by her two Sikh bodyguards in New Delhi], I lived in Manali.

Black smoke came from the bazaar when the crowds [supporters of Prime Minister Indira Gandhi] set fire to a Sikh *gurdwara* [temple], and local youths came into the village with loot under their arms after they looted the Sikh-owned shops.

You can't do much about political disturbances as a foreigner.

Just hope they leave you alone.

Diamonds Today:

I will never forget my 24-hour [train] travel, 3rd class.

From Agra to Patna [north Indian cities], with the Upper India Express in March 1969.

A tough experience, but today a nostalgic and adventurous memory.

Sitting on the [train aisle] floor among crowds of people, a group of hippies were singing, *Lucy In The Sky With Diamonds*.

Under the Galata Bridge:

One time, I spent the entire [3rd class train] trip from Bombay to Delhi shooting cocaine and morphine in the toilets.

Firewood Street:

On those days-long, 3rd class train rides, I used to prefer dropping some *goolies* [handmade pills] of *chandoo* [refined opium] to mellow out.

Together with dexies [Dexedrine] to stay awake.

Late Talk:

Did any of you meet an English guy called Tony?

In Rishikesh [a Hindu holy town on the Ganges River in northwest India's Himalayas], in the late 1970s or early 1980s?

When I met Tony in the late 1970s, he didn't talk.

Something happened to him, when he arrived in India.

He promptly gave all his belongings to poor people.

He was brought to Rishikesh by another Englishman called Richard.

He [Tony] stayed there at an *ashram* [Hindu hermitage].

He was once arrested by the police -- I don't remember why -- but as he didn't speak, he couldn't defend himself. A German man and myself got him out by guaranteeing for him.

I left Rishikesh, but when I came back a couple of years later, I found Tony living in a shack by the river.

He was now speaking again, had grown fat and had a guitar. He told me the locals were looking after him.

I would like to know what became of Tony.

Hot Streams:

I lived for about a year and a half up from Rishikesh, at Laxman Jhula.

Then there was only a walking bridge over the Ganges.

It was full of lepers who had the choice to live in a mud and straw hut -- and be given a bowl of rice a day -- or they could beg on the bridge from the pilgrims.

I would start out on one side, with bananas, and try to give to those most needy.

The *sadhus* would come down from the higher Himalayas to

spend the hot summer on the banks of the Ganges.
They were totally amazing.
Some looked like Chinese mystics with long dreads.
Others, Tibetan.
Others, Indian.
Anytime of the day or night, some would be seen standing on one leg, totally engrossed in some ancient scripture, reading from a handmade tattered book.
Or they would beg along the path beside Ganges.
I remember a very handsome young couple.
He was blind, and she was his sight.
They would chant the most beautiful chants.
All day long.
They were so blown with their own music.
As I walked up the path to the *ashram* higher up the mountain, their songs echoed.
On special celebrations -- such as *Guru Purnima* [a full moon festival honoring gurus] -- the whole village was chanting and, as I went to sleep, it reverberated with the sound of Mother Ganges.
God, it was a space.
Yes, I suppose it will all be different now.
Om Namah Shivaya [an adoration to Shiva].

Late Talk:
In 1977 and 1978, my brother and I, with friends, were on our way up to Badrinath [a Hindu holy town high in the Himalayas].
On the way there -- I believe it was in Joshimath -- we met a man called Doctor X.
He claimed to have been working as a doctor with the World Health Organization, and now he was settled in a cowshed in Joshimath.
He had an all-round remedy that could cure or prevent any kind of illness, so we all had to take it, of course.
We all gulped down a small cup of cow's urine, with raisins in

it.

Big Bottles:
Gomutra [cow urine] is making a big comeback in India.
It even gets sold in bottles.

Late Talk:
Ours was not bottled stuff, it was very fresh.

Very Classic:
Cow urine is a very popular Ayurvedic classic [traditional Hindu medicine], as a Brahmin [the highest Hindu caste] aperitif.

Own Yogic:
Drinking your own urine is a *yogic* practice [a Hindu spiritual discipline] called *Shiva Ambu* [Shiva's Water].

Nostrils Frozen:
Moraji Desai, a prime minister of India [1977 to 1979], used to drink his own, first thing in the morning.

Juice Time:
At that time, there was graffiti on public urinals everywhere: Moraji's Juice Bar.

River Me:
Aloo tikka [vegetable pieces] with the *chola* [chickpea] sauce -- made from the Mandakini River -- was enough for me.
He [an Indian] was rehydrating the sauce with river water, where they had been doing the washing, and burning [cremating] bodies.

Initial This:
I hired a Hindustan Ambassador [an automobile made in India], with a driver from Mandu [a town in central India's

Madhya Pradesh state].

We ended the day at Omkareshwar [a Hindu temple in Madhya Pradesh state, dedicated to Shiva].

The old car was in bad condition.

Frequent stops in small villages to add water to the radiator.

Wires to keep engine parts intact.

The road was a narrow tarmac. Not much traffic.

Driving was slow, but with so much to see, I didn't care.

We passed a large group of tribal people with camels. I asked my driver who they were.

"Gypsies, sir."

Perhaps they were traveling home after the Pushkar fair [a festival including camel-selling in Pushkar a town in India's western Rajasthan state].

After I sat with some *sadhus* [self-declared Hindu holy men], a fake policeman threatened to arrest me for taking drugs.

I threatened him with a violent response.

My driver calmed me down.

"Killing not good, sir!"

We ended up giving the guy a lift, and headed down the road.

Right now, I would give anything for a day like that.

Fabulously Fun:

Defense Colony [a middle and upper class New Delhi neighborhood] was such an extraordinary place to live.

I lived in an [Indian military] Brigadier General K. C. Khanna's *barsati* [rooftop] flat. Beautiful place.

Cool marble terrazzo floors. Enormous wraparound verandah.

General Khanna had an absolutely lovely wife, Mohini. I loved them both.

Very old school, impeccably educated, a son working as a diplomat, I think in Kuala Lumpur [Malaysia]. A daughter in Paris. A darling dachshund named Suzy.

Some of the retired military guys took to interesting hobbies, like one sculpting massive logs into creatures, sitting there on his little tidy lawn.

I remember admiring his creations and being invited in for tea.

So genteel, old fashioned, in a vintage, nice way.

I was a little promiscuous in those days, 1984, had a very brief fling with a fabulously handsome Afghan, Ashraf, with a big motorcycle. He was from Kabul.

He said in his days, the local boys would visit local girls in their Kabul bedrooms, have fun, and leave.

He was very sad about the Taliban's fascism that had taken over his country, with its puritanical fanaticism.

Last I heard, he headed for Germany, married, and had a kid there.

I'm glad for him.

I also had a one night stand with a [U.S.] Marine at the [American Embassy's] Marine House.

Nowhere to have fun. So we did it in the Guard House.

Problem was, I had my period, and the place looked carpet-bombed afterwards.

One New Year's Eve [in New Delhi] -- must have been 1979 after the Soviet takeover of Afghanistan -- a man, an American I think he might have been, sat alone at a nearby [restaurant] table, while I partied with one of the Oberoi kids [from the family of the Indian tycoon and owner of the Oberoi Hotel] and friends.

I sent over some champagne to the solitary man, and went to wish him, "Happy New Year."

We took a walk, sat by the pool, and chatted.

He said he was a journalist, he'd been in Kabul that afternoon.

He was ordered out of his car, and told to stand there. A Soviet soldier took aim, and he heard the bullet zing by his ear. He was told to get in the car, and leave.

He did, arriving in Delhi that day.

He was very shaken by that near-death experience.

He said he had worked in Vietnam during the [U.S.-Vietnam]

war, staying at the Hilton Hotel [in Saigon], driving to the war in the afternoon to report, and coming back to the Hilton for dinner.

He said it was disturbingly surreal, and he was used to scary, dangerous situations.

He seemed sad and jaded.

I wished him good night, and went back to my table.

Dark Talk:
I didn't care about politics, as long as politics left me alone.
I was happy to ignore it.
Still, one heard certain things.
I somehow became aware that the relative absence of street people -- in the part of New Delhi I hung around in -- was due to Mrs. Gandhi's [1975] Emergency measures.

I also became aware of some sort of special relationship between India and the Soviet Union, judging by the ingenuous tone of [India's] newspaper reports, and bits of comical English-language Soviet propaganda that kept popping up in the unlikeliest of places.

Earth Voice:
We arrived in Delhi late at night, in a pre-monsoon heat wave, in 1976.

All the hotels along the main bazaar [in Paharganj] were full, and we spent a few days searching for a place to settle down.

One day, as we fought our way again through the heat and humidity, we heard a voice calling:

"My friends! My friends!"

Looking up, we saw the only Indian person we knew -- a man who had travelled with us on the freaks' bus from Kathmandu to Delhi a few days earlier.

When we told him of our plight, he said:

"Come with me. This is my hotel."

We had helped him out with a problem he had on the bus, and in return he took us to the best room in his hotel [The

Vishal Hotel], on the rooftop, with a 360-degree view.

We ended up staying there for a month.

We used to dash down to The Metropolis [Restaurant and Guest House] between monsoonal downpours.

We lived mainly on omelettes and *chapatis* [flat bread] and jam, but could never really enjoy it because of the young beggars who would press up against the glass windows.

And of course the rats. The biggest ones I have ever seen.

I remember other people who were staying at the Vishal. There was the French junkie who slept outside our room.

He never ate, so we fed him peaches and plums that were plentiful and cheap.

One day he wasn't there when we returned from The Metropolis.

The Delhi police had raided the hotel, and found his stash.

He came back a few days later after paying *baksheesh*.

There was an Australian woman whose daughter was very sick.

We helped restrain the daughter, while her mother administered medicine three times a day -- not a pleasant experience.

Then there was another Australian, a down-to-earth guy who contracted hepatitis A.

He was convinced that a *sadhu* had put a spell on him, after he told others information that the *sadhu* said he shouldn't divulge.

He was put on a flight home after we contacted the Australian Embassy.

We also knew a lot of other travelers who ended up in Delhi at the same time.

Most of them stayed at a hotel down the road -- probably the Vivek.

Night Skin:

I think it was Mr. Jain's [Guest House in New Delhi] where the cockroaches gave me a pedicure during the night.

I woke up, and the dead skin on my feet was chewed off.

Under the Galata Bridge:
You left out -- hanging at The Cellar [disco] downstairs, on the [Connaught Place] circle, and changing money in Mohan Singh Market Shop 23 with Doctor, or going to *subzi mundi* [a vegetable market] to buy my morphine.

Eggs Spaghetti:
And the *char* anna [four anna, less than one rupee] *tongas* [horse-drawn carriages] up Qutab Road, when I came in from Old Delhi [to Connaught Place, also known as Connaught Circle] for ham from The Empire Stores, a pint of milk from The English Dairy, or a great massage for one rupee on the grass park in the middle of Connaught Circle.

Beetroot Voice:
I remember tinned ham and cheese.
And gray sliced bread.
What a treat after months on the road.

Eggs Spaghetti:
They had real cut ham, and sold the ends for a lower price.
So I'd buy a few ounces, bread and butter, and make a sandwich to nosh while I awaited my massage.

Persian Indian:
We grew up on Empire Stores' ham and sausages.
How the world has changed. Now I can order Belgian pork and Spanish ham from my phone, while a large part of the country outside still goes to sleep hungry, sadly.

Unkempt Rocking:
One Saturday evening [in 1971], a bunch of us hired a taxi and headed over to the New Delhi Hilton, where we entered the discotheque they had there.

We were a rather shaggy, unkempt gang, but because we were white -- I guess -- they allowed us inside.

The decor was very plush, as you'd expect.

There was a bar, I believe non-alcoholic, but don't recall exactly.

And a dance floor.

And flashing lights, with smartly dressed young Indian boys and girls having a merry time, dancing to the latest top 10 hits from Britain and America.

Above the dance floor, there was a balcony area where the parents of the teenagers -- even more smartly dressed, and the women mostly pretty chubby, wearing expensive silks and dripping with jewelry -- sat sipping drinks and beaming down on their darling progeny partying below.

We scored a few Cokes and then hit the dance floor ourselves.

The whole scene felt quite surreal after the stoned out shabbiness of The Crown, and the streets of Old Delhi, but still we had a great time.

Good to be rocking to the sounds from back home, even though they didn't play any Jimi [Hendrix], or Pink Floyd, or Grateful Dead.

Totally Challenging:
Usually it was ABBA or Boney M, at least during the early 1980s.

I went to a few, but never high-end joints.

Indian boys -- Kashmiris -- always invited me.

Big Bottles:
In early 1990 there was this place, 13th Mile Stone, just across the Haryana [state] border on the road to Gurgaon [on the outskirts of New Delhi].

It became the place to be, for the hip Indian crowd.

Hardly ever saw foreigners.

Foggy Rock:
It was called 32nd Mile Stone.
I remember looking for it in the winter of 1997. I vividly remember, because of the events that unfolded.

It was the most talked about, in-thing place.

I and a friend, already drunk, decided to visit from Delhi on my motorcycle, on a cold and extremely foggy winter night, in December.

After searching for the place for almost two hours, we reached a huge gate, but couldn't read the sign board because of the heavy fog.

It was the Gurgaon Police Station.

And what luck, the S.H.O. [Station House Officer] was leaving for home, after finishing his shift, and saw us right outside the cop station gate, dazed and confused.

He immediately arrested us, kept us in the cop station the whole night with petty criminals, and filed a case of drunk riding.

My father came the next morning, and bailed us out from the local district court.

No discotheques for me after that.

I stuck to [live] rock and roll gigs.

Music Charmer:
I lived in Nizamuddin East [a New Delhi neighborhood], studied music with a Dagar family [who play ancient classical *dhrupad* music and singing], heard lots of great *qawalis* [Sufi devotional songs from northern India] at the *dargah* [Sufi shrine].

Delhi was sure beautiful in 1973 and 1974.

Many concerts, great bookstores, *chaat* [snack] houses, snake charmer families at the tourist sites, and plenty of cows still wandering.

Persian Indian:
During the magical days of my childhood, I lived in a

government [employees'] neighborhood, not far away from Nizamuddin East.

Even dropped a girl, from the block, off at the Dagar Brothers' house for training in *dhrupad* once, on my Dad's scooter.

Music Charmer [laughing]:
She could've been my girlfriend.

Persian Indian:
We lived in gentle orbit around the bookshops of Khan Market.

Not just part of a city, but an entire country has gone with the wind.

We were the last generation of left-liberal socialist Indians. A small, left-leaning and educated middle class, that mostly worked for the government.

Now the middle class has exploded into millions, who work in the private sector, and are crass consumerists, while right-wing motherfuckers rule.

I hope India finds her soul again.

Music Charmer:
I agree with all you said.

And yes, magical and intelligent leftists, around Khan Market.

I spent so much energy trying to warn people about crass consumerism.

Nobody listened.

Glad at least some of the youth have helped keep some of the old culture alive, and interest has grown in some areas.

Eggs Spaghetti:
I drank the water straight from the [Ganges] river, at Varanasi [a Hindu holy city also known as Benares, Kasi, and Kashi], because folks claimed it could not harm me.

I reckon my guts were doing O.K. before I slurped that handful of *pani* [water] in July 1969, and they were no worse after.

I never ever made it as a religious Hindu, though.

I guess I tried in my young days, and enjoyed roaring through *bhajans* [devotional Hindu songs] like a camp-fire sing-song.

But I'm now tired of them, and would enjoy some of my childhood [Christian] hymns just as much, or more, because some of them contain great poetry.

My path has been Advaitic [Vedantic Hindu], and I soon got over any belief in blue-skinned, many-armed [Hindu] deities.

I remember once talking to a friend about the holy Ganges -- and my strange choice of drink -- and he replied:

"All rivers are holy."

That immediately felt like truth and wisdom.

Enjoy Early:

At Kharkari Ghat in Hardwar [a human cremation site in the Hindu holy city, along the Ganges River] they have an electric crematorium.

Perfect set-up.

The very fine ashes slide right down into the Ganges.

The manager told me that, unfortunately, very few people understand that this is what is needed, if India wants to keep some forest.

I asked him if they used it for the many unidentified corpses, or those of beggars, and he said that the Hardwar Corporation provides low-quality wood for those unfortunates.

Utter madness.

I told him that if I ever ended up there, he better remember that I want electric -- rather than living wood sacrificed -- to burn my dead body.

Begged Lucrative:

The caretakers of the funeral pyres, we saw them especially in Benares.

One guy -- who's job it was to smash down the burning corpse, with a long pole -- had a T-shirt on the pole, waving it across the pyre to dry.

Chants Creator:
Hardwar is the gateway to Badrinath Shrine, dedicated to [Hinduism's] Lord Vishnu, from time immemorial.
So Hardwar is attributed to Lord Vishnu.
The city of Kasi/Kashi/Varanasi/Benares is attributed to Lord Shiva.

Impressive Earth:
Could you feel it, when you stepped into the Ganges River?
When I went into that water [at Varanasi], it was like my mind was washed away.
Lost in the universe.
It was like the believing of millions of Indians over thousands years, turned to reality.
When I stepped out, I was back on earth.

Under Cat:
I went under the [Ganges] water, and when I surfaced, a dead cat floated by.
Best of health ever, since 1984.

So Invaded:
I saw Sikhs' heads on sticks in Delhi in 1984, after the assassination of Indira Gandhi.

Late Talk:
I was living in Delhi at the time, it was very scary times, and the atmosphere in those dramatic days I will never forget -- even if I was stoned at the time.

Abdul Abdul:
In 1976, my wife was seriously ill and needed surgery at

B.H.U. [Benares Hindu University's hospital].
While she was recuperating, a *sadhu* friend did rituals, where we drank Ganges water from a *lota* [a vessel with a spout].
We weren't water boilers, but no [health] problems.

Style All:
Why are you Westerners so fascinated by *sadhus*?
Most of them are not holy.

Rarely Holy:
They don't have to be holy -- they rarely are -- to be interesting.
They usually are.

Shimmering Joy:
The looks, the [hashish] smoke, the wanderings, the freedom.
Above all, the illusion of understanding each other.
These days, there's a weird merging of *Babahood* and *Rastahood*.
But alright, this is just the head-half of the story. As to the heart-half, it typically merges stuff instead.
Take your pick.

Million Million:
I had a million *chillums* with these guys.

Shimmering Joy:
In a forest *mela* [gathering] south of Londa [town] in Karnataka [state], 1978, I met this middle-aged man known as Anjuna Baba and his two young Italian girl devotees.
We sat around in a circle with a few added inquisitive *babas* [male elders], always in the same order, and the *chillum* goes around.
I decline, and pass it on, having stopped some years before.
They stare and stare [at me].
Same day, same ritual, but I change places.

One of the [Italian] girls berates me for having broken the established harmony.

Eventually, we get to some storytelling and ritual matters, in which she says:

"But when *baba* makes love to me, it's nothing physical, all spiritual!"

Next night, an Australian newcomer girl comes and lays besides the *baba*.

I eventually notice that he is fondling her in the dark, all set to go further, all fired-up.

I surprise myself, as I realize that I am standing up, pointing at and screaming to the *baba*:

"*Aur tu, koy baba nahin hote ho, par pagal kota hi!*"

He gawks at me, speechless.

I leave the holy circle.

That Italian girl told me that this *baba* liked girls, and that it was O.K. with them both, even after I had tried to explain just what a *sadhu* was meant to be.

She also affirmed that her proof -- that this *baba* was very especially spiritual -- was the fact that so many other *babas* came to sit around in his *mandal* [circle], attracted by his power.

The mind boggles.

Complicated Incarnation:

Sex is complicated everywhere, with so-called religious people.

In Hindu mythology, there are a few occurrences of a respected saint -- a *rishi, mahatma,* whatever -- jumping on a girl and raping her.

When asked the reason of the rather irreligious act, he will explain that he saw a great invisible soul in search of an incarnation [wanting to reincarnate through an available fertilized ovum].

Nothing to do but help, of course.

On the other end, I knew a young *sadhu* that went crazy, because he had sex repeatedly with a Western woman.

Shimmering Joy:
So many weird or laughable -- take your pick -- stories between *babas* and Western girls.

How many *sadhus* who suddenly regretted to have chosen the *sanyas* [renunciation] path?

How many did suffer anguish and guilt for their forbidden desires?

We will never know.

It is mostly involving a deep misunderstanding between the two cultures. But emotive projection works wonders, and the rationalizing mind always manages to seal and cover the gaps somehow.

Easily, sleazily, done.

It must have been a sort of a status symbol for many hippie girls to be seen with a *sadhu* as a regular fixture.

And then *Bhagwan Shree* Rajneesh [Blessed One, Sir Rajneesh, a guru popular among Westerners and also known as Osho] burst upon the scene, all set for stardom divine.

Complicated Incarnation:
Some Western women sleeping with *sadhus* were spending years in sacred places.

They just fell in love, and some beautiful young *sadhus* couldn't resist.

It was not a difference in culture.

Christian monks and priests had the same issues.

Some still have.

There was a strong link between Goa and the Rajneesh *ashram* in Poona [a city near Bombay].

Lots of so-called Tantric sex [Hindu and Buddhist mystical sex and yoga meditation] and drugs, in both places.

The Heart:
Babas will be *babas*, and do what *babas* do.

[Someone displays a photograph of a naked *sadhu*, smoking a *chillum*]

Sky Sex:
He is called Shiv Raj.
I met him at the 2010 *Kumbh* [the *Kumbh Mela* is a Hindu festival on the Ganges River, attracting hundreds of thousands of devotees] in Hardwar.
He has a friend with elephantitis, and loves Ganesh [Hinduism's elephant-headed god].
God-consciousness has no time for modesty.
I guess that's the point of the *Digambara*, or Sky Clad Ones.
I hung out with them for a couple of days, until he asked me to have sex with him!

Chants Creator:
What?
Are you standing up for him, when he asked you a favor, to sleep with him, when you were hanging with their group?
Who cares if he is a Sky Clad One, or a *Digambara*, or a guru, or any other million sects of *sadhus* out there.
If he cannot have the scruples to act in a right manner towards women -- boom -- everything goes out of the window, and to the drain, along with their values.
They are just ordinary humans, with vices, hoodwinking gullible people, and taking advantage.
That's all there is to it.
Enjoy a free *chillum*, chit chat, have tea, and be respectful, and leave without a care in the world -- is what I do.

Sky Sex [to Chants Creator]:
Loads of men ask me to sleep with them.
Seems absolutely normal to me.
Sometimes I even say yes!
I've even got a daughter.
Sex is real, yo!

I met him, and hung out, because I liked him.
He seemed interesting and unusual.
I was attracted, but at that time celibate.
He obviously isn't.
No biggie -- though it ain't small!

Chants Creator:
There is absolutely nothing wrong in it.
Getting to know as friends, and suggesting sex as fun, is one thing.
But then hiding behind holy and ochre robes, acting pious and godly, and asking the female devotees for sex, is totally a different thing [laughs].
So much for being a guru [laughs].
Sorry to hear that.
Most of these so-called holy men act so godly, only to commit unscrupulous acts against consent, and hide behind their saffron colors and holy powders.

Sky Sex:
Well, he did seek consent.
I replied, "No."
He asked why.
"Because I am a holy woman," I replied.
And he said, "And I am a holy man."
So there we are.
And I don't think there is anything unholy about sex myself. I just wasn't feeling it.
He is, I think, properly into his trip.
He initiated me, and I stood on one leg holding that *trisul* [a trident, also held by Vishnu, a Hindu god] -- while reciting the *Gayatri* mantra [chants dedicated to a Hindu goddess, Gayatri].
But the *baba* business is a bit of a side show, and it wasn't for me.
I think he puts the hours in, if you know what I mean.
A show off, but not a charlatan.

Chants Creator:
Well, open communication and consent is all that matters.
If he can respect consent, and boundaries, and can accept "no" as an answer, then all good.
But sadly in India, it never so happens with men.
It's a sad state of affairs with rape, and especially with violence against women.

Big Bottles:
He [Shiv Raj] loves his foreigners.
Gives him status.
He is such a showoff.
Thrives on attention.

Strange Mountains:
The naked [*sadhus*] are called Sky Clad, and are considered as innocent and pure as little children.
It is usually considered a blessing to see these saints.

Mystical Tantric:
I had some luck. A month with a *Mouni baba* [a devotee of Mouni Baba, born in Kerala, who stayed in *Mouni* -- mystical silence -- for 50 years] at Kyelang [in Himachal Pradesh's Himalayas].
And then, three months in a *Tantric ashram*, between Nagwa and Assi Ghat [in Varanasi].

Strange Mountains:
Sadhus seldom have rules beyond those they impose upon themselves, unless they belong to a *sampraday* [spiritual tradition] that demands certain standards.
Nagas [naked sadhus] are not known for sexual purity.
Nor is it asked of them, usually.
It is no sin to ask a woman for sex, as long as it is not rape, and you have not taken vows to abstain.

Divine Years:
Naga is a title given after many various years of training, service, and initiations.

Not anyone has the prestige to walk freely as such [naked], and not be harassed by police.

Basically -- and this is just one sense of what it means -- it is men devoted to Mother Earth.

Their penis is no weapon, and they have mastered its control.

They do not wish to have family or procreate.

They are in service to the Divine Mother.

Big Bottles:
They are dressed -- they have their holy ashes on.

Being naked is supposed to show their detachment from material things, and things of the flesh.

Enlightenment Guy:
Are regular Indians totally blasé about it?

Or are they similarly shocked that a dude is walking around with his *dong* hanging out?

Is the shock value an intended part of the costume?

I do not have deep knowledge, but I do understand the basic idea behind these guys.

My question is how everyday Indians react to them.

Are they all fully informed and in deep awe and respect for their level of enlightenment?

Or are they like:

"Oh my fucking God, that guy is nude!"

Looks Country:
Dude, there are so many *Naga babas* in our country, and they don't give threats to anyone, and no one is afraid of them.

But yeah, some people just got scared because of their looks.

It not that easy to become *Naga*.

You have to leave everything behind, and do meditation.

So Invaded:
I think God is the ultimate illusion.
The *maya* [illusion] itself.

Sky Sex:
I've read that this world is all God's *maya*, and to experience God-consciousness, you must pierce the veil.
This can be done through years of practice, meditation, fasting, yoga, chanting, renunciation or -- since 1943 -- by taking L.S.D.
Works for me.

So Invaded:
Don't worry, my *Doors of Perception* [a book by British author Aldous Huxley, about his psychedelic experiences] were opened and closed a few times.
I even dipped in *sangam* [unity, flowing in a convergence] for *mauni amavasya* [an auspicious time during a No Moon night] -- full on peyote.

Vision 23:
It has been 41 years that I've been speaking out about sexual abuses by Tibetan lamas.
First, it was Sogyal assaulting me when I was a new Buddhist, age 22, in New York City in 1976.
I got pregnant and miscarried.
Then it was my beloved, and most deeply trusted Geshe Ngawang Dhargyey at the Tibetan Library in Dharamsala, wanting to see my 23-year-old tits.
And his indentured servant, Khedrup, constantly goosing my ass if I walked by him, while doing circumambulations around the Library.
Then it was being assaulted while I was sleeping in 1979, when I was 25, by Lama Topgyal, who had recently married a Danish woman, Pia, who was having his child in Denmark.

I was just recovering from a near fatal bout of hepatitis, and then had an ectopic pregnancy because of his assault -- which almost killed me, and basically ruined my reproductive system.

Then it was being conned into sex with His Holiness Sakya Trizin, who I'd gone to during a broken-hearted time.

I was in a five month meditation retreat, and went to Sakya Trizin, for meditation instruction.

He said he had a vision of him and me *yab-yum* [uniting wisdom and compassion through sexual intercourse], and that I must fulfill his vision tomorrow morning, in my room.

It was transparently bullshit.

His lust, and nothing else.

There were many other smaller, but ugly incidences, like Dodrubchen mash-kissing me, minutes after meeting him, with my boyfriend sitting outside.

Then mashing my hand -- holding my *mala* [Buddhist prayer beads] -- into his crotch.

The Sakya Trizin manipulation was the final straw in 1981.

I was 28 by then.

Yes, both Sogyal and Topgyal got me pregnant.

I had no idea about having sex with either of them, didn't want sex with either of them, was not remotely interested in sex with either of them.

Neither took any responsibility for the pregnancies.

Yes, Dodrubchen is a Sikkimese guy. He is a sleazy lech of a jerk.

When Lama Topgyal attacked me, I was deep asleep, alone in a room, far away from anybody hearing anything if I screamed.

He was big, strong, and fat.

He pinned me, and I just didn't feel like a fight with a person I'd been told was a realized *yogi*.

It was my religion then, Tibetan Buddhism.

I didn't think I had a right to hit him in self defense.

Sogyal had telephoned me -- saying he didn't want to talk on the phone -- when I said I had a dharma question.

Could I come to where he was staying?

I wore a floor length tent dress over a long sleeve turtleneck. My hair was recently cut below my ears.

I wore no jewelry, and went with abject devotion, to speak in person with a *rinpoche* [a respected Tibetan Buddhist teacher].

He opened the door with his shirt off, a beer in his hand, and flung a magazine on the sofa, while he spoke long distance to London.

I was completely shocked, sat down obediently, and waited.

Within a minute of his sitting next to me -- while I started to ask my questions -- he lunged at me, slobbering my face, grunting I was so special.

It felt like some 1950s redneck masher in a pickup truck.

I couldn't think straight.

I was in that devotee mindset, like a kid who sees a priest for comfort.

My heart and mind were in a trusting mindset, seeing a person who was a reincarnation of a lama, reincarnated for the benefit of all sentient beings.

Surely it was an honor just to be in his presence.

I just gave in, hating myself as I did.

Confused, disgusted but wanting to be a Tibetan Buddhist, I couldn't get out of the faith and belief bubble.

I was stuck there.

Firewood Street:
Fake *babas* wouldn't exist if there weren't also real *babas*.

Not so easy to spot maybe, especially not for happily biased Western tourists who don't really know what a *sadhu* is.

So I say:
"*Jab kuch nahin samajta, kuch nahin bolo, bhaya.*"

For a real *baba*, and devotees, the smoke of *charas* is Shiva *prasad* [a Hindu vegetarian holy offering].

Not just a means to get zonked.

Women Amazing:
Real *babas* don't hang on the tourist trail.

They sit alone in caves and meditate, not smoke all day, everyday.

Cave Wonders:
I have been to [cave complexes near Bombay] Ajanta -- once. And Ellora -- it smells like bat shit -- three times.
I have stayed for a few weeks, making yoga in the temples, and staying in the small caves up river, and smoking *chillums* with the *babas* from the Jyotirlinga Temple in Ellora village.
I found a cave, that is behind a waterfall, in the monsoon.
You could sit and chant *Om* [the sounds of the universe], and it would echo for an eternity.
The Kailash Temple is truly one of the wonders of this world.

Shimmering Joy:
I met a Ganesh Baba in Swayambhu, Kathmandu, and went to his *satsang* [gathering of seekers], for two weeks or so.
This man was a total fraud, illogical, and a sex maniac.
His foremost *chella* [disciple] was a fat Swiss girl, who literally believed that he was a reincarnation of Ganesh.
I heard that he went to the U.S.A., and kept on his women-groping game, with the pretext of initiation.

Teaching Meat:
The *Aghoris* are said to eat meat from human corpses.
If they have a teaching to give, I'll hear it.
[*Aghoris* are an extreme Tantric and Pashupata tradition of Shiva *sadhu*, who live at human cremation sites, practice cannabalism, smear their body with cremation ashes, and use a human skull as an eating bowl]

Burning Away:
Not me man. I am staying away from *Aghori babas*.
Got the full experience at the burning *ghat* in Varanasi.

Tongue Rebirth:

I imagined an *Aghori* taking from my dead body, but I felt their bites as if I were alive.

The pain was unbearable.

And then, I imagined my skull, passing to them from hand to hand, and my tongue sliding between the sutures, all over.

I felt the contact now rough, now slippery.

Just before I turned to ashes, I had experienced the untold suffering of fire.

Even when ashes were ashes, I was alive in ashes.

Scattered on their bodies, I was now suffering a new punishment.

And yet I suddenly realized that being alive entails rebirth.

And that I owed it to them.

Tranquility Twisted:

At night, I would go through the tight twisted streets of old Varanasi, to Manikarnika Ghat.

The burning charnel ground.

It's sort of taboo to go there, unless you're part of a family that's in mourning. But I stayed at the far edge, by the [Ganges] river.

There were Shiva *sadhus* there.

After a few nights of sitting quietly by myself, meditating as best I could -- one eye open because I was afraid of the dogs that were feral and ate the pieces of uncremated bodies -- a young *sadhu* befriended me over a well-packed chillum.

We traded stories of how we came to be in the most famous cremation ground on earth, in the middle of the night, smoking hashish.

He was a young kid from Bangladesh who had survived a cyclone that killed his entire family and relatives.

Villagers blown into trees naked.

Drowned in the tidal surge.

Bodies everywhere.

Cows and dead bloated water buffalo. Dogs eating carnage.

The overwhelming smell of rotting death everywhere.

He had freaked out of his mind, walking aimlessly, talking incoherently, shocked.

Some *Aghori sadhus* found him. Adopted him. Brought him to India.

In India, he took *sanyas* [renunciation] and became one of the order [of *Aghoris*].

He said he had been going insane with grief and fear of death.

The senior *sadhu* brought him to the *ghat* at night, to confront his fear and dismantle his attachment to flesh and bone, and to realize spirit as our essence.

I never felt so comfortable in another person's company, like I did sitting next to him.

He appeared fearless, and in deep serenity.

He said he came every night to the *ghat* to do his *sadhana* [spiritual practice], *pranayama* [breath control], and meditation.

He'd leave at dawn, and walk away into the smoky fog, leaving a wake of tranquility behind him.

Fragile Impermanence:
Reminds us of the impermanence of life, and how fragile it is.

Tranquility Twisted:
So fragile.
So fleeting.

Fragile Impermanence:
True.
Maya is too strong.

Touch All:
I met with *Aghoris*, and despite all those horror stories, they were taking care of the sick people, who nobody would touch.

Teaching Meat:

Has anyone else had the funny feeling of being an *Aghori* sadhu in a past life?

It explains a lot, but I don't think that scene would work out very well in America.

Smoking Lepers:

Exhaling, I passed the *chillum* to a happy leper.

His fingers were all rotted off.

White greasy ointment oozed from decaying cracks between his knuckles.

Leprosy opens the way for all sorts of damage, by killing the nerve cells that ordinarily relay pain.

Burns, cuts, and insect bites send no warning. Infection sets in.

Gangrene follows.

Fingers and toes rot away.

The nose can melt into an open sore.

Hands without fingers cannot create an airtight channel for the red-clay *chillum* smoke.

To substitute for the missing digits, the leper wore a bone pipe stem, on a thin chain, around his scrawny neck.

One end of the stem fit into the tight lower lip of the *chillum*.

The other end of the stem is inserted into toothless gums.

I hold the *chillum* upright.

It vibrates as the leper smokes and prays.

Another grizzled leper joins us [at Manikarnika Ghat], *chillum* stem hung from his neck.

Grasping his pipe stem between soiled palms, he fitted one end of the stem and *chillum* together.

The *sadhu* on his far side held the *chillum* steady.

The leper inhaled his hit.

Men muttered, *Ram. Ram. Ram.*

I'd learned to chant the name of *Rama* from the Chishti Order of Sufis, in Marin County, California, whose eclectic mix of sacred traditions belied the Order's Islamic roots, but honored the sensibilities of the hippie converts.

The leper pulled his stem off with a smile, as white goop glistened around the stubs -- where his fingers had vanished.

The *charas* went full circle, and Ram Charand [a *sadhu*] passed it to me.

At that time, science had not yet nailed down any cure or much treatment for leprosy.

Talk on the road held leprosy was contagious and passed through touch -- extending to droplets of moisture released into the air when a leper coughed.

I did not want to be exposed to leprosy.

I did not want to touch or have my lips near the *chillum*, after two lepers had hit on it.

I quietly recoiled.

Getting stoned with the *Ram bhakti yogis* suddenly shifted from being an interesting cross-cultural romp, into a life threatening experience of leprosy-roulette.

I signaled to Ram Charand to pass it on, skipping me. "None for me."

The leper looked stricken.

I shook my head as if to say, "No thank you. I've had enough to smoke."

Ram Charand saw immediately why -- and leaned over to kiss the leper's cheek.

Ram Charand said to me:

"All mans love."

I *toked* [smoked] again.

He put an arm on my shoulder, as I smoked.

"Friend. All mans love."

Ancient Connected [reading]:
This is Neem Karoli Baba [an internationally known guru], quoting the *Gita* [The *Bhagavadgita*, an ancient Hindu poem]:
"O Arjun!
"There is nothing superior to Me.
"Everything existing is connected to Me.

"Like pearls on a thread."

Think Morphed:
He [Neem Karoli Baba] morphed into this [obese] shape, by sitting too long in one position.
Not getting exercise.
I never trusted the guy after I heard he molested young followers, although he claims it was consensual.
If he was so enlightened, why would he need sex, which emits from the first *chakra* [seven centers of spiritual power in the human body]?
I think he was a fraud.

Logical Blessings:
He is an enlightened being.
He has no attachments.
Any form of sexual act was *Maharajji* [a Great King] cleaning his *karma*, that's all.
It might seem inappropriate to us, because we are limited by our separateness.
This is not something we're going to comprehend, with the logical mind.
I am not suggesting you not question others' motives.
But once you start understanding the nature of a guru, the path of *bhakti* [Hindu devotion] and so on, you'll understand that those were blessings.

Think Morphed:
I just get a creepy feeling about him.
He always looks like he needs a good wash.

Healing Imagination:
I'd be dead if it wasn't for him.
In this life, I was born after he died.
But when I was going to kill myself, he came to me in my imagination, crying my own tears for me, and then I burst into

healing tears and cried for an hour.

I was in public, but nobody noticed.

Afterward I felt like a million *bucks*.

It wasn't like I chose for him to appear in my imagination.

It just happened.

Think Morphed:

He [Neem Karoli Baba] actually admitted to having sex with followers.

Lots of them.

The whole *chakra* thing is to bring your mind out, and up -- to the higher *chakras* -- to find Nirvana.

If you stay in the sex *chakra*, you hold yourself back.

I absolutely love sex, but not sex abuse.

Trust Bound:

I don't trust gurus anymore, because of this.

A guru is bound to try and fuck you, or your girlfriend.

Chants Creator:

In his book *Be Here Now* [by Richard Alpert, also known as Baba Ram Dass], he talks about his experience with Neem Karoli Baba, and how he gives him Owsley's acid tabs [L.S.D.], and the Baba remains unaffected by it.

Easily Real:

The guru [Neem Karoli Baba] took one hit of acid, and it appeared not to have any real effect, implying the guy was so spiritual.

But his assistant later told people he [Neem Karoli Baba] had just palmed it.

Old guru tricks, eh?

I hasten to add I have a lot of time for Alpert -- Ram Dass.

But like so many people, who are searching for something, he was easily fooled by those he thought had it.

Established Thriving:
For sure.

All that glitters is not gold. I think the Westerners were extremely naive, with idealistic notions of the mystic East.

They were also frequently very stoned.

Neem Karoli Baba really was an authentic *sadhu*, a Hanuman [a Hindu semi-divine monkey-like being] devotee.

But he allowed, and encouraged, the Westerners to revere him as the guru of gurus.

There were a lot of perks, including the adoring attention of all those beautiful free-spirited hippie women.

The other *yogis* [doing yoga meditation] in *Be Here Now* -- Bhagavan Das the *kirtan* [chanting] master, and especially Baba Hari Dass the silent *sadhu*, who later established a thriving yoga community in the U.S. -- impress me a lot more.

Late Talk:
Did anyone of you meet *baba* Bom Shankar in India or Nepal?

I first met him at Swayambhu [the Buddhist Swayambhu Temple, also known as The Monkey Temple, on Kathmandu's outskirts], and later stayed at his temple in Ajmer [a city in India's western Rajasthan state], and travelled around a bit with him and a Burmese guy.

It was in 1978 or 1979.

Slinging Woman:
Yes in Ibiza [an island off Spain's east coast], a Spanish woman brought him over.

He felt like a caged pet, and made it to England.

He stayed a while with friends in Wiltshire [a county in southwest England].

They took him to the local pub, where he started slinging darts around.

He was ejected.

And they put up a sign above the bar:

NO FAKIRS.

Late Talk:
I remember the Spanish lady who took him to Spain.
I met her in Pushkar.

Slinging Woman:
I don't remember her.
I did like Bom Shankar, he made me laugh. What a character.
I heard he died.
[displays a photograph]
He looks completely out of it in this photo.

Late Talk:
I tried to track him down in 2008 in Ajmer, but was told he died.
Not surprising really, he led a hard life.
His real name was Sampath Nath.
I knew him well, and he showed me his passport, and together with him we met the Spanish lady.

Strange Mountains:
How great to hear all these stories about Nath Bom Shankar.
He is buried in the traditional *Nath* way [Nath is an itinerant, medieval *sadhu* sect worshipping Shiva, mixed with Buddhist and yoga traditions] at his place Nath Ki Bagichi, in Ajmer.
He sheltered me there, during very dark days.
Put some flowers and hash for him, on his grave, if you are passing through town.
The new *mahant* [a devout Hindu in charge] of the place is young, strict, and quite nice.
He had Bom Shankar dug up, and moved into the back lot for disreputable *Naths*.
Jasper Newsome was his sidekick.
They were equally mad, bad, and great to know.
I did not know him in those early days when he went to

Spain, and travelled the entire way without a passport.

He really was a king of the road.

He dedicated his life to the *Nath* principle of *Sahaja* [a Hindu and Tibetan Buddhist meditation and yoga, to awaken internal Kundalini energy and experiences].

And he did it to the hilt.

There is a famous photo taken by Ira Cohen.

His [Bom Shankar's] head is shaved, and he has his tongue reaching into the skull of his great teacher, Parasnath -- taken in the [human cremation] burning ground.

Parasnath once tied him to a tree for two years.

Late Talk:
I've seen that photo.

He showed it to me at his temple, and his *baba* Parasnath was there, so it can't have been his skull.

He was a wild one, but there was also another side to him.

He was like a father to me, and tried his best to advise me, so I would stay safe.

Strange Mountains:
I would say exactly the same about him, both the wildest and the kindest, and even fatherly man, with edges of course.

How wonderful that you met Parasnath.

I wonder who's skull that was, because it was the only time I ever saw his head shaven, for part of the death ritual for very close relatives or the guru.

Late Talk:
I don't know whose skull it was, but I stayed a few times at the temple, and Parasnath was there.

I once witnessed him expelling a demon from a village woman.

Strange Mountains [laughing]:
Naths are never far from magic.

That must have been quite the scene.
He was always deadly serious, under the wildness.
He gave excellent advice.
I am so enjoying our conversation.
I wish we could meet in a *chai* shop on the road, and chat the way only strangers on the road can chat.

Late Talk:
Yes, that would be great.
It was Parasnath who treated the woman with the demon.
A friend of mine -- who was speaking Hindi fluently -- translated the whole thing to me and yes, it was very dramatic.

Strange Mountains [laughing]:
I am also a *Nath*, which was one of our connections, although different branches [sects].
Jasper and Bom Shankar actually initiated me into his *panth* [spiritual path] one drunken afternoon in a hilarious, but completely valid, ceremony.
They did it to bring me into the [Hindu] mainstream, enough to travel among them with a veneer of respectability.
So rich in ironies, I could die laughing.
I knew a young *Nath* who seemed to have spent a good deal of his youth with a band of monkeys.
He taught them to smoke *chillums*, and they protected him from the human race.

Early Sight:
He [Bom Shankar] was my friend in Kashmir [a northwest state in the Himalayas], in the early 1970s.
We walked to Amarnath Cave [a Hindu temple in Kashmir] together.
He took me to Ajmer, his home town.
He always was fun to be with.
I lost sight of him after 1975 in Goa.
Rest in peace, Bom Shankar.

Big Bottles:
I think during the 1960s, into the late 1980s, Kashmir was the place to be.

Lazing on the lake, smoking good dope, eating great food.

Even the poorest hippie got treated like royalty, waited on hand and foot.

It was truly paradise.

Houseboat Beautiful:
One afternoon [on Dal Lake, Srinagar, in Kashmir], the local barber was going from houseboat to houseboat.

Rapunzel -- the beautiful blonde New Yorker I was traveling with -- created quite a stir, and attracted a lot of attention, by pulling up her ankle-length skirt, and having the barber shave her legs.

Which he did.

Initial This:
How many of you met *hijras* [eunuchs] on your travels?

I usually found them to be very friendly with a good sense of humor.

Hijras, as one *sadhu* told me, are neither man nor woman.

Always ready for a good time.

They told me for 100 rupees, they would make sure I had an interesting experience.

On the advice of my trusted associate, Fritz the Cat, I declined their most gracious offer.

One of them, clearly disappointed, blew a kiss as we walked away.

At the *Kumbh Mela*, Allahabad [Uttar Pradesh state], 2001.

Later in the day, while expressing the opinion I had missed out on a unique experience, I asked Fritz what he thought they would have shown me, and should we look for them the next day?

"You are sick," came the reply.

"Are all Americans like you?"

Very People:
I liked them.
The ones I met have been very beautiful people.

Secret Nervous:
I have some film of two of them dancing [as entertainers] at a wedding procession, somewhere near villages near Rawalpindi [a city in Pakistan].

Not being used to film, they held their poses for a few seconds.

It was my first trip in 1968, and I was unaware of their lifestyle.

All part of a massive learning curve for me.

Music Charmer:
There were *hijra* folks living in my neighborhood in Varanasi during 1969 to the 1980s.

All very nice, solid people.

I saw them daily in their lives, out of costume.

Persian Indian:
I was once at the I.S.B.T. -- Inter-State Bus Terminus -- in north Delhi, and had to go to the washroom, where there were a bunch of five guys.

Young lumpens.

There I was. Young too.

A *hijra* in a pink *salwar* suit -- a women's dress of baggy trousers and tunic -- walked in, and the men laughed.

The jokes became pushes and prods and then intrusive mock gropes.

As she-he pushed them away, the jokes became curses, and then the gropes became punches, and they started beating the crap out of her-him.

At risk to myself, I came in the way and yelled at them.

They decided not to escalate the situation by bashing up a *sahib* [a man of status], as I obviously was, and sullenly turned away.

The *hijra*, with bleeding lip and swelling eye, quietly did a *namaste* to me and went away.

Since then I haven't found them creepy.

Just victims.

It's because of Islam that *hijras* are considered a good omen at weddings and births.

Because they are pure of the original sin.

Initial This:

One way to become a *hijra* is to go through a ceremonial castration.

It can happen during or after childhood. Genitalia is removed in a crude operation.

In the following days, hot oil is poured over the wound, as a vaginal type opening is formed.

When I talk about *hijras*, it is this subsection I consider the real *hijras*.

Many became sex workers, catering to men with those tastes.

In this day and age, it [castration] would hardly be the practice.

It is mostly babies -- born that way -- handed over to them [*hijras*].

Their funeral ritual, to the pyre, is quite intense.

The corpse is walked there, being beaten ritually by the procession, so the soul is not reborn as a eunuch in its next birth.

My film-maker friend, Saba, has written a detailed and researched book on the surviving *tawaifs* -- courtesans, dancing girls -- of north India.

They were definitely high-end sex workers, but educated from birth to offer more than that.

Urbane conversation, Indian classical dance and music, and so on. The closest parallel would be Japanese geisha.

But once India fell to the British crown after the [Indian anti-British] Mutiny, unlike previous Britishers who went native with *nautch* [dancing] girls, they [British colonialists] looked at them through the lens of Victorian morality as prostitutes and nothing more, and forced them to mostly shut shop.

Fortress Hovel:
In the notorious Cage District on Bombay's Fauklin Road, impoverished female and eunuch prostitutes displayed themselves in shop fronts, behind vertical bars.

It resembled jail cells because there were no glass windows.

The metal bars enabled them to reach out and touch inquisitive men who stopped and stared at them along the busy street.

Romance:
The Third Sex, they say.

My encounters with them have been brief, but I'm told they used to be a respected group, especially in Moghul India [16th to 19th century].

The British, of course, turned them into outcasts.

But I believe that may be changing.

They have the ability to give [Hindu] blessings, and their history, like most things in India, is fascinating.

The story is they were blessed by [Hinduism's] Lord Rama.

Believe Good:
At a [Indian] train station -- don't remember which one -- I was having a good time with them, and an Indian man broke up our communication.

He tried to make me believe they were dangerous.

Dancing Nowadays:
I've encountered some in the Bombay red-light district.

I went there once for the experience with Indian friends at night time.

The *hijra* smiled at me and made dancing moves.
I liked them.
Later on, I learned in documentaries about their position nowadays, in India and Pakistan.

Big Bottles:
A friend of mine made a very good movie documentary on them, it won many awards.
It's called *Between the Lines: India's Third Gender.*
Look it up.

Struggle Roots:
I witnessed how they extorted a restaurant of a famous chain in Amritsar.
They threatened to enter the place and bother the people, they yelled at the headwaiter at the door, put out some drama, took some money and left.
The headwaiter was begging for them not to enter.
Being a *hijra* -- and hermaphroditism has deep religious roots in Hinduism -- if they would decide, they can very well put out a good show.
People tend not to mess with them.
That means, we can say that they are somehow privileged, comparing to their Western counterparts.
But I can understand their behavior. They must have their own reasons to make their way in the society.
Life is harsh on them, especially in India.
They just struggle to make their way.

Initial This:
Hijras at a carnival beckoned seductively, wandering ascetics and beggars accepted donations, pilgrims added color, men with trained monkies, and snake charmers, worked the crowds during October and November 1998, at the Pushkar Camel Fair.
Legs withered from childhood polio, a man made his living

begging in the street.

As people pitched a few coins or grains of rice, his parrot would hop over to collect them.

As a result of vaccination programs from the W.H.O. [the United Nations' World Health Organization] and the Indian government, polio is now a rare disease in India.

Strange Mountains:
Pushkar is an ancient pilgrimage town, which always makes a place very special, and with special demands on the visitors to remain conscious of where they are, and what they are doing.

Many people are spit out of such places, or run for their lives.

If you love Pushkar, Pushkar loves you first.

Late Talk:
I remember staying in Pushkar in 1978, before all the hotels and shops.

I'd been staying in temples for a while, when I decided to move out to the Samsan Ghat, the place where they burn the dead.

I don't remember why, but it must have been on a spiritual quest.

The only other living person there was a man suffering from leprosy, so we would share our meals together.

How long I stayed, I don't remember.

Maybe only a few days.

But I moved when I got word that my brother had sent me some money to a bank in Bombay.

So onwards to Bombay, with very little money in my pocket.

Under the Galata Bridge:
At The Lotus Social Club [an opium den in Bombay] on Bapti Road, off Shuklaji Street in the 1970s, Rasheed -- the owner -- was my friend.

Bringing Westerners for a kickback, was part of my hustle

back then.

He even let me live free in an apartment downstairs, with my wife and son.

One time, we were hiding out from the police, for a traveler's checks scam.

I was even one of the few Westerners that could roll my own [opium] pipe, a craft that became quite useless as I got clean off all substances in 1982.

Strange Mountains:
That was a famous place.
You [Under the Galata Bridge] are such a former scoundrel, we must have known each other back in the day.
I was the perfect mark. [laughs]

Squalid Dreams:
I remember going with a friend.
Not partaking.
No so-called beautiful dreams.
It was just a surprisingly squalid and unromantic affair.

Solemn and Respectful:
When we would leave the one [opium den] in Bombay, and ride a horse-drawn carriage back to The Carlton [Hotel] at dawn, I felt it was unbelievably romantic.
I still describe it as such.
Crossing Bombay at dawn, 1970, from Kamatipura Road.
The best.

Pillow Thought:
Never thought I could handle the [opium den's] wooden pillow.

Survival Uprisings:
After the first *toke*, it's quite comfortable.

Pillow Thought:
Indeed.
You forgot all about it.

Gentler Ooze:
Shuklaji Street, Kareem Lala's place.
Damn fine stuff.
The thick syrupy opium came in a square little bamboo dish, maybe a centimeter in diameter.
The handler would dip a metal stick into the ooze, and roll it over the flame, until it hardened into a [miniature] donut, which he then stuck onto the pipe and gave it to the user, ready to smoke.
The user then held the pipe over the flame and inhaled deeply.
As opium is a cough suppressor, one could easily inhale and hold a large quantity of smoke.
All the dens were [later] closed down by government order, to be replaced by Brown Sugar heroin from Pakistan and Afghanistan.
End of a gentler era.

History Great:
Great bit of history.

Street Life:
Such a vivid memory.
The scariest moment of my life happened a few minutes before, when we walked into the brothel across the street by accident.

Strange Mountains:
There was a ladies' [opium] den in Bombay.
Not much different, but they put flower-printed cushions and cheap calendars and carpets -- instead of cardboard and newspapers -- as decor.

It was all laughs for us, but these [opium addicts] came to a bad end.

Life has to be awful, and miserable, to get caught up with opium.

Puking and constipation is just too high a price for an evening of fun.

The dreams are lovely.

I think it is easy to go either direction, when faced with a dire necessity.

The poppy is a wonderful medicinal plant, but needs to be respected, and used with care.

Touch Stuff:
Five days on the good stuff [opium] in Benares.
Started *chucking* [vomiting].
Stopped. And didn't touch it since.

Gentler Ooze:
There were dens all over Mother India.
Mostly, but not all, were run by Muslims.
I went to a Hindu one in Rajasthan, where each time someone exhaled, the whole den would yell:
Om Namah Shivaya [Praise Lord Shiva]!
I was a student in Bangalore, and there were two [opium dens] we knew of.
One was in the city market.
But the one we mostly frequented was on Slaughterhoue Road, behind the abatoir, adjacent to Russell Market.
We'd take our guitars and such, and a bottle of *Hercules XXX Rum* for the manager.

Solemn and Respectful:
I can smell it.
So earthy.
So deep.
So ready to take you.

The little copper or *mahjong* tiles [from a Chinese game], that it was served on.
The long needle.
Filling the bowl.
Poking the boiling, black tar.
The first, long draw.
Oh yes.

Smelled Death:
I didn't like the smell of opium smoke.
Smelled like death.
Many folks seemed to like it though.

Street Lost:
Shuklaji Street.
Lost time down there.

Leaving Out:
After leaving, out on the street, *chucking* up in the gutter.

Never Gets:
Never move.
Stay put.
It's the getting up that gets you.

Peanut Horse:
I used to go there [The Lotus Club] after a 37-hour journey in a train from Delhi, have a few cups of *chandoo*, and then take a horse-pulled carriage back to Colaba [a Bombay neighborhood popular with travelers] across the entire city.
Stoned like a peanut.

Eat Rural:
When attending an opium ceremony outside Jodhpur [a city in Rajasthan state] a few years back, there they drank the opium water.

In most parts of rural Rajasthan, they tend to eat little crystallized sweetened nuggets of it.

Strange Mountains:
I heard that when the *Panchayat* -- five worthy men who rule each village -- meet in Rajasthan, by law they must consume the water made from soaking the dried pods of the poppy.
It is surprisingly strong.
Opium is water soluble.

Cool Ritual:
It is their ritual for their guest and friends.
This ritual's name is *Amal ka Dastoor* [The Opium Ritual].
They crush opium poppy with water, and then mix up and filter, and then they drink it.
Kinda cool.
They create an opium water tea.

The Pudding:
Did you ever lose important stuff --- documents or money -- or perhaps get robbed?
Thankfully it never happened to me, but a few times I met travelers who claimed they had been robbed.
Maybe they had just spent all their money.
Anyway, I used to worry a bit -- especially since there was then no embassy I could go to -- how I would survive.

Running Myself:
Never. And I travelled so many times by myself in India and Asia.
Once I bought a bus ticket in Rajasthan.
An Indian man was running behind me. I thought, just another one asking, "Where are you from? Are you married?"
But no, he insisted, because I forget my wallet, and he wanted to give it back to me.

Late Talk:
I lost my passport two times.
I was a bit wild in those days.
I stayed a long time without a passport, and in the end got my hands on a passport -- not mine -- but close enough.

Nearly Spaced:
I nearly always found Indian people to be so trustworthy and kind.
I walked off and left my passport and money bag behind many, many times -- spaced-out kid that I was -- and had people running after me to give it back to me.
Once I left it on the train, which then left the station, but again I got it back intact.
Did once get ripped off by the dodgy travelers' check-changing guys, though.

Shopkeeper's Daughter:
I also got ripped off once by a money-changing guy in [Old Delhi's] Red Fort.
We were with a friend, newly arrived in India, who insisted he had to change money on a Sunday when our regular guy wasn't working.
I knew it was a bad idea, but thought because there were three of us, it would be O.K.
It wasn't.
Within seconds of him handing over the money we had already counted, he got up and ran.
He had done the old trick of switching the notes inside for paper.
The only time, ever, I was ripped off changing money. And should have known better.
In Patna Airport [in the capital of eastern India's Bihar state], flying from Kathmandu with friends, we went to a cafe in the tiny airport, and spent about an hour there eating some Indian food.

Just such a buzz being back in India.

We left the airport to go to town in a cycle rickshaw.

When half-way there, another rickshaw caught us up. We had left a bag with an expensive camera, lenses and film, and they were bringing it to us.

The same guys who we had refused to sell our Scotch and cigarettes to, because we knew we could get a better price.

Most people in India are honest.

It was often the other travelers who were not.

Natives Invited:

I was glad the natives in India were friendly and welcoming to me, although I slept rough sometimes.

I never had to beg.

I was invited.

Those Western junkies were just careless. As careless as they are towards their companions in the West.

I myself never had problems with any Indians, Nepalese or Thais.

Body Target:

We weren't rich.

We lived on a very meager budget of about one dollar a day.

Village Damage:

I lived in a [Indian] village for years.

There were [foreign] people back then that wanted to see as many places as possible, but I preferred knowing one place really well, and learning the language.

The village has changed so much now. They said to me that the village life I knew no longer exists.

It is still nice, but all the fluorescent lights -- and the decimation of local occupations -- is very sad.

The environmental damage really upsets me as well.

Anywhere Main:

It seemed to be O.K. to go [to the toilet in public in India] anywhere.

I once saw a man taking a dump on the main street in Calcutta.

Initial This:
That was me!
I went under a bridge in Delhi.
No option.
Asked my friend to keep guard.
As soon as I squatted, there was a crowd. The typical right-in-your-face stare, hands clasped behind their backs, slack-jawed, buck teeth.
I complained to my friend, but he said the people loved me.
"You're the most interesting thing they've seen all day."
So, I went about my business. When finished, I offered the used paper.
"Oh, no thank you!"

Naked and Barefoot:
It can be a bit of a shock to see.
I remember on the overland trip, starting with Afghanistan to Pakistan and to India, it was a very common thing to witness this happen, in any city or town.

Loved Maybe: I left England with the intention of traveling overland around the world with no money, starting with Africa.
One year later, I arrived in India by boat where I was ripped off.
I got *hep* [hepatitis].
I flipped out.
I travelled around for a few years.
Later I got strung out [addicted to drugs].
I was jailed for eight-and-a-half months, and eventually I was kicked out.
Still it was a fantastic trip.

And I met some really beautiful women.

The Pudding:
Anyone ever spent a night at a train station?
To save money, I guess, I once stayed overnight at the Bombay [Victoria Terminus] train station.
At one point, I looked up and there were hundreds of rats running along the beams.
Yikes.

Truly Overflowing:
I stayed at the Bombay station, and had the same rat story.
I also woke needing to crap.
Overflowing toilets, and no other options, I squatted and took a dump in the gutter right outside the main entry at 8-ish a.m.
Made me feel truly Indian.

Sleeping Forest:
I remember being [in a train station] somewhere in Karnataka [a southern Indian state], nice and snug in my sleeping bag.
Upon waking, there were like a 100 people in a huge circle, squatting down staring at the weird foreigner.
Such is India.

Lovely Railway:
Me too. Many time I spend time in railway.
Waiting train from north to south.
Hundred people around me.
Nobody hurt me.
I was always helped.
Lovely country.

Train Rotting:
I arrived in Ahmedabad [a city in Gujarat state, western

India] and turned left, thus accepting my life with Kathman-don't.

I was tired of riding in the luggage rack of the train car, where below was the corpse of an old Muslim man, surrounded by many wives and children, and thankfully, many flowers which helped death be sweet.

I was not alone in the rack.

My fellow traveler and I slept like two kitchen chairs, stacked on each other -- with our heels at each other's necks -- the dirty socks' perfume mixing with the aroma of patchouli, rotting human flesh, fear sweat, and the excrement bucket.

Such be the pleasures of a 3rd class express train car in India, early 1960s.

Cows' Warmth:
I slept out at Old Delhi train station.
Loads of people sleeping among the numerous cows.
Cows were good for warmth.

Once Upon a Time:
In Pakistan, on the way from Karachi to Lahore, we didn't know that the trip will be so long.

We were very tired to be in the train, and decided to go off, at an unknown town in the middle of the night.

Four girls.

At the small and empty station, we were sitting on the floor, just happy we could stretch legs and lie down.

A man came to us with a huge key and made a sign to follow him.

Two of us did it, and he showed a big room with benches around, and a door to toilets.

Then he show the key and made a gesture to close the main door with it.

We ran out, convinced that he will lock us inside, and who knows what will happen to us?

So we declined very strongly and firmly his offer.

We slept on the dirty floor outside that room, to find out the next morning that it was the Ladies' Waiting Room, by that time full with kids and ladies.

Once upon a time on the hippie trail, there I was, a beautiful young woman, naive, fearful, and confident at the same time.

Reed Times:

Yes I loved my times in Bombay that way, sleeping on my reed mat, and Dutch army sleeping bag as mattress, and my shoulder bag as pillow.

Quite a few times -- in Bombay Victoria [Terminus] station the most -- because hotel prices in Bombay were through the roof, compared to other cities.

Fond Mornings:

I lived there for two weeks in 1977, for the same reason.

Rooms in Bombay were so expensive and disgusting for the price.

I slept on my Goa beach mat, with a large group of other homeless characters.

Very safe and cool.

Chai [milk tea] served to us in the mornings.

They even had showers, and we would leave our bags with the *beedie walla* [seller of tiny cigarettes] during the day.

Fond memories.

Clean Squat:

I slept there, a few nights broke, before found a better spot to squat -- the Central Library porch by night.

The park in front by day.

Luggage in deposit at railway station. One rupee a day charge.

Cheap food also good in Victoria Terminus station restaurant.

And possible to take shower -- even without a booked ticket

-- and go to a clean toilet.

Peanuts All Rough:
I slept rough for almost a year, all around India.
Railway stations, parks, Sikh temples, safe streets.
No money for hotels or much food at 17, but survived on lots of *chai*, *charas*, bananas, *chapati*, and peanuts.

Enjoy Early:
We stayed for five days in the 2nd class waiting room, in Victoria Terminus station in Bombay in February 1968, with quite a few other freaks.
Fairly luxurious in those days.

Heart Unprepared:
On my third trip, mid-1980s, I flew into Bombay with my very beautiful, blonde-haired, blue-eyed girlfriend.
Being from a wealthy North London Jewish background, she was ultra-liberal, until she'd spent a couple of hours being surrounded by dozens of gawping Indian men every time she tried to leave the hotel.
All's well that ends well -- I took her down to Kerala [a southwest state] and Mahabalipuram [a town in south India's Tamil Nadu state], where things were much cooler.

Wondering Yes:
In the old days, I used to like Delhi a lot.
New Delhi with its open spaces and parks, the Handicraft Emporiums, and the Tibetan market on Janpath.
The Indian Coffee House, and it's waiters with big turbans, and white uniforms with red trims.
And the Sikhs driving their Harley Davidson motorcycle rickshaws [taxis] -- between Connaught Place and Old Delhi, to the Red Fort, Jama Masjid [mosque], Chandni Chowk [a main street], the *gurdwara* [Sikh temple] near the fountain, and all the winding little lanes to get lost in.

Living on the roof of The Crown Hotel was like sailing on a ship above the rooftops of the city.

You could see the Indian life happening, on the roofs all around.

People washing. Eating. Sleeping. Kids flying kites.

Marriage parades on the street down below, with the bridegroom riding on a white horse, and a brass band playing hilarious music.

Coolies carrying gas lamps on their heads, to light up the show.

I read *Lord of the Rings* trilogy there, for the first time in 1968.

It somehow fit in with the time and place.

Junkie Crown:
Never stayed in Old Delhi, but I did visit The Crown once.
It had the reputation of being a junkie hotel.

Nearly Spaced:
I took my mother to the Taj [the Taj Mahal in Agra city] in the mid-1980s.

We took a cycle rickshaw and arrived before dawn and -- luckily I could speak Hindi -- managed to persuade the guards to let us in, before opening time, so we had the place to ourselves for awhile.

Serene and peaceful. So beautiful.

On the way, we heard the first cry of a newborn baby, coming from a shanty hut built of flattened oil tins and cardboard boxes, on the pavement.

The rickshaw *walla* [worker] turned to us and said:

"A child born in India is a child born into hell."

I've never forgotten.

Romance:
Charming.

Hard Boot:

I lived in Calcutta for nearly two years, and it is still my favorite Indian city.

Arts, politics, and music are still strong.

No aircon in 1968. A ceiling fan when lucky.

One got used to it.

In Old Delhi, when staying at The Crown, I'd buy a whole slab of ice and put it under the fan.

Aircon.

Romance:
Calcutta is pretty harsh for me.

Chants Creator:
The poet [Allen Ginsberg] was especially intrigued by the scene of burning funeral pyres [in Calcutta and Varanasi] and said:

"There they just lay it out and burn it and the family watches the dissolution / they see the emptiness in front of them / the emptiness of the body in front of them.

"So I had the opportunity to see the inside of the human body / to see the face cracked and torn / fallen off / the brains bubbling and burning."

He visited crematories wherever he went, often spending nights, watching bodies decompose.

Big Bottles [to Chants Creator]:
Weird fascination.

But yes, in the West we didn't -- and still don't -- get confronted with the suffering of human existence.

In India, it is right in your face.

It's almost like the Buddha stepping out of his sheltered life -- for the first time -- and seeing old age, sickness, and death.

The human condition.

I lived and worked in India for over 45 years. I've seen babies born, loved ones lost in the fog of dementia, and cancer patients die in my arms.

Sleeping Horses:
He [Ginsberg] sounds like he was a pretty sick dude, to me.
I lived in Cambodia for two-and-a-half years.
There were families totally naked living on cardboard, on the sidewalks.
There were dead bodies in the streets.
There are tours to the Killing Fields [Pol Pot's Khmer Rouge mass graves, on the outskirts of Phnom Penh] in Cambodia.
I never went to the place where so much death happened.
I'm a Jew, and never had any interest in going to the death camps, like so many people do.
When I travel, I want to capture the joy of a place, and it does exist even in the poorest areas.

Big Bottles:
The hottest thing to do, in Bombay nowadays, is to take a tour of the slums.
It's a difficult moral, ethical question.

Chants Creator:
He [Ginsberg] spent lots of time in Varanasi too, where there are dead bodies floating on the [Ganges] river, and corpses half-eaten by feral dogs.

Sleeping Horses:
What bothers me about him is, you said he sought out similar horrors in other countries he visited.

Chants Creator:
No, what I meant was at the time he travelled to India, it was more seen as an exotic land of snake charmers, Hinduism, and poverty and stuff.
During his time in Varanasi, he observed how people treated death as normal, and life moves on.
If you see at the burning *ghats*' funeral pyres, there would be a

funeral procession going, but at the same time you might see some other festivity in a corner.

So he saw it as a deeply philosophical concept.

He realised that the country treated death as a part of normal, everyday life.

He saw how Hindus understood it as merely the burning of the body, and how a funeral is treated in the West.

Allen Ginsberg was into Buddhism and Zen before he travelled to India.

So he had this philosophical, and deep introspective, view of the world, and it showed in his poetry and journals.

Understand Three:
I think Ginsberg is an O.K. kind of guy.
He's one of the three poets I can understand.

Chants Creator:
One more important thing to note, is that Allen Ginsberg's visit to India was after publishing his poem *Howl* -- which got him embroiled in controversy, and put him on trial -- as the mass was not ready for it at that time.

He was way advanced for his time.

The trial was the last straw, after which he packed bags to India.

Early Picture:
Walking across [Calcutta's] Howrah Bridge, I saw a body with rats going in and out of the body's asshole.

As I walked by I saw, to my horror, the old man was still alive.

I gave him water and a prayer. 1970.

Live Anything:
I can take anything. But not rats.
And not rats in an asshole.
And not rats in a live asshole.

Begged Lucrative:
There was a guy with a wooden cart, going around picking up the dead off the sidewalk.
And Howrah Bridge was unbelievable.
Thousands of people living on it!
Calcutta in 1965 was quite the scene.

Houseboat Beautiful:
Robin -- my beautiful female blonde traveling companion -- and I dropped acid one night, and went to have a spiritual experience by the [Ganges] river, and burning bodies.
But the Indians were too fascinated with her, to leave us alone.
So it was a disappointing night.
On top of that, a couple days later, I bought some morphine to take to Goa -- and it was brutal shit.

Clean Squat:
Pharmaceutical?
Palfium? [also known as Dextromoramide, about three times stronger than morphine]

Houseboat Beautiful:
It's been 45 years my friend, I can't remember.
Perhaps pharmaceutical.
What I do remember is that it was brutal on the nose.

Clean Squat:
In Calcutta, you had *pousse pousse* [a person pulling a two-wheeled rickshaw].
The guy just running in front, like in China before.
Cycle rickshaws [a rickshaw attached to a three-wheeled bicycle, pedaled by a person] were modern compared to them.

Big Bottles:

Yes, the human-drawn ones were usually barefoot Muslim migrants from Bangladesh.

The poorest of the poor.

They even have to rent their rickshaw.

In Dacca [Bangladesh's capital], it's all cycle rickshaws, and most of them have a small electric motor, to help pedal.

Narrow High:
There are still some lanes [in Calcutta] that are too narrow, even for a cycle rickshaw.

When the streets are flooded by monsoon rains -- and the taxis cannot operate -- rickshaw is king.

Because the pullers will run through deep water, while the passenger rides high above the flood.

Clean Squat:
The Kali Temple in Kalicutta [Calcutta] was also attracting me.

Goat sacrifices and blood.

I was 24 then, and still full of *maya*.

A foreign *charsi*, tripping in a *sadhu* outfit.

Narrow High:
In those days, it was hard not to get in a rickshaw [pulled by a person] in Calcutta.

While we may have been uncomfortable with the image, the ride was important for the rickshaw *wallah*, who needed the money -- usually resolved by doubling the fare as a tip.

Beetroot Voice:
You had to avoid communist marches in Calcutta, and they were huge.

We even had stones thrown at us, by kids who thought we were American.

Despite these demonstrations occasionally, I absolutely loved Calcutta.

It was a good base for Varanasi, East Pakistan, and Nepal.

Heart Unprepared:
One time when I was in India -- I can't remember where or when -- I was eating *samosas* [fried stuffed dough] on the street, from a stall that handed out big leaves as plates.

A cow wandered over, and tried to chew on the leaf plate of the Indian guy next to me.

He punched it hard, right between the eyes -- BLAM -- and it wandered off again.

Cow Holy:
Holy cow!

Eating Marigolds:
I had marigolds around my neck, and a cow came up and started eating them.

Window Cows:
I loved the cows window-shopping for a handout at night.

Retreat First:
When I first stepped out of the airport in Bombay, I was overwhelmed by the situation, and I remained standing for a few moments, taking in the star-studded sky, and feeling the warm air of the night enveloping me.

Whereupon a skinny, dirty, one-armed beggar rushed up to me, and stuck his stump in my face -- all the time babbling something I couldn't understand.

My impulse was to retreat back into the airport but luckily, before I did, another man told off the beggar, and I proceeded down the stairs, and began my love story with India.

Totally Challenging:
Now they take one look at me, and they know I am not a virgin to India, and I am snarly.

The advantages of age.

Fortress Hovel:
Living in India was like living in medieval times.
Minarets gently moaning on the horizon.
Skeletons begging in the backstreets.
We rambled through tribal Himalayas and turban-strewn deserts, with fill-in-the-blank as our only companions.
India. The journey through life and death.
In New Delhi, I lived in a dome-topped slum among strange bloated lizards and soft voices:
"No momma, no poppa."
"No arms, no legs."
We heard wild stories about that fantastic land we remembered as America, which had shrunk and now glowed in the dark.

Initial This [displays a photograph of a beggar]:
Deformed or mentally ill babies, are often sold to people who run strings of beggars.
The owner of this beggar [in Badrinath, a Hindu holy town on the Ganges River] had about a dozen others [begging] in 2002.
We got into a confrontation, and I gave serious thought to beating him up.
Fritz, my Dutch friend, talked me out of it.
In 2004, I had a bag of coins to exchange for dollars, as I was leaving the country.
I complained to the bank that beggars refused coins. Staff members started telling their stories:
"This is big problem, sir."
"The beggars have it too easy!"
"They have been spoiled!"
"They will not accept coins from us either."
"But the Bank of India is proud to take your coins, sir."

Telephone Promising:
Back in the 1970s, waiting to make an international telephone call in India was an ordeal.

You soon found out - even for a booked call -- it could take hours, and on some occasions longer.

Inevitably, hunger got the better of you.

But fear of leaving the Telephone Exchange Office -- in case you missed your slot -- prevented you from leaving.

The solution was to ask a street boy to get some food, like *bhajis* [fried onion fritters] or some *samosas* and *ek glass chai* [one glass of tea] from the street vendor -- *walla* -- outside the compound.

The trick was to stop the boy absconding with your money.

So you gave him the money for the food, and one half of a one-rupee note -- promising the other half of the note when he returned with your *chai*, and the now much-needed *bhajis*.

A good deal for both sides.

Unkempt Rocking:
One thing I remember, from being in Manali, were the little balls of *charas* you could buy from young boys, who would go and hand rub it from wild plants early in the morning.

Enough for one or maybe two *chillums*.

Each ball would cost you exactly one rupee.

Best Hand:
Hand-pressed is the best.

Survival Uprisings:
Rubbing and pressing pollen.
Too many blisters, until you get tough skin.

Million Million:
Do you remember the ball of *bhang* [edible marijuana], which cost 10 paisa [one-tenth of a rupee]?

With one ball, you were stoned all day long.

Ice One:
Good deal.
The ones I bought in Pushkar where very strong.
Like tripping.
Unlike the *bhang* ice cream for the kids at Shiva Ratri [a Hindu festival dedicated to the god Shiva].
Needed two of them.

Touch All:
My first was my last.
It completly blew me out of my mind, and I was unable to move for 28 hours.
I got one presented from my favorite shopkeeper in the Kathmandu vegetable market, for Shiva Ratri.
She put it right into my mouth, laughing, and that was it.

Million Million:
My first one was in the little *mandir* [Hindu temple] behind the Taj Mahal.

Heart and Soul:
Bhang lassis [*bhang* mixed into liquid yogurt to drink] in Pushkar.
Epics of epic.

Very Classic:
We drank *bhang* with Pushkar lake water.
And when, in 1984, Indira Gandhi's ashes were scattered in the lake, every time we drank we screamed:
"Indiraaa!"

Never Silver:
For me, too strong.
I was tripping.
It was never pleasant trips.

I really lost it.

They were dragging me away from the Oberoi [Hotel] swimming pool in Bombay.

I didn't stay there.

I didn't know how I got there.

And I didn't remember how I got back to my hotel in Colaba.

All I know is had a *bhang lassie* in a temple compound, somewhere in Bombay, just next to, or behind, a silver shop street.

Sitars There:

I had one at a temple, then went to see Ravi Shankar in Bombay.

Sitars were in my head for two days.

Visa Feeding:

In 1972, I was going to travel [from India] to America, with a woman from New York, who I met here in India.

I was still trying to get a U.S. visa, but her money was running out, and she was still in India.

She had already bought two donkeys for trekking around Manali.

But the monkeys, I mean donkeys, didn't go up the mountain.

So now she was in Manali, trying to sell those donkeys.

A big one, and its child.

She complained to me that all her energy and money, she was spending on those donkeys.

All the time feeding them.

So I told her:

"Sure man, you buying donkeys, you have to spend time and money like that."

Bite Rush:

I had one [monkey] rush me, and try to bite me in Kashi.

Fucker.

Enjoy Early:
Rhesus are the worst.
At least the langurs are handsome.
Try growing salad, or fruit trees, in the mountains, and you'll dislike them both.
And watch out for the flowers in your garden.
Of course we are to blame for stealing their habitat.

Strange Mountains:
The macaques used to be O.K., but when their population pressures grew, the monkeys got meaner and meaner.
Now villages pay monkey hunters to remove them to the jungle, where nobody has to listen to them die in jungle monkey wars.

Women Amazing:
Langurs, by the way, raided my house every year, and broke off the whole papaya tree.
I never got a single banana from all my years of planting.
When I chased them, they threw roof tiles at me, or sat up in the trees, and *wanked* [masturbated] to drive my dogs nuts.

Groovy Bamboo:
When I lived in the jungle [in Thailand], I lived in a small hut on stilts, and slept on a bamboo mat.
A monkey got into my house, and stole my camera and binoculars, climbed up on the roof of the house, and looked at me as he swung them wildly, back and forth, banging them loudly.
He knew what he was doing.
That son of a bitch was actually smiling at me.

Clothes Rip:
My girlfriend, Tralala, and I were having a picnic on the

hillside of Swayambhu in 1972, and a monkey got my camera bag.

Tralala and the monkey had a tug-of-war, both showing their teeth and growling and howling.

Tralala got the bag back.

Initial This:
In Nepal, 1982, a monkey stole my camera.
When I demanded it's return, he showed me his teeth.
His rather long, sharp teeth, to be precise.
My friends laughed, saying it looked like I'd lost a camera.
But I saved the day by offering an orange.
Mister Monkey accepted the offer, the trade was made, and everyone was happy.
I have never trusted a monkey since.

Fortress Hovel:
Midnight. 104 degree heat.
A steamy breeze cuts through our train across India.
People sleep like gas chamber corpses -- arms dangling, bodies tangled on the floor, crunched into corners, and heaped onto one another.
Outside, in the darkened countryside, fever wars take their toll.
Uttar Pradesh [a northern state], 1972.
Scrawled in red paint on old village walls, huge signs warn: GET BLOOD TESTS FOR ALL FEVER CASES.

Calcutta Puri [introduces an elderly Indian man in ragged clothes]:
This old man is a wise bastard.
He's been all over the world.
To every country that is, and has been.
Ain't that right, old man?
[the elderly man grins]
He was in the British Navy for 20 years.

And now look at him.
He's a fucking rickshaw driver.
In Calcutta.
At his age.
After being all over the world like Christopher Columbus, he has to pull a bloody rickshaw in Calcutta.

Initial This:
After World War Two, there was a labor shortage [in England], and workers from Pakistan were brought in.
Eventually, those [textile] mills shut down, and the legacy is cities like Bradford [in England].
Friends I met gave me a look at Bradford, a few years ago.
Run down.
Closed factories.
Elderly Muslim men walking around.
And an excellent Kashmiri restaurant.

Calcutta Puri:
We learned the Earth is round from the British.
They also taught us to always tell the truth.
In this country, under the British, if any one of us lied to a colonial officer, the colonialist would tie him on the end of a bloody cannon, and blow him to bloody pieces.
We don't mind about being hung, but to be blown to bits, that's too bloody much, man.

Skull Press:
In Manali, the [Kulu tribe] ladies wanted to show me how to press my two-week-old son's skull -- into the desired shape.
I wasn't on board with that one.

Amoebic Sun Rise:
On a trip between Dharamsala and Manali -- a long train ride through Simla [a town in the Himalayas], and then up on a bus to Manali -- I got amoebic dysentery.

The bus driver gave me some opium.

At every stop, I'd get out and retch.

Arriving in Manali, I had to be pulled off the bus, and made my way to one of the old hotels.

That night, I thought it would be my last one on Earth.

I sent my girlfriend out to find a Tibetan doctor.

She came back with some herbal remedy which made me even worse.

Puking blood, gasping for breath, and blood gushing from my butt, I prayed that all that I wanted to do was to see the sun rise one more time, and I would be content to die.

That morning, my girlfriend went out again to find help.

She found a British doctor, who when he first saw me laughed and said:

"I thought you Americans were smart people. You've been drinking the water."

Fortress Hovel:

On the lawn of New Delhi's fabled Imperial Hotel, huge crows swoop down and snatch your *nan* [flat bread] whenever they can.

While eating at the outdoor restaurant there, I often told people who had just arrived in India for the first time, that the crows were vultures.

"Be careful, because the vultures will fly down and bite your ears off."

That would always freak people out, because the crows continually swooped really close by.

And when the Yugoslavian leader Tito was perishing on his deathbed in May 1980, I was languishing on a sweaty bed in the Imperial, suffering dysentery or some slowly twisting illness.

For several days I lay there, listening to my transistor radio broadcasting the B.B.C., which was filled with updates and mournful stories about Tito slowly dying.

It was like a soundtrack describing my plight.

It was really freaky when Tito died and, all through my fever and delirium, they kept describing the intricacies and consequences of his funeral.

Eight Ball:
By the way, did you ever get your ears cleaned by the guy in Connaught [Connaught Place]?
He used an eight-inch metal rod, and kept a golf ball-sized lump of ear wax in his pocket, which he told gullible folk he had just dug out of their ears.
God help anyone if he got nudged while he had that thing stuck in their ear.
Free brain surgery?

Blue Prayer:
Never did it.
I was told they drop a little stone in your ear, and demand more money when they fish it out.

Orange Thing:
Met one in Bombay once, and before I could resist, he was inside my ear with a metal instrument telling me that I had stones.
"You been to Goa? That explains it. Always stones when you swim in sea. I'll take them out, 25 paisa a piece."
And then he moved his thing around in my ear, and I heard and felt that he was hitting against something hard in there.
Then he dug out a little white mineral stone, and then another.
What he really was doing was flipping his nail on the end of the metal thing and it felt, and sounded, as if he hit something in there.
Can't remember if I gave him any money, but I knew I was being taken for a ride.
Left me with a nice, orange color in my ear though.

Practicing Sleep [laughing]:

I was practicing my sitar, playing in the park after a daily lesson at Rikki Rahm [the famous Rikki Rahm Music Shop where the Beatles bought instruments when they visited India], next to Connaught.

Suddenly this guy is getting in to my ear.

I shouted, "Hey, stop it!"

Two seconds of ear work, and he produced -- guess what -- a stone.

I told him bullshit.

And he said without no shame, "What is your country?"

So I said Sweden.

"Ah ha! Switzterland. Mmmmmm money!"

"No, no, Sweden!"

He said, "Tell me something specific about Sweden."

So I told him about the midnight sun, in the summer, that the sun wouldn't go down for some time, and it would be bright and light 24 hours a day.

He looked at me like a child who just heard an amazing story.

He said with big eyes:

"People never sleep?"

Hard Boot:

All I know is since 1968, I had it done [ears cleaned] a few times by the right people, and never complained.

I miss them sorely.

Their only critics are those who never spent enough time to find the difference between honest traders and scammers.

Fortress Hovel:

Bombay's first TV station began broadcasting one day in 1972, while we were staying in the wretched Rex Hotel.

So the hotel manager brought a black-and-white TV into the dark lobby.

Plugged it in.

Turned it on.

All the Indians sat there, staring transfixed, seeing a TV

broadcast for the first time in their lives.

They watched pure visual static.

For some reason, that first broadcast either didn't happen exactly then, or the TV's antennae was fucked.

But they excitedly watched that static for a really long time.

Dancing Surly:
Oh, the Rex [on Bombay's Mereweather Road], right around the corner from Leopold's -- and the tasty *biryani* [rice cooked with other ingredients].

And the gorgeous, dark, wood-trimmed Olympia Coffee House, across the street.

The Rex, with its surly management, paper thin walls, and bug-infested beds, was only somewhat redeemed by tiny, private balconies overlooking the street scene below -- including the action just outside iconic Dipti's [a cheap cafe popular with travelers], across the street.

And occasional shows by cruel sidewalk beggars, exploiting their dancing bears, just for a hippie toss of meager paisa.

Candle War:
The Rex Hotel, we stayed there several times.

I remember waking up to a rat on the bed post, looking at me.

Some windows at The Rex looked down onto a sort of courtyard, or just nothing, and everyone seemed to toss their trash out the window, and the rats would be down there having a great time.

Lots of them.

We also stayed at Buckley Court near there, which I really liked.

We were staying there during the India-Pakistan war, or whatever it was, and had to run outside.

Total blackout.

Someone in our group hired a taxi without headlights, to go to Jailhouse Road to get cocaine and more hash, so we could stay in inner hallways with a candle burning, staying stoned.

It was a scary time for us.

Roof People:
I remember that night.

Before we went into the halls, we lit candles in the rooms.

But people outside started throwing stones, because they could see the light out the windows -- and it was a blackout, on account of the air raids.

The next day, they painted the windows black.

Me and a companion went up to the roof to watch the A.A. [anti-aircraft] fire.

A stupid thing to do, because the next day we read of injuries from falling shrapnel.

What a time.

Pleasure Asia:
I remember huge rats in the toilet at night.

I had to hold off going, until morning.

I used to stay at The Carlton around the corner sometimes.

Plenty of rats there too.

Very Classic:
In the early 1980s, I lived among the mice of the Indian Guest House.

But after 20 *chillums*, you sleep everywhere.

Million Million:
In Agra [a city in Rajasthan state], behind the Taj Mahal, there was a small temple.

It was right on the edge of the Yamuna [River], and there we saw the corpses of the poor floating in the water.

After a while the current, which was weak in front of the temple, carried the corpses a little further, where the stray dogs came to eat them.

The dogs were very fat and disgusting.

Women Amazing:
There was a story told to me, by a fellow traveler who saw -- driving by in the middle of India, in some obscure place -- what looked like a re-enaction of the death of Jesus.

A man on a cross, and a whole group of people around it.

So he stopped to check it out.

And the man on the cross was rolling his eyes in a terrible way, and writhing around on the cross.

He was told that this man was dying of rabies, and the villagers tied him up there so he could not hurt himself, or anyone else.

Dan White:
It is January 2001, and I am in Delhi.

It is absolutely freezing.

I would go out and try and pick up one of those hippie chicks, but I have forgotten all that rich-kid-in-India hippie lingo.

You know, all the stuff about what drug is what, and getting it badly wrong about what Hindu god is, like, really cool.

Dead Water:
I carried a sheet of blotters [L.S.D.-soaked perforated paper] in Varanasi, and held the sheet over the water jugs set out for a dinner for Indira Gandhi, and her full cabinet [of ministers], but didn't carry out the mission.

Sunshine and Sandoz [L.S.D. brands].

In the room itself, I was talked down by my friend, a Bengali *Brahmin* [the highest Hindu caste] from London, clearly stating that I, he, our mutual friend -- a grandson of a minister, in whose house the dinner was prepared -- and residents of a house housing numerous escapees from Benares Hindu University -- would all be dead by the morning.

Naked and Barefoot:

Near Puri [an east coast town in Orissa state], miles of beach in either direction, yet the children choose to play in the village's open sewer.

It was couple of miles north of Puri -- I forget the name of the village -- and was a popular foreigner hangout through the 1970s and early 1980s.

But it's one of those places that gets no tourist trade anymore.

Does anyone remember the name of this village? We used to have to walk to it from Puri.

Many Europeans, living the dream there.

Local *ganja* [marijuana], quite good.

Long ago.

Only one beach hut.

A fisherman's family.

Everyday, pomfret fish, absolutely the best, some big-sized and a good price.

And the underrated, I think, truly superb [Konark] Sun Temple, with the [temple's Hindu *devdasi*] prostitutes, in a little road, behind the temple.

Maybe it's a bygone thing.

Big Bottles:
I remember a guest house called Xanadu, and all the fishing villages lining the seafront.

And they all shit on the beach.

The high tide would take it away.

Never swam there.

Fishmarket Experience:
That's my experience as well. I was there in 1997.
They held the fish market on the same beach.

Enjoy Early:
I heard in the early 1970s that the Puri beach was full of excrement, so I never understood why anyone would want to

go there.

Nothing Shacks:
All beaches in India are basic toilets for the locals.
Nothing surprising when you know that latrines are non-existent in their house or shacks.
Along the rail tracks, if no beach.

Sun Think:
I personally think it's the most environmentally friendly to do.
The beach is not of any use to the local community, just because we like lying there.
Just up the road is the magnificent Konark Sun Temple. We went for a visit and stayed two weeks.
Can't say I remember the prostitutes, but not my interest.

Naked and Barefoot:
Not my interest either, but the temple -- being for the Sun God -- the story was that they [*devdasi*s] were a historical part of the place.

Sun Think:
There are many stories about [Hindu] prostitution within temples.
Unless you are a born Hindu, you couldn't get into the temple.
Wonderful beach with turtles -- usually dead -- but very busy with Indian tourists.
You used to be able to find government *bhang* shops.
The lovely *bhang*, for a peaceful day.
The [*bhang* shop] owner got us to sign a letter saying that we were quite happy with the opium or grass, but would never touch hashish.

Naked and Barefoot:

Even in 1980, the locals were a bit pushy over the local *ganja*.
They didn't like tourists turning up with *charas*.
The main temple in Puri had an opium shop as well.

Sun Think:
But very poor quality opium.
Was fine if you mixed it with the *bhang*.

Ice One:
In the government *ganja* shop, they always tried to cheat you.
Better to go to the fishing village.

Nearly Spaced:
We came upon a traveling circus in the early 1980s while cruising Orissa on our bikes.
A family affair, from Gujarat [a west coast state], on the road with their many animals.
A string of goats, elephants, and camels -- and carrying all their tents and gear on about a dozen ox-drawn carts, which were very old and heavy, and beautifully carved and embossed with brass and bells.
We hooked up with them, and camped with them for a couple of nights on the road.
Hilarious campfire situations every evening, with the oldies smoking opium, kids running around everywhere, teenagers playing with all the smaller animals -- which included tame monkeys, snakes, and a baby elephant.
Fun times
Wish I had had a camera.

Fortress Hovel:
Bikes?
Bicycles or motorcycles?

Nearly Spaced:
Bicycles!

I absolutely loved it as a way to travel through rural India.

Always peaceful, and moving at the same pace as the locals.

Instant welcome to stay in any village or temple, and punctures could be fixed at pretty much any household, for free.

My bike was an old Indian one, an Atlas, with no gears.

It cost me 25 rupees.

Inside Scoundrels:

I grew up in Madras [the capital of Tamil Nadu, a southeast state, along the Bay of Bengal and Andaman Sea].

"All my changes were there," as Neil Young would sing.

The [Broadlands Hotel] was one of those segregated places. They did not allow Indians inside.

No big shit for me, but a white friend of ours staying there wanted some *shrooms* [psychedelic mushrooms] we'd got back from Kodai [Kodaikanal, a hill town in Tamil Nadu state].

When we landed up at Broadlands, the snooty [Indian] reception guy was discouraging to say the least, until we told him we were doing his guest a favor.

I know for a fact that *smack* dealers and other scoundrels had no problems entering.

We weren't dealers.

Squalid Dreams:
Run by Indians, but Indian nationals not allowed.

Sad Level:
The level of insult of Indians by an Indian.
Sad.

Inside Scoundrels:
Except *smack* dealers.
I'm talking about the early 1980s.

Naked and Barefoot:

Shrooms.
There are stories there.
I was picking handfuls of them soon after Madras.

Up From the Plains:
I came up from the plains, as the heat and dust rose below.
Stellar time.
Kodaikanal 1982.
In the morning, a young boy would walk from a nearby village with a box on his head.
The baker.
He would get to my residence, and slowly unwrap its contents.
Bread on top.
Below that, sweet rolls.
Then, with a quick look around, he'd unwrap the lower level.
Jars of mushroom jam.
Magic jam.
350 *shrooms* per jar.
The 11 Italians, in the room next to me, had it for breakfast every morning, toasting bread over an open flame.
This was lunch:
Fresh tomatoes, carrots, local cheese and bread, and more *shrooms*.
Country living.

Fishmarket Experience:
I stayed [in Madras] for one week in January 1986, and saw Ravi Shankar playing [classical sitar music] in a modern, but really cool, town hall.
I found it boring then. I had no idea of Indian classical music.
Luckily that changed.

Street Shocked:
On New Year's Eve 1989, I saw him too in Madras.

I was invited to sit on stage, and I dropped strong L.S.D. before the concert.

Truly mind-blowing.

Sleeping Horse:
I'll take Brian Eno's *Baby's On Fire* any day of the week, over any Eastern music I've ever heard.

If that makes me blasphemous or unsophisticated, makes no difference to me.

I'd need a whole lot of acid to listen to sitar for more than five minutes.

Paper Mouth:
In New Delhi, there was a boy who showed me a piece of paper, which claimed he was a beggar who could not speak.

I was a bit suspicious.

So I asked him:

"Let me your tongue."

And he opened his mouth, and he had no tongue.

He probably rolled it back in his mouth, but hell, if he can do that trick it's worth something.

So I gave him 10 rupees.

Dirt Curry:
I miss the curry with the dirt, on the streets of Bombay.

In 1973, they asked me:

"Hey, white monkey, what is your name?

"Why are you here?"

"Where are you going?"

"What are your qualifications?"

Bipping in and out of [hepatitis] recovery was miraculous.

My religion is:

Wash after defecating.

Remember, if you're on the toilet seven or eight times a day, it's dysentery that you have.

But if you can't get off the toilet, it's cholera.

Have lepers crawled down the aisles on your 3rd class train?
Never go anywhere without one.
They stuck their stumps in my meals.

Initial This:
Soon after I arrived in India, a leper chased me down the street, waving what was left of a bloody arm, in my face.
I ran back to my room and cried.
Why him, and not me?
Feelings of guilt and confusion.
I realized I had a choice.
Admit I could not deal with India, give up, and go back to America.
Or come to terms with reality, realize it was not my fault -- and I couldn't do much to change things -- and continue the journey.
Eventually, I saw the grim people in the streets as a lesson.
Be grateful for what you have, and be kind to those who suffer.
I saw them as people, and was often comfortable around them.

Never Gets:
Same kind of experience I had.
First time arrival in Madras, 1969. So many lepers everywhere.
They camped out on sidewalks and traffic islands.
I hardly got out of my room for days.
I had sort of a breakdown.
Wrote to the girlfriend I left behind, moaning that I felt helpless.
She wrote back, "Maybe the only way to handle it," was to "go and do something about it."
But I could not, it was too overwhelming.
Mind you, I had been in the country a year already, but it still got me.

The sheer size of the problem, the hopelessness.
I don't know what helped me accept it, and deal with it.

Strange Mountains:
On my way to Fatehpur Sikri [an abandoned 16th century royal Moghul city near the Taj Mahal], I actually saw a group of lepers, with 10-foot poles, for begging at a distance.
Now leprosy seems easily handled, and they are rare to see.

On the Border:
When we crossed, by foot, the no man's land -- between India and Pakistan -- in 1973, thousands of refugees from Bangladesh were there, entering Pakistan.
Most were in very bad condition and needed food and medical treatment.
I gave a family my U.S. Army mess kit and canteen.
We gave blankets, and my girlfriend gave her sleeping bag.
We were devastated and had never seen anything like it.
By the time we went through Benares and Calcutta, we were shell-shocked and numb.
We came from a place of white picket fences and lawnmowers.
Nothing prepared us.

Best Bad:
While recovering from bad belly in Bangalore [a southern city], I developed a routine.
In the morning, I would listen for the mango lady. She would come to the door with two huge, incredible, ripe, ripe, mangoes.
I would take them to the fridge, and swap them for two cold ones from yesterday.
I'd grab a wooden board and knife, and go to the shower.
I'd sit and eat, and make an unmerciful mess, with juice running to my elbows.
Then I'd turn on the shower.
Best breakfast ever.

The Saint:
Bhaila [Dipti's restaurant manager], was literally my best friend in Bombay, and helped me, by fronting me food and drinks for almost a month in 1975.

Strange Mountains:
He was better than the Post Office for saving mail and messages, and delivering them correctly.
Dipti's was a wonderful haven.

The Saint:
Bhaila, the Saint of Colaba.

Eat Rural:
A gorgeous man, and friend to many.
Aside from those delicious, life-saving juices.
Dipti's was like a lifeline.

Juice Me:
Red grape juice, and brown bread with cheese, was my favorite.
Thanks to Bhaila.

Forget Not:
Do not forget The Baghdadi [a nearby restaurant].

Strange Mountains:
Pretty sure the *keema* [usually lamb or goat meat] at The Baghdadi was rat meat.
On the other hand, meat was hard to find for a price like that.

Survived Struggling:
I was broke, and on the street -- by Dipti's -- when you [Wondered Big] helped me out.

I was an 18-year-old, struggling musician.
Nothing but love, I'll always respect that, Wondered Big.
Before that, I was at Sher-e-Punjab [Hotel], in Paharganj in Delhi, with Big Pierre.
What a junk monkey dive that was.
Well, anyway, we paid our dues and survived.

Wondered Big:
I can't remember a thing.

Survived Struggling:
It's just life, some things one remembers, some things one doesn't.
Best to leave it at that, and carry on.
I am -- and I'm sure you are -- in better spaces in life now.

Wondered Big:
I am.

Broke Insane:
I'll never forget one of the most insane bus rides I've ever been on, and -- like Survived Struggling -- I was broke and in a bad way in The Crown annex, and you [Wondered Big] helped me out too.
I'll never forget.

Wondered Big:
I remember [that bus ride].
I woke up, with the asshole's -- in the seat behind -- hand down the front of my dress.

Women Amazing:
The hierarchy of the [*sadhus'* hashish] smoke circle was also interesting, as it was my job, as a foreigner, to supply the *dope* [drugs].
The *chillum* was then offered to me with many bows and

compliments, and faked wonderment that a beautiful woman like me could *toke* like a freight train.

I was a bit shocked that these compliments gave me a dopamine rush, even though I knew they were total bullshit.

The [*sadhus'*] musical chairs game started long before the *chillum* was ready.

Best *tokes* are at the beginning.

So after lighting, I would of course pass it to *baba* [an elder male].

Some were not allowed to sit down and participate at all.

Tiny hand movements by *baba* directed all this, almost unnoticeable.

The chased away would pretend to enjoy just watching.

This all started to piss me off a bit, considering they smoked my *dope*.

So I patted the place next to me, and invited a poor disheveled-looking fellow to sit there.

Not a great seat, considering the *chillum* had gone around once already before it got to him.

But *baba* was pissed.

Usually if there were other foreigners with me, we had to whisper to each other and -- on the signal -- all get up at once, very fast, to get out of there [laughs].

Otherwise these greedy holy so-and-sos would have smoked all our stash.

[someone displays a photograph of Subramani Chillum Baba, a *sadhu* in Hampi, a town near Goa]

Broken Chillums:
He [Subramani Chillum Baba] made beautifully decorated clay *chillums*.

It had four cobra heads looking at you, each snake with its own little cobra egg on the chest.

All the tails were spiraling around, down the *chillum*.

I had one given to me at Chapora beach [in Goa] during

1971 or 1972.

I wanted to save and keep it -- used of course -- and sent it off to New York City with half-a-dozen others.

Different-sized Bombay black ones.

Another one from Varanasi, looking like stone.

One like marble.

They all arrived.

But every singe one was badly broken.

I suspect on purpose.

Never seen one again, not even on the Internet.

Orange Thing:

When I was there in 1975, it was him [Subramani Chillum Baba] and an older *baba* living there.

I seem to remember that the old guy was the original Chillum Baba.

Am I wrong?

Right On:

You are right, he was Gopal Swami.

Subramani was his *chella*.

Survival Uprisings:

For a masterpiece, you had to go and see him, in a town away from Hampi.

He only made one a day.

And if he had a previous order, you had to wait for him to finish that.

So he told me to go and wait in Hampi, and come back in five days.

Right On probably remembers the name of the city.

I ordered three.

Lost one in India, broken.

And another, that I had kept in Sweden, I left in a train in Copenhagen.

[displays a photograph of a *chillum*]

This is the third, that I left with a friend.
I think he still has it.
When Gopal died, apparently most of his *chillums* cracked.

[someone displays a photo of a different *chillum*]

Right On:
I'm not familiar with Subramani's *chillums* -- it's been a long time -- but I'm quite sure this is one of Gopal's five-heads snake *chillum*.

He died in 1976, and was less productive toward the end.

Lots of time and work gathering what he needed to make his special mixture of clay and, of course, lots of cow shit and branches to fire them.

The black color was done with smoke of banana leaves.

And yes, as far as I know, most of his *chillums* broke when he passed away.

On the two I still have, the rings broke in two, and a snake has a chip on the cobra's nose.

I mailed them to Canada and they arrived broken, so I'm not sure exactly when they broke.

But when Gopal passed away, I was in Manali, sitting cleaning two of them. I had them on my *lungi* [sarong].

Don't ask me why I stood up.

The *chillums* went flying and broke.

Survival Uprisings:
Yes, the broken or vanished *chillums*, after the maker left his earthly existence.

The town I went to see him in, was further away from Hampi than Hospet.

Looking at the map -- Bellary [a city in Karnataka state] maybe?

Right On:
Or Hubli?

Back then, you had to go first to Hubli then Hospet, to go to Hampi.

Survival Uprisings:
I kind of remember it was further northeast. And not too far away.
That's why I think Bellary.
But I also see Kollapur [a city in Maharashtra state].
Thing is, I went to Hampi many times, and did trips around.
Once to a *fakir mela* [ascetics' festival].
Trippy to say the least.

Right On:
I was there once for that *mela*.
Don't remember when.
I think something to do with the moon?
Gopal took me there.
He told me most of the *sadhus*, living in caves around Hampi, came out only for that *mela*, at the magical Virupaksha Temple.

Survival Uprisings:
The deity was Devi [a powerful Hindu goddess also known as Durga, or Shakti], riding on a tiger.
I think I still have the idol's framed picture somewhere.

Right On:
Durga was very important in Hampi.
The small temple by the river where Gopal was staying during the dry season, it's a Durga temple.
She's often portrayed sitting on a tiger.

Died Intact:
I still have one [a *chillum* made by Gopal] with three rings.
It is still intact, although it has been resting in its *chillum* bag for quite some time.
Got it in the beginning of 1976.

Only few weeks before Baba Gopal died.

Begged Lucrative:
I used to hang out on the [Ganges] river with the *sadhus*.
It was clear that they had their society conned into believing they were holy, and thus were taken care of, as far as food and alms go.
I certainly did not meet any genuine holy ones, sitting smoking hash with them.
What I found far more interesting were the Muslim holy men -- and rarely women.
They called them, in Pakistan, *Malang* [devotees of Muslim saints, and similar to Persian Sufis].
They are called *majnoon* [crazy] or God Mad.

Greenish Invalids:
The mark of our infamy has become embedded.
Many invalids wandered around -- with dark eyes, in the bus station -- fleeing deformed faces, inhumane, crazy-eyed.
The mother breastfed her child.
I turned away to let her do it peacefully. But the child burped, and then swelled with a continuous, gigantic, excruciating cry.
I looked at him and discovered that the mother was carrying a monster with a prematurely aged face -- he even had a grotesque beard -- with counterfeit, twisted limbs.
His gaze, and his cry, seemed to be inhuman.
He was staring at me, but did he see me?
I wanted to say something to the mother, but her fixed eye of infinite resignation nailed all the words to the bottom of my throat.
Then they left, bending under the weight of their painful mysteries.
A greenish lake reflected the palace, and the polychrome statues of Indian gods that surrounded it.

Totally Everyone:
I met one guy in Poona who totally lost it, he wrote all over the walls in his room. Weird stuff.
And he kept talking to an imaginary audience, nonstop.
In Lakshmi Villas. I don't know what happened to him.
And another guy who jumped off a rooftop.
We can't save everyone.

Wonderful Hanging:
I was a 15-year-old, hanging out in a opium den, located near the railway station in Poona, in 1978.
The opium *baba* was named Moltilal.
It was a mini U.N. -- Iranians, Iraqis, Muslims, Hindus, Jews.
Frankly, it was a wonderful place.

My Legs:
Many people could not handle the total freedom.
Locals had absolutely no expectations, or boundaries, on our behavior.

Just East:
Often glamorized, but there was a dark side to the trail too.

Hard Flipped:
So many flipped away.
Some returned.
I stayed out in Asia for five great years. Wonderful times.
Yes.
I never had anything to do with hard drugs.

Dark Talk:
The dark side was always hovering nearby, wasn't it?
As I suppose it is everywhere.
It frightened me, and kept me more or less on the straight and narrow.
I got sick enough as it was, and saw many who were much

worse off.

Mystic Tantric:
There were people, who seemed to not be able to handle the total freedom, of having no infrastructure, or safety net.

There was a German guy, in Varanasi when I was there in 1996, who had been shot in the arm in Parvati Valley, when he was trying to rob *ganja* crops.

He came down from the mountains, with his infected arm all bandaged up.

And he was sleeping in abandoned temples.

And scoring heroin and opium when he could.

People were begging him to go to the embassy, and get flown home, but he decided to head to Goa instead.

Never saw him again.

At the same time, a Dutch girl was found wandering naked in the streets, babbling.

Apparently she had been smoking a [hallucinogenic plant] datura-infused *charas* mix, with *sadhus*.

The police took her away, never to be heard from again.

As well a young man in his 20s, died at the International Ashram in Assi Ghat [along the Ganges River in Varanasi].

I think it was drug-related.

Nearly Spaced:
The datura story was, sadly, not so rare.

I came across it a few times, and got involved in repatriating people who had entered deep psychosis as a result.

Sometimes it seems fake *sadhus* poisoned them with datura on purpose, in order to rob them of their passport and money.

One of the classic symptoms of datura madness is throwing away your clothes and possessions.

Very sad and distressing.

Skull Press:
I was three months pregnant, and left Goa for Manali with

100 dollars, which I kept in a little drawstring purse, around my waist.

Yet somehow, somewhere, walking from The Crown Hotel and back, it disappeared -- and I still have no idea how.

Luckily I still had my cassette player, which I was able to sell, and use the money for a bus ticket to Manali, with a bit left over to survive for a week or so.

Once there, I started to make apricot jam, and sold it for five rupees a pot.

In no time, I was selling 20 or 30 pots a day, so it all ended well.

Probably was a blessing in disguise, because I'd never really been alone before that -- and realized I could hustle a living, if need be.

Slinging Woman:
I haven't heard [Indians asking], "What is your purpose?" -- for years.
It's a tough question.
I do get asked, "Where is your husband?"
I usually say, "Dead."
Conversation stopper.

Ice One:
"Madam what are you?"
"Are you married?"
"Are you a disco dancer?"

And What:
And the classic:
"What is your qualification?"

Future Aura:
A turbaned fortune teller approached me, apparently to check my aura.
"You very lucky man. I see your past, I see your future.

Which country you from?"

    Given Leave:
    "Where do you hail from?"
    "What is your purpose in coming here?"
    "Has your father given you leave to go?"

    Country Invention:
    "What is your mother country?"

    Juice Time:
    "Sir, excuse me, but are you being a hippie?
    "Are you practicing free love?"

6 • GOA, THE CHILLUM COAST

Women Amazing:
The terrible thing about Cleo [Cleo Odzer, an American heroin dealer and author], she teamed up with Sam Biryani [a Bombay gangster, also known as Gurbux Biryani, and Anand Ram Biryani] -- a *smack* [heroin] dealer from Bombay -- and introduced *smack* into the Anjuna community [a beach in Goa], in a big way.

She seduced young men, and then her and Sam used them, sent them on *smack* runs.

She was so pretty.

She didn't look like a junkie.

So people started to think, "How bad can it be, this *smack*?"

She was a bad, bad woman.

I know people who survived their *smack* addiction, and are still daily battling with it mentally.

Most junkies felt very clever thinking that no one knew they were junkies, even while they were nodding out in the *chai* shops and we were giggling behind their backs.

I heard from several reliable people that she died from AIDS, that she had contracted from her [Thai] pimp.

She worked in the sex trade in Bangkok.

My friend, who was her neighbor [in Goa], says she had a very perverse sex trip going.

He could hear her through the walls of the house.

She had no interest in women, or any female friends that I heard of.

She definitely seduced lots of young men, and turned them on to *smack*.

And then her, and Sam, sent them off on scams.

There are always a lot of people in our circles who say we

shouldn't be judgmental, everyone makes their own choices, but I am not one of them.

If Cleo had just quietly taken her *smack*, I could not have cared one way or another.

But seducing people, and then turning them on with it, is a crime in my opinion, a big crime.

Better just take them outside, and shoot them in the head.

People who had to care for junkies, or had some in their family, might understand my extreme stance on this.

I personally never met Cleo.

My husband knew her.

And never mind the fucking book [Cleo Odzer's confessional autobiography, *Goa Freaks*].

It certainly was not our Goa she was talking about.

Nicely Wonderful:

Cleo was like any one of us, at the time.

She was a girl in search of happiness.

Life was wonderful in Anjuna until *smack* showed up.

Some of us were smart enough and avoided those poisons, and some of us let it invade our lives.

It's easy to look back at those times and say, "She was a bad girl."

At the time, we didn't know the effects of those drugs. There was no information, everything was an experiment.

And many of us were so young.

Cleo helped me, and let me stay at her house when I had a bad breakup with my ex.

She was a sweet and positive girl, whether you like her or not.

She was lost like many of us.

Influenced by what was going on in Anjuna at the time.

We learned a sad and devastating lesson when we watched our friends die, one by one, from drugs.

Cleo told it like it is [in *Goa Freaks*].

She maybe said too much?

And she should not have used people's real names.

Thank God, we didn't know each other's last names at the time.

We all had nicknames.

Some friends -- who were mentioned in the book in a bad way -- are very upset she would write such things about them. I totally understand.

You can say all you want about the book. She wrote it in the 1970s, and people are still talking about it.

Every year, this [book] comes up. I think she would have liked that.

Rest in peace, my old friend.

I was lucky, I was on her good side and was mentioned nicely.

True, if she had written bad things, I would also say her book is crap.

Women Amazing:
The Queen that Brought *Smack* to Goa.

And got everyone, young and able, to do [heroin smuggling] runs for Sam Biryani.

That destroyed the scene, and left behind many O.D.s, many, many prisoners, and suicides.

I always hoped she'd be cursed.

And she was.

Died of AIDS.

Her pretty smile got her everywhere, even got a lift with the devil's handcart.

She was pretty once.

That was her weapon.

Life and Death:
She did not die of AIDS.

She was only HIV positive, and that was only in the last months of her life.

She might have died of that, after many years, if she had

survived.

She had a stroke.

She was only doing a bit of opium before she died.

I know this as a fact, because I was the one who opened her room, as well as being the person who talked to the doctor who presided over her death.

I was allowed to do that because she was a cousin.

Buried Idea:
Any idea where she is buried?

Be Cremated:
You have to be a Catholic or Muslim to get buried in this part of India [Goa].

All others are cremated.

True Yes:
Yes that's true.
She got cremated.

Immediately White:
I knew her well, we both stayed at The White Negro [a hotel in Anjuna beach], and I was with her the day she passed away.

As you may know, she had enormous health problems.

That day [she died], she fell at home, and hit her head.

She was unconscious for several hours before me and the guy from White Negro, Raji, found her on the floor.

We immediately called an ambulance.

They took her to hospital.

She opened her eyes for the last time, a few hours later, and passed away.

Buried Idea:
She was such a free spirit.
And she has inspired many people.

Immediately White:
Yes, she was indeed, we had the best time together.
She was living in the house on the left side of The White Negro.

Life and Death:
When I went to her room, to visit her, The White Negro told me to go to Mapusa Hospital.
Upon arriving and asking for her, after they asked who I was -- and telling them, I am her cousin -- they directed me to the doctor's office, where he said:
"Sit down. She just died a few hours ago of brain damage from a stroke."
When I returned to open her room, I found the note she had started and tried to write -- in her hammock -- saying that she thought she was having a stroke also.
Found the puddle of opium on the chair, next to her bed.
I also saved her hard drives, with her writings, from her Mac computer -- one of the earliest.
Her friend, the doctor, said she had tested positive for HIV, but only was very recently infected, as he had checked six months before, and she was negative then.
She had the new French boyfriend, who was also positive.
I had to organize her affairs with her "Mumsie" [mother] in New York.
Very sad affair.

Human Money:
Cleo made big money with white [the best heroin] and brown [less refined].
I know she helped some.
But still, she made big money with that stuff.
And she had a very bad opinion of most travelers. But she wasn't stupid, and knew how to look cool at some point.
Of course I knew her. And I knew also many people from Vagator village [a beach in Goa].

And many of those didn't like her.
And no, I wasn't one of those junkies.
I also didn't like this person.
I wasn't the only one. May I mention it?
She was greedy.
She was hypocritical.
But she was a human, so she certainly had good sides.

Think Much:
In the 1984 to 1985 season, they didn't sell much food, only brown [heroin].
I avoided that place like hell.
Many shops were selling *smack* that time, but not all.
Ramdas, Primrose, and Day Night were exceptions. I think.

Very Snake:
I rented her house, The Snake House.
Behind Pasquale and Filomena restaurant.
Very *shanti* [peaceful] place in 1980.

Normal Super:
Why you call it The Snake House?
I always heard something big sliding around on the roof, when I was super stoned.
But I thought it was normal paranoia.

New Red:
I met her in New York City, a year or two before her death.
I remember that her apartment there was almost entirely done in red.

Woman There:
I'm in there [*Goa Freaks*] as the other woman.

Early Picture:
I liked my chapter.

Enjoy Early:
I thought it terribly amusing that she wrote her PhD on prostitution in Bangkok.

Before I heard this, a friend showed me a flyer he found in his Bangkok hotel room, with photos of escorts to hire.

And she was one of them.

We Who:
We accepted everyone as they were.

It was up to each individual as to who they wanted to spend time with, and we all knew who was who.

Garden Seasons:
A time we chose to love everybody without money, the simplest way was the best direction, to value our beautiful chance to be a beautiful useful helpful healthy hero, or a beautiful doomed villain.

We all danced and went to the beach together, and are still here to talk about it.

Outrageously Invited:
But the *smack* still cost 60 dollars a gram, at a time when you could live comfortably on the beach for 15 dollars a week.

And I don't think many were giving it away.

Thus the culture of robbery proliferated.

Much Friendlier:
The wannabe Queen of the Junkies of Goa.

She got her sticky fingers on a big jar of *smack*, that some smuggler had left behind, when he got busted and ran.

She planned to start distributing it.

However, some other members of the Western community objected, and took the *smack* from her and dumped it into the sea.

She was furious, but many of us congratulated the two guys

that did it.

Sleeping Horses:
In the first chapter [of *Goa Freaks*], she claims to have ripped off tourists of their traveler's checks.
Sounds like she was a piece of shit chick.
I know she got out of being busted by fucking a cop, but to be honest, I wish she had to go to prison.

Garden Seasons:
The robbery of your soul, while compassion is still too cheap.
The robber of life is always another devil.

Mind Moon:
I have the book signed by Cleo, right off the press in New York City in 1985.
And it's my photo on the front cover. The morning after a Full Moon Party.
And inside some of my photos also. I have the originals.
She asked if I wanted photo credits, I and declined, due to circumstances in my life in 1985.
I wanted to keep a very low profile, for reasons.
She was a very, very dear close friend of mine. I miss her all the time.
It was me who telephoned her "Mumsie" to tell her Cleo died in Goa.
Was the hardest phone call I ever made at the time, and still is in my mind.

Outrageously Invited:
The first rot was the Thai White influence.

Rocked Time:
I think you might find that heroin had been in India for quite some time, before she rocked up.

Much Friendlier:
However she was someone who thought it was cool to turn people on to *smack*, who had never tried it, and then develop a new customer.

Street Shocked:
Cleo the *smack* dealer.

Loved Maybe:
Stupid, liar, and rip-off.
But maybe, for a very brief time, we loved her.

Waste City:
I bought a copy [of *Goa Freaks*] in New York City a few years back.
Read just a few pages, and stopped soon after in disgust.
I despised her racist attitude towards my fellow [Indian] countrymen.
Complete waste of time and money.

Melted Time:
She never understood anything what was going on, where it was going, and why things happened like they did.
Her only interest she had, it was all only, only Cleo.
And she was certainly not the only one like that there, in that time, in Goa.
They saw the world only like they wanted, not like it was and is.
Living their own dreams, not the reality of every day.
What actually was a fantastic thing to do in those days in Goa -- I did it every day and every night, in my hut and on that beach -- was to be with the people around me.
Goans. Indians. Foreigners.
Some people lost in themselves.
Thinkers and thieves.

The searchers.

And the ones who had found themselves.

Together we had a great time, in that remote paradise.

It did not last long, because some people thought that they were better, and had more rights than others.

That stupid game of some humans, who always start to play that.

If there ever was a place in the world to get rid of that, where that was easy, then it was Goa and India, in the early 1970s.

I lived nearly two years without money and a passport in India, mostly on the road to nowhere, in the early 1970s.

Sometimes hard and sobering, you learn fast what you are and what not.

But I had some of the greatest times of my life.

End of my first monsoon, I came to Goa. It was like a little friendly paradise.

All the hopelessness, the dirtiness, and insignificance of the road you have met, melted slowly away.

The friendly Goans didn't hassle you, and left you alone if you wanted to.

A luxury you only find up in the Himalayan mountains, and on the beaches of northern Goa.

Beautiful Tribe:

I read her book before it was published.

Cleo was slowly dying at the time, she'd always had a problem with her legs, she refused to eat vegetables, and only ate meat.

She was beautiful, and had come to terms with her twisted past and fading future.

She was working with [Thai] girls who had fallen ill in the sex trade, mostly around Patpong [a tourist-friendly, red-light road in Bangkok].

The opening chapter of her book is shocking in its way, which is what Cleo wanted.

Her point of view was limited to a certain crowd she hung

out with.

I had been in Goa, coinciding with her time there, and although the dealers and smugglers had a scene, there were a lot of other people enjoying the sun and freedom too.

Personally, I grew tired of the freak tourist fantasy land, even if it was cool.

I met some real interesting people there, but I wanted to venture forth into Hindustan [traditional India], and delve into the many cultures.

But Cleo wanted to be with her tribe, and why not?

It was her life and her decision.

Rest in peace, Cleo.

The *Bom Shankars* Clan:

In the beginning, there was unity in the tribe.

The hash *chillums* were king.

Then later on, someone brought *smack* to the Goa scene.

Soon after, the unity broke up into two tribes.

The *chillum* smoking *Bom Shankars* Clan, and the downtown Chinatown *Smack Bongs* [pipe for smoking] Clan.

Cleo was in the *bong* tribe.

Embraced Her:

I'm in her book, with my real name.

But then I lived with her, off and on, in Goa and in Bombay for a while.

She lied about me in the book, as she did with others, but my personal opinion of Cleo doesn't matter here.

The main reason I didn't like the book was the very negative and partial image she painted of Anjuna.

I lived between India and Nepal from 1971 to 1980, and spent all the winters in Goa.

There was a lot more going on in Anjuna, lots of people were not into heavy drugs.

And I was amazed too when going back in 2010, I was recognized and embraced by the Anjuna Goans.

They remembered me more than some of the Westerners did.

My Girlfriend:
She [Cleo] was my girlfriend, during the period of her book.

Bravo Unforgettable:
Bravo, sir?
So did you supply the *smack*?
Unforgettable are bodies lying with needles still in their arms, the morning after an Anjuna party, in the early 1970s.

My Girlfriend:
No, I did not.
I also didn't use it.

Nice Photos:
Yes, she mentions you in her book.
And also a couple of photos of you.
Nice to meet you.

Slinging Woman:
Luckily I was no longer in Goa, when she arrived.
I heard she was responsible for lots of people getting into *smack*.
Bad news.
I read the book. It's fairly clear.
Smack was not unheard of in Goa, but she turned it into a party drug, and was selling it.

Clean Squat:
I read the book also.
Selling, smuggling, using.
Classic.

Young Monsoon:

My time in Goa 1972 to 1973 was not at all like that.
Yes we smoked hash and grass.
Yes there was L.S.D. also around.
But so far as I know, no heroin or other hard drugs.
Those days, freaks were very much against hard drugs.

It was just traveling young people from all over the world, who spent some time there, resting, having a good time meeting other travelers for a while.

And most of us continued to travel to other places, around India.

Some ended up staying in Goa, and going up north [into India's Himalayas or Nepal] during monsoon time.

Things changed in later years.

Black Proof:
Most of the people that lived there [Goa] had experience with *smack*, and Peshawar [Pakistan's pharmaceutical] pills, Benares pharmacies, and the Crown Hotel in Delhi.

Most of the people that judge Cleo were not even there in her time, or just passing through.

Anyway, she is remembered and loved. Never mind good or bad.

The man from *Smack* Palace [Biryani], she mentions him.

When they [travelers] were broke, they wanted to work for him [smuggling], or with him.

His lieutenant was Jimmy the Knife.
Died in Bombay under strange circumstances.
Long blonde hair, British.
Sometimes a D.J. on stage, in his Saville Row suit.
Loved his acid and booze then.
Later something else.

Enjoy Early:
She brought Sam Biryani down from Bombay, and installed him in her place, in the center of Goa.

One had to be extremely naive and irresponsible to do that.

Biryani caused more damage to our [Goa beach] scene, even before then.

And afterwards.

Biryani was the lord of traveler's check scams, *smack* dealing, and other activities.

She also published real names [in *Goa Freaks*], which could have endangered people.

Not cool.

Not insider behavior.

Cool Fire:
Very bad form.
Don't like *grasses* [informants].

Enjoy Early:
Exactly, and that is what she was, an *effing* [fucking] *grass*.

She was trouble from the moment she arrived.

And stayed trouble after she left.

And she was a disaster for my dear friend [redacted], and partly responsible for his death.

Partly.

He was also an idiot for having fallen under her spell, while his girlfriend and little daughter were with him.

And how [in *Goa Freaks*] she slags the girlfriend.

Black Proof:
He [Biryani] began to hustle in Delhi, walking kilometers to change foreign currency.

Embraced Her:
I arrived in Bombay by ship, from Kenya, in June 1971.

The second day I was there, Sam stole all my traveler's checks.

I initially didn't mean to go to Goa, but there I was, in India with no money.

And I knew I had some friends of friends from London in

Goa.
So there I went.
The rest is history.

Loved Maybe:
I was not in India in the 1980s, so I only knew his beginnings as a Bombay street hustler.
But I was friends with Jimmy the Knife.
So I knew what was going on, and I had personal reasons not to be upset by his [Biryani's] death.
He was strangled and hung.
It's not sure if by inmates, or wardens, or both.

Black Proof:
When was he killed in Delhi prison, he was there waiting for judgment, and heard the death sentence might be his destiny by the judge.
In 2012, he was still alive.
Remember when Fara's Road Gang ambushed him and his people, and beat them up?
He [Biryani] thought he was God of Bombay, and told Muslims not to run [crime] business.
But they did not take a shit from him.
Rashid, Shakur Bai, Gara's Road Gang near Shuklaji, were tough nuts to break.
And Mohammed Ali's Road did not give a damn about him.

Slowly Bananas:
I stayed with Joe Bananas in 1998 to 2002, and Cleo came in many times.
Had some great talks with her, but she got into some bad habits, and she slowly went down hill.
But a lovely lady.

Embraced Her:
Once a girlfriend of ours jumped in Joe Bananas' drinking-

water well.

She broke a leg badly, and bled in it.

Somebody had to go down and tie her, so that we could pull her up.

For Joe, it was a nuisance.

He poured disinfectant in the water.

But for many months, he could not use the well for drinking or cooking water.

Chocolate Looks:

I only had a brief conversation with Cleo, when I was a Sysop on the Travel Forum of CompuServe.

[displays text]

I'm in the last message:

12-Feb-95 09:41:52
Sb: #622277-Goa
Fm: Cleo Odzer 70233,623
To: *********
Been to Goa?
I lived there for 6 years.

#: 624011 S7/Asia
14-Feb-95 00:00:42
Sb: #623549-Goa
Fm: Cleo Odzer 70233,623
To: *********

And I don't know much about Europeans found dead in hedges, but they found a dead junkie in my well once.

He must have stumbled into it in the middle of the night and couldn't get out, so drowned.

It was really annoying.

The natives were superstitious and they insisted on dredging up all the water from the well, and even some of the mud underneath.

Then they wouldn't use it for the next 2 years.

That well was right next to my house.

The second closest was pretty far to lug buckets of water from, over and over.

I had built the first flush toilet on Anjuna beach.

It had a water tank on the roof and the Goans would fill it from the well every few days.

After we found the body in the well, it was real difficult to get someone willing to lug water back and forth from that other well.

#: 627006 S7/Asia
16-Feb-95 23:43:22
Sb: #626876-Goa
Fm: Cleo Odzer 70233,623
To: *********

When you had a pig snuffling under you only inches away [in village outhouse toilets], waiting in hopeful anticipation for a yummy meal, and all you did was pee on its head -- kinda made you feel sad.

Never Silver:
In Goa, they had the pig toilets.

Mind Moon:
You had to go armed with big rocks, to fight off the pigs eating your shit hanging out of your ass.

Stones Go:
Yes, you have to go in the toilet with stones.

Sitars There:
My husband had a stick to beat back the greedy big pig, and give the smaller pigs a chance.

Tongue Stick:
I was in Arambol [a Goa beach] and, in the beginning, I was

going without the stick.

Once the pig came so near, I almost felt her tongue in my ass.

And she grabbed in the air for her food.

After that, I was carrying my stick always.

Best Bad:
It's something I don't miss, to be honest.

[Human Money displays a photograph of a pig with its snout sticking into the drain of a Goa outhouse, seen from the user's view -- looking down into the toilet at the pig. The pig's face is captioned: "So patiently it waits."]

Open Under:
Ah yes, they were fighting under there for a good position as soon as they heard the door open.

Hot First:
The first time shitting, I was very afraid by the pig eating my hot.

Bite Soon:
I sometimes was scared they'd bite my ass.

Hey Lick: [laughing at the pig in the photograph]:
Hey!
Don't lick my ass.

Stick Always:
Always take a stick.

Face View:
In Chapora, in Sea View Guest House until few years ago, there was a toilet like this.

When low tide, pigs were there.

I got super scared the first time it happened.
I couldn't understand what it was -- that sound -- until I saw the pig face.

I Remember:
I remember my first shit in Goa [laughs].

Especially Still:
I certainly do.

Morning Yes:
Yes, good morning, piggy.

Forget the Impossible:
Impossible to forget.

Little Noses:
We took little stones in with us, and kept popping on their noses, so they could not lick our ass in the process.

Twinkle Well:
Yes, I remember it well.
When you see the twinkle in their eyes, how can you say no?

Candle War:
Oh yeah, I remember seeing the snouts beneath me.

Spattered Proper:
I once spattered a pig's face with diarrhea, and he licked it up good and proper.
Loved it.

Strange Heart:
It gave me almost a heart attack the first time.
I just heard a strange noise.
Under my butt.

Shiny Wild:
With wild open mouth, and shiny eyes.

Hard Flipped:
The best system.

Rosy Party:
She was called Rosy.
We needed a stick sometimes. Especially after party.
She knew what to expect.

Betsy Lashes:
Mine was Betsy.
Her lashes always dripping shit.

Really Eaten:
Oh fuck yeah.
Shit really really fast, or have your ass eaten out.
I remember all too well.

Breath Warm:
The warm breath.

Late Talk [laughing]:
Fond memories.

Discover Tongue:
That was when you discover how long their tongue is!

Stoned Newspaper:
In 1975 and 1976, there was a newspaper [a zine by travelers in Goa] called *Stoned Pig*.
They could be stoned pigs, because of all the drugs in the shit.

Humbled Hard:

I remember two pigs fighting over my crap one morning.

Such a strange experience, having to use the bathroom, while tripping hard on *shrooms*.

It was the most disgusting experience of my life.

This was my first time.

Pigs in Ireland don't run after you squealing with delight, over dinner about to be served [in your toilet].

It stripped me, a lot, of my natural reservations.

It's crazy.

They smell you, and "oink" with delight.

I found myself laughing a lot too.

Especially if I was altered off my face -- especially if I was on *ket* [ketamine] or acid, or whatever.

Maybe the pigs got high off the human waste, and they were really all just addicts?

I know for a fact they get more excited about foreigners taking a dump [laughs].

I couldn't help but laugh in Arambol in 1996, because as soon as the pigs saw me with a towel, soap, and a water bottle, they came running over.

Oh, the indignity.

But maybe it humbled us too.

Golden Sharp:

Remember the big [Indian] Mafia Mama, with the sharp tongue and the golden heart?

Anytime New:

I remember when some new police walked in, and she went mad.

Grabbed the *chillum* from someone, and was very angry with the police.

They became very afraid and left.

She was good to us, but strict about some things.

I asked if I could smoke a *joint*, and she said:

"Of course anytime."
Good times.

Nose Years:
She was my landlady for a lot of years. So I knew her well.
Rented me a nine-room house, with big garden, behind Pasquale restaurant in Vagator.
She was a good friend to me, and quite a character.
I stayed there with Irish Sean, and English Thunder Nose.
Nicest times of my life.
She did a lot of good things for us. Never any police.
And breakfast in Pasquale restaurant every morning.

Alive Thunder:
Thunder Nose?
Does anyone know anything about him?
Is he still alive?

Four Five:
He was in Chapora, four or five years ago.
Somebody said he passed away, a couple of years ago.

Peace Too:
Yes. Thunder Nose has moved on too.
Rest in peace.

Normal Super:
Bless him.
He was fun to be with.

Priest Happened:
What happened to the priest?
Was he called Father [redacted]?
He was also into black market and dodgy dealing.
Do you remember him?

He lived in Baga [a Goa beach].

Enjoy Early:
Father [redacted]. We used to call him Father Piranha.
He was Mickey Mouse compared to Biryani.
Money changing and -- I've heard, but not 100 percent confirmed -- renting out some girl.
And probably a bit of thievery.
He had a guesthouse.
Not the worst place. One of the first.

Priest Happened:
You have a good memory.
Yes, he was the local money changer and, I think, organized some smuggling.
Fairly harmless I think, but unusual for a priest.

Enjoy Early:
The best is, when he came by at Christmas, and told us that God had a Christmas present for us -- namely, that the rate for the dollar had gone up, by 10 paisa [one-tenth of a rupee].
We just cracked up.
Still, he was handy to have.

Priest Happened [laughing]:
A present from God -- that's hilarious.
I guess he's gone to meet his maker, if Saint Peter let him enter the Pearly Gates [of heaven].
Maybe not?
He was naughty.

Early Picture:
We were safely hidden on Anjuna for years.
As soon as the [travelers'] flea market showed up, we exposed ourselves to a nation of shopkeepers.
As soon as they knew they could make paisa, the Bombay

wallahs poured in, and change took place quickly.
I left in 1976.

Cave Wonders:
They used to sell [tour] packages in Bombay for Indian tourists, to come and see the naked hippie girls.
Plus half-price booze in Goa.

Under the Galata Bridge:
I remember busloads of Indians showing up in the end, to see the nude Westerners.

Early Picture:
Did you see the fat Indian, waddling down the beach, to check out the naked chicks?

Slinging Woman:
Electronic music ruined it for me.
Then came the rave scene.
But I was gone by then, 1972.

Best Bad:
The spoiling of a special place is very relative.
My wife is from Arambol, and I know hippie folks who lived lakeside in the 1970s.
The locals thought the lake was haunted, because young lads encountered mud-bathing, acid dropping hippies at sunset.
Between them, and their adrenaline fuelled imaginations, the legend of the ghosts began.
My brother-in-law was one of those kids.
They lived in Indian poverty.
No life.
But enough to eat.
Mom and dad roamed the baking hot hillsides, collecting cashews to supplement meager incomes.
My good lady wife had to move to Mapusa when she began

secondary school, as Arambol was still without power, and she could not study after sunset.

But word was spreading, and every year more hippies came.

Then the Israelis discovered Goa, and Arambol became famous.

Today there's litter, pollution, and development.

It's easy to say, "How terrible."

But my cousin runs one of the lakeside restaurants, and his brother works here in Wicklow [a county town in Ireland] after my wife got him a work permit.

Their kids are massively advantaged, compared to the previous generation.

Many of them have travelled to Europe and beyond. Some have settled, but all will tell, "Life is good."

Sure the village is bursting, and the litter is terrible. But from their perspective, the *Lonely Planet* was a godsend.

We, the white privileged Westerners, need to be patient. These things take time to settle.

I'm an Irishman.

And I have watched tourism here [in Ireland] for 50 years develop from effectively fleecing the *Yanks* [Americans], to a very sophisticated, empathetic tourism model.

But it takes money and time.

Big Bottles:

A whole generation -- of very naive, mostly girls -- has [recently] descended on Goa.

Either they get dead drunk and walk off with any guy, or they get into yoga and spiritual New Age stuff, and fall in love or get abused by their teacher.

There have been quite a few rape and murder cases.

I find that young backpackers seem so much more trusting, naive, and fragile than early travelers.

Jungle Tripping:

I've been once in Arambol. I was completely Vagator and

Chapora.

In 1980, people were really tripping in jungle nature, if you know what I mean.

My Spanish good friend Kosmos, and his beautiful girlfriend from Canada, received me there, with much love.

I heard he is dead. Many datura.

Danced Dream:

I used to tell people back in the U.S.A. that I danced 40 hours a week, outdoors, on or near a beach, while they spent 40 hours a week in a tiny cubicle, in an airless office.

Of course, they are all now retired, and get big fat checks monthly.

But I would never dream of trading with them.

Naked Moon:

Dancing Naked Under Palm Trees. It's a song [by Sedrick the MC] which always reminds me of the wonderful Full Moon Parties on Vagator and Anjuna beach in the 1970s.

Sure Doses:

Were most of you taking Sunshine L.S.D.?

I was there in 1971 the first time, and sure enough, just about every late night gathering started -- and continued -- high on big doses of pure acid.

Hooo weee.

What a time it was.

Under the Galata Bridge:

I still remember walking down the beach [in Goa], in the early 1970s, to the sound of our local band playing *Sympathy For the Devil.*

And then when I got there, I'd see Liquid Tongues with his bottle of liquid acid, and eye-dropper, putting drops on the tongues of all the people in line.

I didn't participate, because by then I was into much stronger drugs, and my saying was, "Acid's for kids."

I did have fun dancing on the stage, in my long black velvet cape, with Kali embroidered on the back -- and jumping off into crowd, with my cape blowing in the wind.

It was a great time, and I was privileged to be there in the beginning.

Blue Prayer:
I lived in a palm leaf *teepee*, south end Anjuna, 1974 and 1975.
A party every night, all night Christmas Eve until New Year's.
Free acid.
A little stage. Guitars, amps and a tiny drum kit from Goa, because no one brought one overland.
Sympathy For the Devil all night long.

Danced Dream [displaying a photograph of nearly-naked travelers sitting on a beach]:
Another photo I just stumbled upon, in my copious photo albums.
This one is how we used to spend relaxed, unstressed days in Goa, back in the times.

Dark Talk:
Unstressed and undressed.
Maybe they are connected.

Scrawny:
Some scrawny folks there.

Danced Dream:
No McDonald's nearby anywhere.

On the Border:
Oh, those lazy naked *chillum* afternoons of our misspent youth.

Danced Dream:
Yes, we all retired in our 20s, but now have to work until we die.

I'd rather work now, and know I had a well-spent and very stress-free youth.

Much Friendlier:
I knew Brian Glass very well in Swayambhu in the 1970s, and in Bali in 1975, and later in the States.

I met him, for the first time, on the beach in Puri [an east coast city in Orissa state] in 1971.

He was freshly released from an Indian jail, where he was locked up with Bombay Brian for smuggling car parts from Nepal to India.

He said the worst part of jail was when he was in the same cell as Brian.

In November 1970, I got a ride from Kabul to Delhi with Acid Nicholas, who blah-blah'ed endlessly about the Brotherhood [The Brotherhood of Eternal Love, which began in Laguna Beach, California, and included influential L.S.D. enthusiasts, manufacturers, and distributors].

Laguna Beach:
I remember Laguna Beach.

Cute Beaches:
I'm sure that we must have been in Laguna in the 1960s, and Goa, at the same time, and probably crossed paths.

Too many cute guys in Laguna for me to remember every one.

In Goa, we stayed on Vagator beach with our own stash of Sunshine and Afghani, so we rarely went to Anjuna, and didn't socialize much.

I was always too high, anyway [laughs].

I never went back to Goa after 1972.

Too many other places to explore.
Nice beaches, and nice people, wherever we went.
I only remember a couple of places [in Laguna Beach].
A record store, and Mystic Arts [Mystic Arts World, a psychedelic gallery in 1967 to 1970] -- where there was a room in back, for chilling out.

Pure Tribe:
Acid Nicholas met his old friend Timothy Leary in Afghanistan [in January 1973], and Timothy then gave Acid Nicholas a handful of pure L.S.D, enough acid for thousands of trips, with the instructions not to sell it, but return to Goa, and share it freely with the Goa tribe.

Bravo Unforgettable:
In 1973, he [Acid Nicholas] had his dog and himself with colored hair -- light violet.
That's when I saw him first time, and received his gift.

Especially Still:
I remember a Full Moon Party in Anjuna, when a guy gave away free L.S.D., in January or February 1973.

Clear Years:
He certainly shared it with me.
Whoa, what a trip.
Liquid clear pure acid from Timothy lasted years within me.

Sunshine Shouted:
Oh yes, with eye-dropper bottles.
Acid Eric, I remember him arriving, making an ad hoc *teepee*, and someone shouted:
"The Sunshine Acid is here."

Many Was I:
I was there.

Best acid ever.
Many trips.

Pure Tribe:
Orange Sunshine.

Younger Uncanny [indicating a photograph]:
This photo does look a lot like Brian Glass, but it is Acid Nicholas.
The likeness is uncanny.
They looked very much alike, when they were younger.
But it's Acid Nicholas.
I can tell by the necklace he's wearing.
Plus, Brian Glass had not been to Goa yet, when this photo was taken.
He did not get there until the late 1970s.
This photo was taken in the early 1970s on Anjuna Beach.
It is an old photo of Acid Nicholas, rolling a *jay* [cannabis cigarette].

Many Decadent:
What decadent great times we had, my dear.
Those were the days.
Without many responsibilities.

Cave Wonders:
I think most of us were trying to escape from world politics in our 20s.
I met a few [American anti-Vietnam War] draft dodgers in Goa.
It's been a pirate port [since the 15th century].
They used to harass Dutch, French and British ships, and were known as the Malabar Pirates.
Way back in the 17th century, Margao [a city in Goa on the Sal River] was the largest settlement on the [Indian] subcontinent.

After India liberated Goa from the Portuguese [in 1961], there was only one road into the state, from Hubli Junction.

Or the boat from Bombay.

Most of the first people to arrive were draft dodgers, or people on the run.

Then came the overland travelers.

Tourism started in earnest in 1986, with the first package tourists' direct flights.

Enjoy Early:

The coastal Goans did not see it as a liberation [from Portuguese colonialism] but as an invasion [by India].

We once had a heated discussion on this topic with a Punjabi friend and his aunt, whose brother or husband was the general leading the invasion.

And the wonderful Gerson da Cunha and me on the other side of the debate.

The Sikh auntie was terribly upset when the incredibly cultured Goan -- Gerson -- called it an invasion.

Early Picture:

Did you ever read of Vasco's arrival [Portuguese explorer Vasco da Gama, circa 1498]?

First thing he did was kill and behead all the fishermen.

Then he hung them from the [ship's] mast, and sailed along the coast, firing cannons into the villages.

Landed in Kerala and butchered everyone.

Strange Mountains:

By the 1980s, Goa was nothing but a holiday getaway.

Mostly naked before that.

Nakedness was important to us hippies.

Fashion came after that. And private, invitation-only parties.

In the beginning, it was R & R [rest and recreation] for those brave people who had ruined themselves with hard travel to remote and difficult places -- mostly to find the best *charas* in the world.

Bathe Nostalgic [responding to a photograph of Indians staring at a traveler pouring water over the head and body of a topless Western girl, next to a village well in Goa]:
Nostalgic.
But don't bathe next to the well.

Naked Looking:
That's why the Indians are looking at her so weirdly.
Not because she's naked.

Sitars There:
The soapy water filters into the well.
Bad.

Lovely Railway:
Living there for many years, this was what bothered me.
The disrespect for the local population, and the soap that went into the well.
Water we drank!
Freedom is not this.
Freedom is respecting the places, and the people who live there.

Soap Well:
I dropped the soap in the well.

Clean and True:
True, don't bathe too close to the well.
I remember using those communal wells.
Worst thing was, when you filled a bucket and -- while your back is turned -- a cow sticks its head in, and drinks the lot.
Then you need to clean it, before you can refill it.

Clothes Rip:

My girlfriend passed out in Colva beach [in Goa].
I took her to the hospital.
She stayed a few days. They said she had phlebitis -- water on the lungs.
All the sick women were in the same room, with their different ailments.
One woman gave birth, and the newborn baby was passed around among all of us.
Only the strong survive.

Disturbed Love:
The truth is, I wasn't planning to go to India, but I fell in love with a man, older than me.
I left home, and a few months later I was there.
After Dwarka [a coastal city in Gujarat state] -- a very fine sandy beach -- we had arrived in paradise [Goa] and we chose Arambol, because of its beautiful name.
I was stoned by everything.
It was my first trip abroad.
Local people climbing the palm trees.
Pigs cleaning the toilets.
The early-riser roosters.
The beauty of the tropical landscape, with the colonial remains of Portugal.
The [Goa] women with flowers in their hair.
And all the amazing people from all over the world, staying there.
I didn't speak English, and I was dying of envy, seeing those experienced hippies.
But soon we started to copy them, buying some freak clothes, and immediately made friends with a Brazilian couple, and later a group of Italians and French, and we started our own band.
After a week, we had transformed into some neo-hippies, and we attended the Chapora parties, and the Anjuna flea market, where we sold all the useless things we brought for the

trip.

I was captivated by the relaxed atmosphere.

But not everything was perfect.

The parties and the acids touched more than one.

And the day after, it was normal to find somebody who lost his mind, usually wondering who he was, or talking to a palm tree.

This added to [more] police, who were always looking for *baksheesh* from us.

But speaking of police and acids, surely some of you will know the story of the murder, after a party on the lake's beach.

It was said that one night, a tourist from Eastern Europe, preyed on by madness, killed three or four tourists who slept on the beach -- with his ax.

The fact is that he escaped into the jungle, and was never caught, increasing the legends about the nationality of the murderer and where he was hiding.

Somebody said he knew the killer.

Local people said he was still in the jungle.

Others said that he was in Cambodia.

Who knows?

Maybe one of you have the right version?

Anyway, it was a mysterious terror and good story to hear around the fire in Arambol.

Late Talk: I remember the story of the ax murderer in Arambol.

I knew someone who was there at the time.

I remember them saying that the man was Polish, but I don't know.

Nearly Spaced:
Czech.

I was there that night in Arambol, asleep alone in my little camp in the jungle, when the murders happened.

I was woken by a stranger, in the middle of the night, and

quickly ran down to the beach, where we all gathered.

Sleeping Friend:
There was an Australian woman, her Indian friend, and one European tourist [murdered].
They were sleeping on the beach.

Ice One:
The Indian guy was Ramsroet or Ram, no?
Selling *chillums* in the Anjuna market?

Sleeping Friend:
Yes, Ram Swaroop.
I knew him.
I met them in Manali, a few months before this happened.

Ice One:
I met him in different places in India, selling his *chillums*.

Golden Sharp:
All I heard, it was a Russian [murderer].
There had been a group, training in yoga and martial arts.
Seems the teacher fed them psychedelics, and this one man went on the rampage.
Strange thing though, while on the run, some of the V.I.P. hippies gave him shelter, and helped him to cross the Goa border [and escape].
But nobody tells why they were doing that.
Another mystery in the clouds.

Squalid Dreams:
It was a big guy called Thomas.
He had been behaving oddly.
Who didn't?
He made his own fire, by himself, on top of the hill for New Year's Eve.

At the time [of the murders], I was staying in the Banana House in Vagator.

People, terrified, came over from Arambol to stay with me.

They thought that it was Mira, a big English friend who went a bit crazy every year, but it wasn't.

I believe he was from Czechoslovakia.

Nearly Spaced:
He [Mira] used to follow me around, had a bit of a fixation on me it seemed, and it really frightened me.

I was very young.

I'd never met anybody in his state before.

Now I am old, and I've been working in mental health, and I understand what he was experiencing.

But at that time, I was young, and sometimes scared he was going to hurt me.

Is he still living?

Complicated Incarnation:
Mira died a very long time ago.

He committed a kind of ritual suicide, as he was obsessed with Shiva and Kali.

He was not that crazy, but played the role well.

He was an amazing bluesman as well, played beautiful harmonica, and had a gift with words.

I remember him singing in one of our fabulous acoustic parties, happening in the Arambol jungle:

"They want you to believe you got to be famous / They are fools / You want to be like the rocks in the river / Nobody knows them."

Sand Ax:
Thomas, from Czechoslovakia, was the man wielding the ax.

He killed his best friend Ruben, a backpacker who was sleeping on the sand.

And an Indian guy, who also happened to be there by

chance.
He ran away, and was never caught.
We never saw him again.

Nearly Spaced:
The guy who was sleeping in the sand, I found his body.
Trying to wake him up, and warn him what had happened, I realized he was dead.
A very frightening moment for young me.

Very Snake:
I met Ruben, a Russian soldier who escaped from Afghanistan. 1982?
We smoked *chillums*.
Then I went to Tirakol Fort.
The day after, I came back to Arambol.
Policemen everywhere.
That very night, Thomas from Czechoslovakia had assassinated three people.
Ruben was strangulated with a chain, and drowned in the lake.
Since then, I do not like the idea to take a bath there [in the lake].

Told One:
The one who was killed by Thomas -- Ruben -- he was from Armenia, he told me.

Complicated Incarnation:
I was there too. Long and complicated story.
Thomas, a Czech -- tall, very strong and muscular -- had a rivalry with Ruben, the guy from Armenia.
They were practicing martial arts with some other people as well.
Ruben was the teacher.
Around Christmas time, Thomas was very perturbed by a

very short love with a French woman, that turned out badly.

Then, during the crazy night, he ate with this Indian guy and his girlfriend.

I talked with her the next day.

It's not clear if he was fed datura.

Anyway, he killed him with his knife.

Then he took an ax and killed a French man sleeping on the beach -- a martial artist.

Then he went for Ruben.

Ruben came out of his hut in some bushes, near the lake, with nunchucks [a chain-and-sticks weapon] and Thomas strangled him with it.

There is much more to the story.

Thomas tried to kidnap a baby.

But these are the facts about the murders.

After that he escaped by swimming.

We heard he was busted in Germany later.

Mad Warning:
Mad ax man, killed his karate teacher and others.

There was a wanted and warning poster of him, in our *chai* shop in Colva.

I didn't want to frighten you [Girl Warning].

Girl Warning:
I'm a big girl now, daddy.
I think I can handle it.

Mad Warning [laughing]:
Yeah, you were little at the time, though.

Is Is:
I went to Panjim [Goa's capital] police headquarters, to renew my visa, and they thought I was the ax man.

They had a photograph of the guy and fortunately he had no tattoos, but I have.

Hairy few minutes back then.
Got the visa extension.

Big Bottles:
He was never caught.
Remains one of the unsolved horrors.

So Invaded:
I remember Thomas, I didn't like the guy.
Bad vibes.
I was in Arambol two days prior to the murders.

Four Five:
It was February 1982.
We having party on Vagator Beach. Somebody came to me, to tell me.
And then asked me to stop the music.
We said:
"No way. People are all tripping [on L.S.D.], so don't panic them."

Dark Talk:
How awful that is.
Murder in paradise.
The worst I ever saw was some Italian guy trying to bash another fellow, with a two-meter-long flaming piece of wood he took out of the bonfire at Anjuna, during one of the all-night parties there.
It was an awful shock to see that break out, in what was otherwise a very peaceful scene.

Firewood Street:
Weird things happen, and places like Goa have always attracted craziness at times.
I wouldn't particularly focus on these tragedies too much, though.

They are few and far apart, and shouldn't be allowed to overshadow the beautiful, and enchanting, character of that place.
Or any place at all.

Disturbed Love:
I remember once speaking with a mother of a young Israeli.
She was looking for him in Manikaran [in Parvati Valley, Himachal Pradesh state], hanging his photo in the village.

Carnival Dude:
In 1973 Goa. Me 13 [years old].
Some hippie dude comes up to only me --not the adults -- and says:
"Ya wanna buy some acid?"
Weird as fuck.
He then came up to me again, months later, in Kathmandu.
And finally Kuta Beach [in Bali, Indonesia].
1974, by then.
Only me.
And that same carnival barker line.
My first stalker.

Disappeared Looking:
You wouldn't find any psychedelics, if you weren't looking.
I first arrived [in Baga beach] in 1979.
There was a lot of Brown Sugar [less refined heroin] around then, lots of junkies, and many people getting robbed and burgled by *smack* heads.
They mostly had O.D.'d, been busted, or disappeared by the mid-1980s.

Under the Galata Bridge:
I had a few dry times for morphine.
I remember not being able to score on November 25th 1970, the day my son was born.

But never saw Goa without lots of [hashish] smoke -- maybe in monsoon season, when we all went north to Manali, Kashmir, or Nepal?

The *Bom Shankars* Clan:
Those were some of the best times in my life.
We were all pure hedonists, without any shame.

Hot Streams:
We certainly were.
Living on a straw mat. Right next to the ocean.
Most were naked.
Baked fresh by the sun.
Lulled by the moon.
Walking along the beach from Vagator around to Anjuna, to dance under the stars.
An occasional trip for supplies.
The [Goa] children bringing [selling] bananas and pawpaws.
Another dimension.

Dancing Nowadays:
I don't agree on the naked thing.
We were topless.
And men were wearing a kind of improvised G-string.
Most of us were skinny. Living a simple life near the beach.
But we all had a *lungi* as our dress, scarf, towel, or hair turban.

Sleeping Horses:
Reminds me of every beach I stayed at during the early 1970s.
Hedonism was the driving force for all of us.

Idyllic Atrocious:
I arrived in Goa in 1970, and left for Bombay and [Bollywood's] Sun City studios in 1972, to get away from the

atrocious behavior of most of the hippies -- many of whom were on the run from the authorities in their own countries.

The drug war in Calangute -- between the Italians and the French -- ended with a shootout and one dead.

We were lucky to live in a calm little part of Baga, with great fishing people, and musicians from Shantiniketan [a university near Calcutta].

It was idyllic where we lived.

Marvelous Blood:
I was there [Anjuna] during the dry season of 1971.
Had no money, and slept on a straw mat on the beach.
Survived on bananas, and whatever those peanut candies were.

Firewood Street:
So magnificent.
I once knew every stone of the path down to it [Anjuna beach].
And on my second year there, had my *teepee* right on the ridge.

Shack Nirvana:
Before living on Anjuna for two months during the end of 1976, it was my vision of Nirvana for hippies and freaks.

After some people and friends went swimming out [in the Arabian Sea] on acid -- who never showed up again -- and other friends in straitjackets after a stroll naked in Panjim.

Others proclaiming themselves Shiva and ripping [stealing] money and passports.

And The Children of God [an American-led cult] having a field-day for weeks and years.

I finally gave up my preconceptions about India and Asia.
And then my real trip began.
I was free.
Most of the time.

Fully stoned.
Near the beautiful church on Anjuna beach just behind our shack.

Involved and Beautiful:
One time, I met a beautiful Israeli girl who everybody said had taken too much acid in Goa, and was absolutely out of it, and broke.
The *chai wallahs* were taking turns in the caves, paying with a cup and a *chapati*.
I tried talking to her, but she made no sense at all, as if in another world.
And no other foreigner wanted to get involved.

Very People:
I remember three guys I met in Ceylon [the island nation later known as Sri Lanka], and Almora [a Himalayan foothill town, in Uttarakhand state].
All lost their lives in tragic circumstances, in India.
Drug use was the cause.
I always had great respect for hard drugs, they frightened me.
That was one of the reasons why I didn't want to go to Goa, because it was known for its drug excesses.
And one of them died there.
Another one walked all the way down from Almora to Delhi.
He had apparently no money any more, and his woman left him at one point.
And later I came to know, he literally starved in Delhi.
In 1979, I spent some weeks in Calcutta.
At that time, I met an older German who occasionally worked for the consulate.
He buried Germans and Europeans who died there, in a cemetery.
Imagine.
This was his job.

Dancing Nowadays:

Before going on the road, my mother had warned me about heroin.

She was dead right to warn me.

I stayed at a large distance from junkies, at least I tried to.

To survive myself.

Sometimes, very interesting people. Also back home in Amsterdam.

This was a big reason not to go to Goa anymore, between 1976 and 1985.

It was all so depressing.

Street Shocked:

I was pretty shocked when I arrived overland to Goa in 1978, to see the mindless drug addiction.

I smoked pure *dope* [cannabis] -- with no tobacco -- and still do.

Once daily.

And then two hours tai chi to music.

But never, through my 36 years now in India, have I felt any interest in any of all those synthetic drugs.

The last station on the journey of self-pity.

I recall seeing, in Delhi, hordes of lost [Western] junkies.

In bandages.

Begging.

Skeletons, crap, and a dead body sometimes, lying on the street during early mornings, outside some guest house in Paharganj.

Revolting.

Gross.

Enjoy Early:

It was not easy to say no, in our scene.

Although Eddie [Eight Finger Eddie, a popular traveler based in Goa] didn't smoke.

Stuff Time:
Did he have only eight fingers?

Begged Lucrative:
Yes he was born that way.
On his right hand, he was missing the ring and middle finger.
But the hand looked normal, just narrow.

Trance Eight:
In 1977 and 1978, we [with Eight Finger Eddie] used to sit, and talk for hours.
He had the most fantastic stories, and held me in a trance, for days at a time.
When I went back in 2004 or so, he said they were all lies.
Good stories.
But.

Begged Lucrative:
I understand.
What he wrote about me, in his book, was wrong as well.

Under the Galata Bridge:
I stayed a week on a rented houseboat [on the Ganges River in Varanasi, 1970].
I was on my way to Kathmandu from Goa to *cop* some hash to sell by the *tola* for my season in Goa.
I'd left a very pregnant Angelique in the house we had rented for six months [in Goa], and she would birth our son in that house after I got back.
I met Eight Finger Eddie who was renting the boat next to me on the Ganges.
He became a good friend.

Tree Characters:
Was Vagator the next beach up, north of Anjuna?
A little river to cross?

And a jungle on the other side?
Where that [French] guy lived in a tree on a platform?
I spent a few days there with him.
No one else.
Peace.
Unforgettable.
In my days, 1976, no need to buy *charas*.
That French guy would sweep the [party] beach the following morning, gathering all the goodies folks had lost there.
Half an ounce, an ounce, whatever money.
And he'd come to me and roll [cannabis cigarettes], and we'd go have lunch.
I'll never forget that beautiful slim Goanese woman, with her huge basket of exotic fruit, passing by every morning, and we'd stuff ourselves with mangoes.
The pigs [at the toilets] were happy.
What a shock the first time, hearing that munching, until I looked through the [toilet] hole, and saw two or three of them chomping happily.
Couldn't help bursting into laughter.
What I loved of India was, I took everything as it came.
Which is quite impossible in the Western world, at least for me.
Everything makes me uneasy here [in the West].
Angry.
I was often [in India] taken for a local.
I'm from Italy, I am dark, and had my hair up.
My toddler loved pulling my hair.
I started dressing local as well, from Afghanistan.
How to resist?
And how to resist giving away anything plastic, or jeans, on the way?
It was easy to give. Still is.
Anyone comes around and says, "I love this" -- and if we don't need it, I immediately put whatever they liked in their hands, and thank them.

My things I love, but pile up.
They go to a good home.
I really do believe we are one.
That trip to India gave me -- I understood life looks after itself.
We all needed each other, one way or another.
Discovering together.
I met such characters everywhere, all the way.
I love you all.
Namaste.

The Heart:
Yes, many layers.
India is a different story if it was a watering hole on your way from A to Z, or a holiday resort where you went every winter after you worked the handicraft markets in the West or did your scam.

Or if you were stuck there [in India] -- year in, year out -- in your little village, tied down by your cats and dogs and children and garden, and your lack of valid travel documents.

I remember monsoons, where we hadn't got 10 rupees between the six of us.

Monsoons we survived only by the grace of the village grocers giving credit.

Until the jet set came back after the rains, throwing lavish dinners, buying what [handicrafts] we made during monsoon.

The tourists would buy a bit of *dope*, and we could even our scores with the shop and innkeepers, until the next rains.

For us, who lived there all year round, the local people were a genuine village community, and we experienced great solidarity from them.

I didn't have kids in Goa.

But I experienced how well the community, locals and foreigners alike, took care of kids in trouble.

One thing you could be sure of, as a parent, was that your kids will be taken care of -- if you broke a leg -- one way or the other.

Beedi Travel:
In Goa, when I was about to travel around India, the *beedi* [a tiny cigarette] makers made me packets, with grass inside, which was nice to travel around with.

Needed Body:
You know when people get the bridge of their nose pierced?
But it's always just the skin part?
He, Bone Pierced, pierced his own, but went through the bone.
Through the bone!
At one point he literally lived on *lassi*.
Nothing else.
He said it was all the body needed.
The memories [laughs].

Cool Fire:
The *chillum* ceremonies used to get on my tits at times because -- due to all the ceremonials, "*Bom Shiva Shanka shamboo*" and all that bollocks -- you had to wait an age before you got a *chug* [smoke], and they had to keep relighting it.

[The Navhind Times, India]:
"11 January 1970 -- We can give you only verbal pictures, because if we print real pictures of the hippy 'scene' at Calangute beach, it would invite the wrath of the anti-obscenity laws on our heads.
"Picture a nude girl lying on the sands, her legs spread wide, and reading an Agatha Christie novel.
"Picture a voluptuous bouncing girl, sprinting like a gazelle across the sands, and plonking herself down at the sleeping young man, in the altogether, and smiling up to us with a sauciness that pushed up our pulse rate.
"We saw sights straight out of the fables of Sodom and

Gomorrah, scenes that reminded us of chapters in banned books and blue films -- a surfeit of sex and the white man's fall on the entire beach, from the Tourist Resort to Baga chapel.

"These closely-knit -- they do not mix with local people for the simple reason that in their lexicon, Indians are disgusting -- tribalistic and obscene young men and women are plundering with impunity the traditional and honored morality of this peaceful territory.

"These white men and women with fair skin and dark minds, are today posing a grave menace -- because they feel that the 'damn ruthless Indians' can take it."

7 • KATHMANDU & NEPAL

Her Naked:

[China's] military was trying to arrest a bus load of us traveling out of Lhasa [Tibet's capital] to the Nepalese border, when Tibet was kicking all foreigners out, circa 1987, give or take a year.

So I stripped completely naked in front of two of the soldiers, and they got so embarrassed they ran off -- threatening to imprison me as they ran off -- and left us all alone.

Sold Survival:

I travelled dirt poor and, on occasion, not even sleeping indoors.

We had my family send, via postal service, the last of my few hundreds in savings.

In Nepal, we stayed with friends.

We lived on pennies really.

And, one time, we were truly desperate and -- it's not something I like to admit -- I sold myself.

I prostituted myself to a well-educated Westerner, and two of his associates.

All clean.

But I had to think of it as survival sex.

Worms:

I've taken acid. I've taken Mandrex pills [Methaqualone, also known as Quaaludes].

The Kathmandu government hospital has 200 beds.

Do you know about worms?

If I can get to Hong Kong, I could have a lot of medicine.

One load of Mandrex, and I slept for three days.//
I did not die.
But my mouth was so bitter.
I have pus on my head [scratches his head hard and wildly].
A housewife threw urine out of the window yesterday, and it landed right on my head.

Fortress Hovel:
There was an American junkie from Flint, Michigan, snorting heroin on the top floor of the Everest Lodge, on the corner of Freak Street in 1972.
He would merrily sing whenever he scored more:
"Heroin / makes a good wife / because when you're married to H / you're married for life."

Street Reasons:
There were reasons, other than drugs, to be on this street [Freak Street in Kathmandu].

Under the Galata Bridge:
Maybe, but scoring some *keys* [kilograms] from the Eden Hotel, was my whole purpose of going to Nepal the first time, in 1970.

Much Friendlier:
I -- a hippie traveler -- and a friend who was starting to get interested in buying antiques, were invited to dinner at the Yak and Yeti [an upmarket Kathmandu hotel] by General Singha Shamsher Rana, the oldest member of all the Rana [dynasty] royalty.
He was very interested in why young travelers were in Nepal, and what they had to say.
He was a very educated man, and had travelled and lived in Europe several times.
He liked to answer our questions about Nepal, and also loved to discuss art and literature.

With great amusement, he said some of his family did not approve of his hanging out with the hippies, and attending our parties, but they could not say so directly or stop him because he was the oldest Rana.

What an honor, and so entertaining to talk to him.

He was 80-plus, and knew all the tales, gossip, and palace intrigue of those years.

He said he liked to talk to us, because we were different and interesting, and artistic and free thinkers.

Fresh Staying:
Aunt Jane's was a restaurant opened by a lady named Jane Martin.

She was the wife of a Peace Corps official.

The restaurant was located on the 2nd floor of a building on Freak Street.

I will never forget the buffalo meat, and chocolate cake, with peanut butter ice cream.

The place was like a little piece of home.

Early Picture:
Please don't remind me that I actually ate a *buff* steak.

When you hear the cook pounding on your [water buffalo] steak, it's time to change your order.

My Legs:
Loved the peanut ice cream, and chocolate cake.

Candy Kilometers:
Aunt Jane befriended my gal and I, and invited us over to her house, which was a piece of America.

Real bathrooms with toilets and running water, and mirrors, and a kitchen that looked like it came from America.

Since her husband was the head of the Peace Corps, they had their whole home furnishings shipped over [to Nepal].

Beautiful lady, and terribly fun to hang out with.

She would insist we take showers, and by then a great dinner was served.

Incredible Vice:
We were taken to an opium den in Kathmandu by an Australian pharmacist we met there, who prided himself on traveling between vice cities -- Hong Kong, Bangkok, etcetera.

We learned an incredible amount in a couple of days with him.

Shimmering Joy:
I met this Ganesh Baba [an elder, devoted to Ganesh] in Swayambhu, and went to his *satsang* [gathering of spiritual seekers] for two weeks or so.

This man was a total fraud, illogical, and a sex maniac.

His foremost *chella* was a fat Swiss girl who literally believed that he was a reincarnation of Ganesh.

I heard that he went to the U.S.A. and kept on his women-groping game, with the pretext of initiation.

Generously Revered:
Are you sure?

Ganesh Baba had a lot of devotees, and I was generously given a book by one of them, by Eve Baumohl Neuhaus, *The Crazy Wisdom of Ganesh Baba*.

Control Eye:
I met Ganesh Baba in New York.

Paul and some other people brought him to New York for an eye operation.

Yes he was a control freak, and a womanizer.

Shimmering Joy:
And he had nothing new of value to say.

Among his group of devotees -- or just hangers-on trying to check him out -- there was a French girl named Holy Tits, with whom I had a brief affair.

It must have been 1979.

When he gave his initiation, Ganesh Baba gave a long hug to the person, while muttering some stuff.

After her initiation, Holy Tits started to have serious doubts about the holy man, and she told me:

"I don't understand why he had to fondle my tits as he hugged me?"

Generously Revered:
Speak up for Ganesh Baba someone, preferably female!

Shimmering Joy [in a mimicking voice]:
"Speak up for Ganesh Baba, someone, preferably girls!"

You mean, those who have been fondled, fooled, fouled, and abused by him, via their own immature gullibility?

And loved every moment of it?

[again in a mocking tone, but about an Italian devotee of Anjuna Baba in 1978 Karnataka state]:

"When Baba makes love to me, it is nothing material, but all spiritual, you can't understand!"

[laughs]

Strange Mountains:
The Ganesh Baba of the profound and hilarious one-liners?

Shimmering Joy:
Why even mention this fat fucker, or the ego-tripping holy wannabees buzzing around him?

Are we that desperate for entertainment?

Any ridiculous Bollywood flop will do that, heaps better for anyone.

Enjoy Early:
It is perfectly O.K. to have different opinions about Ganesh Baba, but it is absolutely unacceptable to scream at people you

know nothing about.

You don't know Generously Revered, who is no flake by any definition.

Generously Revered:
Ganesh Baba did not make love to any women.

They revered him, and he revered them.

I think we've heard enough of your put-down of Ganesh Baba.

Why are you so jealous of those very good and real people?

Firewood Street:
There were -- and also are -- quite a few Ganesh Babas.

The only one I specifically met, was living in a old little temple in Hampi [ancient ruins in southwest India's Karnataka state], as I was too, in 1974.

Hampi was still deserted then, and an abode of monkeys and bats.

Ganesh Baba was a real nice *baba* who used to make beautifully crafted *chillums*.

They were decorated with cobras and tridents.

If he liked you, he gave them away, Indian fashion, expecting a small gift in return.

Women Amazing:
Sadly, Ganesh Baba is as common a name as Mr. Smith, so maybe you should make sure first, about who you are all talking about?

All *babas* that fraternize with Western hippies are most suspect, that's for sure.

According to the rules, a *baba* should not even look at any woman -- especially a Western one.

To touch one, for whatever reason, is totally out of order, unless he is saving her life pulling her from a raging stream.

Generously Revered:

Pterodactyl [Generously Revered's brother] went to India first in 1963, as an ornithologist, and was turned on [to hashish] just before he left [India], to come back to study at Oxford.

Cannabis of course changed his life.

Ganesh Baba was his guru.

But Pterodactyl was a *Naga* brother, and was considered by them to be a reincarnation of one of them.

Fortunately, he didn't go through with the final rite of the *Nagas* [castration or mutilation to end sexual desire].

He liked women, and even married.

But fortunately divorced his lunatic wife.

No children.

Slinging Woman:

I moved into a house with Pterodactyl and Michael Hollingshead [a British L.S.D. enthusiast from Oxford University] in Kathmandu.

Women Amazing:

We knew Pterodactyl, but not well.

He was always drunk when we encountered him -- very drunk.

I know you probably don't want to hear this, but maybe it helps to explain the chaos of his letters and general confusion.

Sorry you lost him.

Generously Revered:

I don't know who you are, or where you met Pterodactyl.

Of course I know alcohol got the better of him, and killed him.

I feel very guilty myself for not looking after him and preventing that.

It is a continuous source of grief.

I don't think Pterodactyl's fate affects the Ganesh Baba who was his guru, and obviously not the *baba* that dreadful Shimmering Joy is talking about.

Poor Pterodactyl's last years in Oxford were very unhappy and chaotic.

He didn't look after himself, or his possessions.

A tragedy, for which I feel partly responsible.

Which is why I am trying to salvage the better parts of his life for him, now.

Women Amazing:

Very sorry to hear this. So sad. I didn't know.

We were both Anjuna residents.

I met Pterodactyl in 1979, and Mister Amazing knew him longer because he grew up in Anjuna.

I don't really want to comment on the *baba* thing too much.

I am agnostic.

I do know that many associate with Western followers, but as far as their scriptures go, they shouldn't.

So I admit, I quite mistrust those that do.

I met too many fake ones. In 25 years, only two seemed trustworthy.

Both of them lived in the high Himalayas, and didn't associate with Western people. Locals took me there to visit.

Shimmering Joy actually knows a lot about Asian traditions, and speaks and writes many languages.

And no, I don't think he is mad.

He just likes to play with words a bit too much sometimes.

I don't think he says, whatever he does, to upset you, or anyone.

He was around in Kathmandu at the time.

So if you are really researching, don't dismiss him as a nutter so easily.

Please don't blame yourself for Pterodactyl's fate. We are all responsible for our own.

But please remember that all of the people that are telling you stories were heavily into drugs.

Something they would probably like to deny now, or not mention.

But their testimonies are skewed because of this.

I smoked a bit. But Mister Amazing, nothing.

The sad fate of his [Mister Amazing's] family, and so many of his childhood friends dying, convinced him that it wasn't a good idea.

Just remember how gullible we all were.

And a particular breed of neglected kids is attracted to the so-called spiritual path.

They find what they imagined, be it real or not.

I do not think that Pterodactyl's fate affects Ganesh Baba.

He should have been the one helping Pterodactyl with his alcohol problem early on.

It was very obvious.

Shimmering Joy:

Indeed, no one has got a remotely accurate knowledge of the enormous number of Indian men known as Ganesh Baba in any particular span of time.

But as for me, all indications I have gathered from different sources here, do point to the same individual.

Ganesh Baba was in Kathmandu in 1978 and, later on, flown to the U.S., continuing to fondle women's tits and more, while talking nonsensical spiritual clichés.

Women Amazing:

I remember vaguely hearing some such stories -- I was in Kathmandu at the same time -- but I don't remember them well enough to really testify to it.

But usually -- when there are abuse allegations -- they are only the tip of the iceberg, because it is so painful for people to recall them.

Especially if they are half-brainwashed by religious mumbo jumbo.

So they keep quiet.

It's very embarrassing.

And the worst kind of crime is to abuse someone who is

seeking spirituality.

Shimmering Joy:
I am lamenting the dramatic downfall of so many kids from the Flower Power era, who all began their journeys eastwards -- or simply inwards -- with eyes wide open, but who have fallen deep in the pit trap of woo-woo beliefs, pseudo-sciences, and established religious identifications.

The more arcane and little-known -- and dark in appearance -- the more attractive.

They are deluding themselves, that they finally are now somebody, belonging to some higher orb of consciousness.

Or the chosen few.

Old as the Bronze Age, this mind trick was meant to be spotted -- and avoided -- as these kids escaped the narrow and rigid institutionalized dogmas, and mentalities, of the Western world -- only to ensconce their insecure mind into similar, or worse, pit holes.

All blissfully unaware.

Late Talk:
You seem really bothered about other people's beliefs.

Why not just be at peace with your own belief, and leave others to theirs?

Shimmering Joy:
Because any belief of the religious kind is potentially highly dangerous, as human history has consistently proved.

Other people's beliefs are to be broken down, in order for deluded believers to understand their historical and psychological process.

You simply won't get that from any insider.

Trouble is, precious few people are willing to ever begin looking at the status of their mind's manipulation.

People like me do not have any belief.

Learn Fun:
Today would have been the 83rd birthday of the great *baba*, Paul Babes.

And I will always think of March 17th not as just Saint Patrick's Day, but also Saint Paul Babes's Day.

I hope he and Ira [Cohen], and Eight Finger Eddie, and Peanut Butter Harry, and Angus, and Hetty, and Swayambhu Billy -- and all the dearly departed, original Kathmandu hipsters -- are having a groovy party in heaven today.

Paul was once a New York City taxi driver, and became a well known world traveler in Kathmandu in the 1970s, starting the Eclipse night club, financing Bardo Matrix poetry publications, and raising a family with Pippy in Swayambhu, and Bali, and Goa.

I met him in Woodstock in the 1980s, and I tried to absorb as much wisdom from him as possible, until he passed on into the great unknown in 2010.

Eggs Spaghetti:
In 1975, I was writing poetry and reading it with Ira, Petra, Hettie and Angus, who printed some of my words on their Bardo Matrix Press [in Kathmandu].

They influenced me greatly in later printing my own works, one of which had one of Petra's photographs -- on the cover -- of me made-up in clown face, holding a skull, while on acid.

I think it was at a party at the Balaju swimming pool [a neighborhood near Kathmandu].

We used to hang out and do our readings at *Eat At Joe*'s [an inexpensive restaurant popular with travelers] in Freak Street.

A lot of us were eating O daily at that time.

But the *I-Ching* told me to move on, and I did so, after three months in Kathmandu.

Sugar Skulls:
I'm remembering one party in The Rose Garden [an inexpensive Kathmandu restaurant].

The foliage was adorned with small skulls made of sugar, slowly disintegrating through the afternoon.

Personal Hush:
Ira and Petra, they knew my family in Tangier [Morocco], and invited me to a dinner party, which was eccentric and wild.

The Italian ambassador doing heroin, while across from him, some smuggler and his sexy chick were snorting coke, a *bubbly bubbly* going full steam, and a cloud of smoke.

Retreat First:
Sometime in the early 1980s, my travels took me to Kathmandu where I, on occasion, took a photo of a *sadhu*.

He also reached out to receive a gratification.

He was not satisfied with the amount I offered, and made it clear that if I should fail to give him a satisfactory amount, I would not get his photo.

Since I had already taken it, I disregarded his displeasure, and went on with my journey.

On subsequently having the film developed, I recalled the *sadhu* and his decree.

Sure enough, his photo was not found.

Fortress Hovel:
I was holed up in a five-dollar a night, florescent room, in the Kathmandu Guest House [in 1982], listening to a Nepali version of *Hotel California* pouring out of a Tibetan girl's face.

Swayambhu's Monkey Temple bubbled on the horizon.

Freak Street and Durbar Square were smeared and blurred.

The Shiva Pagoda's stripped-down hunchback -- a horrible-eyed kid -- liked to spew incantations at the sky.

Gods, demons, and revolutionaries were all drooling intrigue in the bricked backstreets, while the Tibetan girl wiggled her tongue, playing a xylophone on her hand-carved teeth.

Strange Mountains:

I spent some evenings with Ngakpa Keith in Swayambhu, towards the end of his life.

He started traveling at 12 years old, and gave his life to adventure, and the magical side of the spiritual life.

Poverty got to him in the end.

End Point:
Did you know Raj Colonial?
He would have been there from about 1975 to 1980.
He was in Kashmir at one point.

A Brit, raised in the Raj [British colonial] times in India, he took refuge [in a Buddhist temple] at some point, and was in robes [as a Buddhist monk].

And then out of robes, and rather at sea towards the end, in Kathmandu and Bodh Gaya [the birthplace of Buddha, now a town in India's northern Bihar state] and elsewhere.

Shocking Semites:
When I was in Kathmandu as a 20-year-old in 1973, I stayed at a guest lodge.

One day, I was talking to a guy who worked there and he asked me if I was a Christian.

I said, "No, I'm Jewish."

He said "No! You can't be! I've heard that Jews kill Christian babies and eat them."

It was shocking to hear that, especially there.

I knew that was a theme among European anti-Semites.

But I couldn't believe it had made its way to then-remote Nepal.

I told him to tell whoever told him that that it was a terrible lie.

But I doubt I changed anyone's mind.

Honey Hand:
After I left Kabul, I flew to Delhi, crashed at a flea bag hotel

near the airport, and woke up in the middle of the night with terrible stomach pains.

I crawled into a rickshaw, and asked the driver to take me to the nearest hospital.

We arrived at Safdarjang [a free hospital for mostly poor people in New Delhi].

And I passed out in the emergency room.

Next thing I knew, I was in a ward with an IV [an intravenous drip] in my arm.

I thought I was dying.

It turned out to be a case of gastroenteritis from polluted water in a cooler, where the Coke at the hotel was kept.

I spent three days in the hospital, cared for by the family members of the other women in my ward.

They were so kind.

The nurses couldn't believe I was on my own.

My friends from the dance company were on their way overland at that point.

When I got out, I looked up the only person I knew in Delhi whose name had been given to me in Amsterdam -- a Dutch woman, who was involved with the Sufi community there.

She brought me to the Tomb of Nizamuddin [the Sufi saint Khywaja Nizamuddin Auliya's tomb in New Delhi] where there was a deep water tank, covered with green scum, and suggested I immerse myself to recover from the gastroenteritis.

I gave it a pass.

It was the last day of Ramadan, when they were feeding the poor.

Hundreds lined up on the floor, waiting for rice and *dal*, to be placed on their banana leaf plates.

When a gun was fired off to signal the end of the day, pandemonium broke out with people scrambling to be fed.

When my friends caught up with me in Delhi, some of us decided to leave right away for Nepal.

Good plan. We set off on the train, 3rd class.

Which meant that we had people sitting on top of us --

dodging the police who swept through the train car, beating and ejecting people without tickets.

Hundreds more travelled on the rooftops, and jumped off when they came to their villages along the route.

Fortunately, after that, I had the opportunity to stay at Kopan Monastery [in Nepal] for a one-month meditation course, which completely changed my life.

Red Entering:
It's virtually impossible to explain the journey to someone who wasn't attracted to join its flow.

Does the river hesitate becoming the sea?

Could we open your presents for you, even if we could?

Street Shocked:
I arrived [in Nepal] during February 1978, and just stayed.

I am still here, supporting myself teaching tai chi in magical places.

[Now in] Pokhara.

Shroom Melt:
I got off the bus.

A young boy sold me a bag of mushrooms.

I walked into a cafe, and gave the bag to the cook for my first *shroom* omelette.

I sat outside and watched the mountains melt into Lake Pokhara. 1978.

Splendor:
Every morning I would lie in bed, kick the door open, and bask in the splendor of that mountain.

1978, Pokhara.

A lady lived in the compound, taught me how to thresh millet with a stick, and smoked my cigarettes -- all with a delightful smile.

Robes Dance:
I remember meeting this guy on the way up to Everest. He was the only guy I knew who had a porter.

He shows me a ball of O the size of a grapefruit, and asks if I think it's enough for him to make the trek.

I assured him that would do, if he paced himself.

That was a weird time to be headed to the top of the world -- a full moon over Everest.

Five rising planets.

If you're into that, apparently it was a pretty special time.

Ran into Goose and Betty who'd come up, to be as close to the stars as possible.

They got dressed in magic robes, and were dancing a dance that has no name.

Honey Hand:
Two of us came out of Tibet, at the border with Nepal, in 1987 -- right when the monsoon was going full bore.

After crossing the Friendship Bridge [spanning the China-Nepal border] at Tatopani [a frontier town in northern Nepal], and spending the night in a small hotel, we hired porters to carry our backpacks, and lead us out of the valley.

There were moving landslides on the route, and the road was closed to vehicular traffic.

So we had to walk about 50 kilometers to the nearest bus stop.

We walked for hours through driving rain, trusting our porters to know how to cross the landslides safely.

We continued in the dark, with the sound of things collapsing around us.

Finally, we came to a small village and our porter arranged for us to stay in the home of a local family.

They very kindly gave us a lovely soup to warm up.

The father, who spoke a little English, translated for us, so we could learn more about our porters.

I asked the one, who had been carrying my pack, about his

family.

He said his house had been washed downstream along with his village, but his wife and children had been visiting relatives, so were spared.

I asked what he was going to do, and he said that the Nepali government had given each man the equivalent of 1.50 dollars, and a shirt.

And with that, he was supposed to rebuild his life.

It was well known at the time that the royal family was sucking up foreign money, and using it on themselves.

One member of the royal family had an apartment on Sutton Place in New York City, an expensive address in the city.

It was sickening to hear this [porter] man's story, knowing it was typical for the Sherpas in Nepal.

My Legs:
I was pregnant.
So we decided to take a fairly easy hike, for just a few days out, in the Annapurna [a Himalayan mountain] area.

A couple of days in, we got to our second guest house.

As those of you who were there in those days [1981] would remember, there was a guest house an easy five or six hour walk from one another.

There was just one room, with maybe four beds.

As I walked into the dark cold room to throw my stuff on a bed, I saw the bed furthest in was occupied.

The owner said the boy was sick.

He was feverish when I talked to him.

He was an American on break from Harvard -- so in theory not entirely stupid.

He told me he had decided not to stay in the first guest house, but to keep walking, but it got dark, so he decided to camp.

When he woke up, he said he had leeches all over him.

He got to the second guest house, but couldn't go any further.

He said he had contracted hepatitis in Kathmandu, but the doctor had cleared him to travel.

I told him we would arrange for him to be carried out.

I am not sure what it is like now, but in those days, the only way out was to be carried in a basket, on someone's back.

He said no.

He wanted to be carried further in, toward Annapurna.

We tried to talk him out of it, since he was obviously very sick.

But when we couldn't, I asked for his information and told him we would contact the [American] consulate when we got back to Kathmandu.

A few days later, when we returned to Kathmandu, I called the consulate.

The woman on the phone groaned when I told her his name. She said,

"Oh no. We thought he had gone home. The doctor didn't clear him to travel. He was cleared to go home."

She said he had contacted cholera, in Bombay.

The consulate there helped him out.

Then he got robbed of everything on the way to Calcutta.

The consulate there helped him out.

Then he came to Kathmandu.

I have often wondered what happened to him.

I did my share of stupid things when I was a young traveler, and I survived more through luck than good judgment.

But I saw people who didn't make it.

Usually it was because of drugs, but also there were people who seemed to not be able to handle the total freedom of having no infrastructure or safety net.

A foreigner had no social mores to prop them up, they could act totally crazy.

Everything except serious crime.

There was, and still is, a dark side if you removed yourself as far as possible from your culture.

But it is also addictively rewarding.

I consider myself lucky because I saw junkies, before I had hard drugs readily available.

In the top layer of my memory, everything was wonderful, but I can remember the details.

Touch Stuff:
I wound up with *hep* A [hepatitis A] in Pokhara in 1978, after buying a bicycle in Varanasi and cycling to Pokhara.

I didn't know I had it, until I peed Coca-Cola colored.

I put the bike on a bus, and went to Kathmandu's Institute for Contagious Diseases.

They told me I could stay there, and get well, but I decided to return to Europe.

I sold the bike -- Hero brand -- in Freak Street, and took a flight to Delhi.

On the way from the airport [in New Delhi] to the Ringo Guest House in Connaught Circus, I lost my passport.

Song: *Dum Maro Dum*
Film: *Hare Rama Hare Krishna*
Director: Dev Anand
Music: R. D. Burman
Singer: Asha Bhosle
Lyrics: Anand Bakshi

My Legs:
I was first in Kathmandu in early spring 1971.

While I was there, I worked for a few days as an extra in the movie, *Hare Rama Hare Krishna*.

I played a hippie.

Big stretch.

The days when I was working, were actually night shots.

We were sitting and smoking [hashish], while some of the cast danced around a fire.

The extras [in real life] had mostly travelled overland, and our clothes were a uniform shade of grunge.

The Indian cast had on these new, clean hippie clothes.

The part I remember the most, the director had several of us in a semi-circle, smoking *chillums*.

We each had one.

And he wanted us to all be smoking at the same time.

As some of you might remember, *chillums* are usually passed around, not smoked by one person.

So as we smoked, someone's *chillum* would go out.

The rest of us *toked* away, keeping our *chillum* going, while the person filled and lit his *chillum*.

Then someone else's *chillum* would go out.

Finally the director said:

"Stop. Dump out your *chillum*.

"OK, fill the *chillum*.

"Light the *chillum*."

By this time, most of us were almost comatose.

I can see myself [in *Hare Rama, Hare Krishna*] in a couple of quick pan shots.

I had a cheesy line, but I think it got cut. Something like, "Cool, man" or "Far out, man."

It was cool because it was kind of an otherworldly thing, in an otherworldly place.

I remember the Indian cast.

The lead was a bit arrogant -- drank a lot of booze while the foreigners smoked hash.

They hadn't figured out the ending while I was there.

I know the movie ended up being a big success, but we thought of it as a bit of a joke.

I've never seen the whole thing, but the parts I saw came together much better than we would have imagined.

Do you remember the commune Hog Farm was there?

They were filming the filming.

I would love to see those movies.

Broke Fun:
I was there. It was 1971.

We got 10 rupees a night, as extras.
About one dollar.
It was fun.
We were so broke.
But it did feel a little like a sell out.

Free:
Why a sell out?
And was the *dope* free?

Broke Fun:
I think the *dope* was free.
At least I don't remember paying for it.
Sell out, because we knew the intent of the film was to show hippies in an unflattering light.
Towards the end of the movie, one of the Indian characters went crazy [in real life] from the *reefer* [marijuana], and had a fight with another character.
I was a stand-in for the lead female actor -- as I had long black hair -- and had to watch the fight while freaking out.
It was lots of fun.
We worked all through the night.
I had no money.
We were literally hungry.
After six months on the road from England through Turkey, Iran, Afghanistan, Pakistan and India, finally to Nepal, my clothes were rags.
I don't regret a minute of it.
It was great.

My Legs:
I worked for a few days on that film in Kathmandu.
We got a dollar a day, which was more than most of us needed.

Free:

Hippies got paid back in the 1970s to be in Bollywood movies, as extras.

It gave the movies a flavor of the exotic, having foreigners -- better known as freaks -- with long hair, smoking *dope* among the brown actors of the movie.

Too bad I was on my way to Goa, and didn't hang around Bombay long enough to be on the set.

My few moments of glory, passed up for a beach.

Fortress Hovel:
Any English translation of the film's *Dum Maro Dum* hashish-smoking song?

I think the lyrics say:

"Smoke, smoke / All sorrows are scraped away."

Shimmering Joy:
Dum Maro Dum means "a hit," or in this case, "a puff".

Maro is the injunctive form of the verb *marna* which means "to beat" or "to hit".

I need to see the original Devanagari [ancient script] writing to be sure.

Basically -- and without having the full lyrics -- the song and the film paints hippies as an amoral, lost, at times violent, careless lot of selfish drifters.

"Why care about anything? Just take another hit!" is the main message here.

Shimmering Joy:
An utterly surreal, silly, ridiculous, biased, ignorant and damaging *flick* [movie].

Mister Border:
If you were wandering around rural India at that time, it would be very tiresome.

The minute you were spotted as a Westerner, the hordes would break out with that refrain:

Dum Maro Dum!
And I can tell you, it was done incessantly, in a very depreciative fashion.

Applaud Time [laughing]:
It's a wonder they let any Western hippies over the border after this.

Fortress Hovel:
I love the song because, like many of the Bollywood "*filmi* playback singers," Asha Bhosle hits those sublimely screeching, mosquito voice's high pitch -- which sounds so India 1970s through ear-splitting tinny speakers, just as you are being blasted by the heat.
She is such a great singer.
Her and Lata Mangeshkar.

Merge Sleeves:
She [Asha Bhosle] later married the [song's] composer R. D. Burman.
He probably was the first to merge Western music to Indian music scene -- this later on became his hallmark -- although he does have some awesome classical pieces under his sleeves.
His father was a great classical musician and composer, S. D. Burman, who wrote and composed many hits in the 1960s and the 1970s.
Oh and by the way, Lata Mangeshkar and Asha Bhosle are sisters.

Fortress Hovel: I also like *ghazals* [traditional songs of devotion].

Shimmering Joy:
Ghazal and *bhajaan* [devotional religious songs], they've got soul.
Ghazal saw a huge revival in north India around the 1980s

among the middle class, although the genre is generally pooh-poohed by classical *sangeet khyal* [music in an imaginative, ornamental style] musicians for being way too syrupy, over sentimental, and lacking transcendental sublimity.

Not the view of Urdu [language] poetry buffs, nor [mystical Muslim] Sufi-minded folks, of course.

Not so with *bhajans*, which exude devotion -- *bhakti* -- of a more divine nature, at least for Hindus, which may be sung by renown *khyal* singers such as Bade Ghulam Ali Khan, Kesar Bai Kerkar, Kishori Amonkar, Parveen Sultana or Lakshmi Shankar.

Fortress Hovel:
I'm listening to the Dagar Brothers' *dhrupad* now.

Shimmering Joy:
Bitter stuff, this *dhrupad*, with all these weird microtones.

Not that appealing today to most Indians or *videshi* [foreigners].

The melodic zeitgeist has come and gone.

But music that feels hermetic at first-hear, can stick to the head and heart a lot tighter than its opposite, when familiar.

A universal principle it seems.

Or rather, an in-built functional peculiarity of the mind.

Early Picture:
Shimmering Joy, Where did you learn Hindi?

Shimmering Joy:
In Hindu-situ and at a Paris university.

I graduated after three years at INALCO [Institut National des Langues et Civilisations Orientales], in which I also upgraded my knowledge of Hindu civilization and general topics about India and Nepal, together with the languages Nepali, Thai, and Indonesian.

Anyone is very welcome to point any errors of mine, or provide source-based information when contesting, in English or any other lingo.

What should prevail is personal improvement over fear to offend.

As for me, I am all-round unfuckwithable, and wish the liberating same to everyone.

I still make mistakes though, especially when I cannot check my reference books.

But basically, I do not rely on available Western transliteration of Sanskrit and Hindi vocabulary -- my source being via Devanagari.

I try to appropriately match that alphabet, with the corresponding sounds in English.

The result may at times not correspond to the official written rendering, because there are many inaccurate stereotypes with that, I also avoid.

The Western suffixation of "s" -- for plural -- calls for automatic pronunciation errors, so I always keep that "s" separate.

Free:
Can you translate some of the lyrics, and what she's singing about, in *Dum Maro Dum*?

Shimmering Joy:
I have trouble with making sense of lyrics in Bollywood songs, due to the typical high-pitched voice, and the way words are linked together in this style of singing.

I can only get some of it right, and often have to guess the rest.

But I usually can translate accurately from original written text.

Can we get this from somewhere?

Free:
I love this song and the hippies in the film, even two of them kissing in the background, which must of been very erotic in the

1970s for Indian movie-goers.

I'm interested in the translation because of the *Hare Rama Hare Krishna* [chorus] in the lyrics, and what Krishna [a Hindu god] has got to do with everything.

Shimmering Joy:
Yes, the use of this [*Hare Rama Hare Krishna*] mantra is a tad puzzling.

I think it is meant as the expression of a fatalistic attitude -- or rather a distancing -- an escape from the mundane world these hippies are supposed to espouse, as a way of life.

But it is not related to [Hindu guru] Bhaktivedanta's ISKCON [the New York-based International Society for Krishna Consciousness] -- made famous later on with the same mantra.

Free:
Maybe, or just a devotion song of the culture the character is struggling with?

The film was a star-making vehicle for Zeenat Aman, who played a Westernized hippie.

The movie dealt with the decadence of the hippie culture.

It aimed to have an anti-drug message.

And also depicts some problems associated with Westernization, such as divorce.

Shimmering Joy:
The hippie-infected girl [played by Zeenat] -- who her brother attempts to save -- is singing a kind of anthem to hippiedom -- Indian version.

She shrieks:
"*Dunya men, kya?*"
"In this world, what?"

Followed by [the lyrics'] injunctions for yet another puff.

The scenes depicted, are so far from the real thing, as to appear totally ludicrous.

This shows a fundamental misconception of the spirit, and antics, of the phenomena.

Fortress Hovel:
The *Hare Krishna* chanting may be just some stereotype of hippies doing a West-meets-East thing -- as imagined by the script writer -- because especially in those years, there were a lot of guru followers.

Shimmering Joy:
That too, without a doubt.

My Legs:
Yes I agree, stereotype chanting.
I heard so many people [travelers] around that time invoking the *Hare Krishna Hare Ram* thing.
I always suspected most didn't have a clue of the real meaning.
But there were lots of pseudo-Hindus at that time amongst Westerners.

Young First:
I was an extra in the movie during 1971 in Kathmandu.
I quit after the first day, as the director kept shouting like a great dictator.
Dum Maro Dum, I remember, was the song about a young girl who ran away and joined a bunch of hippies.

Shimmering Joy:
The first part is this:
Dum Maro Dum / Mitti jae gham / Bolo suboh sham / Hare Krishna Hare Ram.
I am not quite sure of the *mitti* -- meaning "ground" -- but my guess is that the word is used to mean "interred," or "gone".
The literal translation would then be:
"A hit, take a hit / In the ground goes sorrow / Say from

morning to night / Hare Krishna Hare Ram!"

> Free:
> I love this song.
> Don't quite know why.
>
> My Legs:
> I actually love it too.
> Invokes that era.
>
> Clothes Rip:
> It must be played so loud, that the speakers are distorted.
>
> Free:
> And here it is, the song translated:
>
> Take another hit,
> Take another hit,
> All your worries will disappear.
> From morning to night sing,
> Hare Krishna Hare Ram!
>
> What has the world given us?
> What have we taken from the world?
> Why should we worry about anyone?
> What has anyone done for us?
>
> Take another hit,
> Take another hit,
> All your worries will disappear.
> From morning to night sing,
> Hare Krishna Hare Ram!
>
> Whether we want to live or die,
> We won't be afraid of anyone.
> The world won't be able to stop us,

For we will do what we want.

Beard's Shadow:
I loved that song because everybody was singing it, all over [India].
They taught me the lyrics, and they wanted me to sing along.
Fifty years later, I saw the film and -- I have to say -- a fake perception of the hippie way of being.
I knew the guys and chicks being hired to do the film.

Busy Minding:
The amount of times that damn song was sung to me, while I was busy minding my own business.

Chai Guitar:
Although I hated the song, I learned to play it on guitar and sing it.
It earned me lots of free meals, cups of *chai* and *chillums*.

Future Aura:
Dum Maro Dum was blaring from radios everywhere, during those days.

Strange Mountains:
We had such a good thing happening, until that movie came out, and the population learned our true nature, and that we were not supernatural beings.
So sad.

Burst Spontaneously:
Everywhere we went in India during the early 1970s, the local young men would spontaneously burst into this song, as soon as they saw us.

Firewood Street:
I hated that film.

It was the cause of totally fucked up ideas about hippies and freaks in India.

Especially Still:
I remember that film caused us travelers from the West -- especially girls -- a lot of problems.
The film was presenting Western hippies, as very dangerous to the Indian youth, a bad influence.
And the [movie's hippie] girls seemed like they were just screwing around with everybody.
We did not.
But we did decide with who, when, and how often ourselves. No one else had the right to decide over our bodies.
That's a big difference to the situation many Indian women are facing -- and in other parts of the world -- still.

Basic Nepal:
The basic message of the movie was, don't throw your life away on drugs.
And it was the story of a broken home, and the consequences on the children.
The hippies were a device.
Because hippies were big those days.
For this and other songs and scenes, the producers rounded up hippies in Nepal and paid them, and everyone had a good time.

Under the Galata Bridge:
So many foreign girls worked as extras in Bollywood.
They paid them very little, and their roles were usually just stand around as hookers.
Lots of my excess girlfriends got this kind of work in Bombay.

Fond Morning:
That movie made every Indian a critic, and popularized the

consensus that hippies were immoral purveyors of drug culture and free love.

Which to them was a taboo.

Clothes Rip:
They just looked at us, and started singing it:
Dum Maro Dum.

Believe Good:
I have written a whole piece, which is part of my memoir, about the girl who was the muse for *Hare Rama Hare Krishna*.

She is Indo-Canadian and lives in Vancouver.

She met Dev Anand in the bar of the Soaltee Hotel [a Kathmandu upmarket hotel], and the rest is history.

I lived in Kathmandu at the time, and I helped her find some work.

Mini Days:
I was the girl in the mini-dress, dancing with the heroine Zeenat.

Loved those days.

Fortress Hovel:
Bollywood's magazines loved to call her "Zeeny Baby!"

Beard's Shadow:
In the beginning, she sings *Dum Maro Dum*.

The [movie's] intent was a fake hippie tale.

They hired a few freaks around, for good money, playing to smoke *chillums* in a sort of disco-pub, with all Indians around, and showing a shitty shade on the hippie style.

Then she sung the famous song, acting half-stoned and half-sexy -- ignoring those who follow [Hinduism's devout] *Hare Rama Hare Krishna* path, don't use drugs.

All of the film that comes later, is just an early Bollywood production, with almost no artistic value.

In 1972, I had not watched the film, but I knew very well the song, being sung everywhere.

I still remember most of the lyrics my Indian friends taught me.

The [Indian] actors became famous.

People would stay in a queue for many hours, to have a ticket for the few big cinema halls.

It was a real big fake, but they made lots of money with it.

Big Breath:

In the spring of 1969, some French or Italian movie-makers rounded up about two dozen freaks, as extras on their film, *Les Chemins de Katmandou* [starring Jane Birkin].

We also smoked *chillums* for the movie.

We were at a temple complex near Kathmandu, but I don't remember exactly where.

We got paid 100 rupees per day, for two days.

Quite a handsome sum back then.

Early Picture:

They took us to Swayambhu and Pashupati [Buddhist and Hindu temple complexes on Kathmandu's outskirts].

At Pashupati, we had the burning *ghat* scene.

And we had to sing a horrid song.

When we figured out than Jane [Birkin] had O.D.'d, we were not happy with the scene, and chaos ensued.

I used the 200 rupees to go to Everest, but ended up in a *Chong* joint [Early Picture's slang for a Chinese building], with some *Tibooti* chicks [Early Picture's slang for Tibetan females].

Then I ran back to Kathmandu, with *Tibooti* crabs and lice.

I went to the doctor.

And he sprayed me with Peace Corps' DDT.

We should be dead.

I went to the M [morphine] Doctor, who had the contraption to tie you off [tighten a tourniquet on his arm].

It had little gears he tightened.

Medieval.

Big Breath:
Oh Lordy, I loved going there.

I met a French couple named Danse Macabre and Can Can, and they took my great friend Glenn -- rest in peace -- and me there.

The doctor slowly went through his deliberations, and Glenn passed out briefly, just watching the whole scene.

Some mornings, we'd take a bicycle rickshaw to the doctor's office, and Glenn would stand up and exhort the driver like Ben Hur in the great chariot race.

What a blast of a time to be in Nepal.

Clothes Rip [displays a photograph of Himalayas, forests, and glacier-covered peaks]:
A lovely day hiking in the Nepalese Himalaya, 1972.

Tralala offered a friendly chillum to a passer by.

She [Tralala] had two kilos of *charas* from Balkh in her backpack.

We got five pounds for 29 dollars up in Balkh.

Hand-pressed at the fort.

We got snowed in at Tengboche [the Buddhist Tengboche Monastery in eastern Nepal], for a couple of days.

Our caretaker monk made fun of us because we all smoked, wanted to sleep, and always had the munchies.

We would bug him to conjure us up food.

He would say the food is sleeping.

Love Face:
So many of us fell in love with Nepal in the late 1960s and early 1970s, and our memories have stuck, and hopefully made us better people.

Early Picture:
I was headed for Tibet when I left Haight Ashbury [San

Francisco's hippie neighborhood], but by the time I got to Kathmandu in 1969, the Cultural Revolution [in Mao Tse-tung's China] was in full craziness, and the [Nepal-China] border was closed.

Kicking back in our yard in Manali one day, and a Navajo brave [Native American tribesman] -- wearing turquoise and coral beads -- stepped out of the forest.

Turns out he was Tibetan.

But looked just like the Navajos I knew from Arizona.

Then his whole clan came out of the forest.

They had escaped Tibet.

And we were the first people they saw in India.

A bunch of half-naked freaks.

8 • LOST

Street Shocked:
I woke up one morning in 1978 in Chapora, and someone I knew -- French lady -- was tied to a tree.
Almost naked.
Hair disheveled.
Been mad three days, on datura.
Done all sorts of crazy things.
Now back, but with very little memories of what happened.
When released, she shaved her hair and walked into the jungle, and we never saw her again.
I've never been tempted to try this plant!
I know a few women who went with bad *babas*.
Datura mixed in their food, and then they got raped.
Rats.

My Legs:
I remember being in a Railroad Guest House somewhere in rural northern India.
There was a foreign guy who was totally freaked out.
People in the market beat him, because he would overturn things in the stalls.
The foreigners wanted to figure out where he was from, so they could alert his consulate.
He wasn't native English-speaking, but probably from northern Europe.
A couple of other people staying there suggested I sit with him at dinner -- because I was a woman -- and try to get some information. So I went over to sit at his table.

I think I said a couple of sentences, and he stood up screaming at me about women and God and evil, and then starting throwing plates at me.

I decided he was way beyond my ability to help.

He is another one who probably didn't make it.

Village Damage:
Sadly not a unique story.
I heard of quite a few people who died while on datura.
Some were spiked with it.
A lot of people who survived were hallucinating for a long time and never really recovered.
Dangerous stuff I think.

Strange Mountains:
I think the ones who went mad, for more than a short while, suffered the highest mortality rate.
They lived on the fringes, slept in the corners, and ate the scraps -- until they disappeared one day.
Sometimes they came back with amazing stories, but that was rare.
Accidental, or novice, datura trips killed plenty.
And apparently disease killed lots of us.
Personally I lived in a bubble where nobody died, and the sun always shone [laughs].

Nostrils Frozen:
Datura was a big problem.

The Pudding:
Did you ever meet someone who was looking for a lost son or daughter?
Or friend?
Twice I met someone in anguish, whose child seemed to have disappeared.
Maybe the person was actually avoiding them?

Who knows?
But it was sad.

Slinging Woman:
In Kathmandu in 1969, and I still remember it -- a man walking around with a photo of his daughter.

Very People:
A German youngster was missing in Goa.
When I was back in Germany, I got to know it.
The parents went to Goa to look for him.

Nothing Completely:
In 1979 in Nepal, my Tasmanian friend went trekking with her friend and Sherpas, but didn't reach one of the sections.
Completely disappeared.
No trace.
Her parents also went and tried to continue the search.
Nothing.

Late Talk:
In Pushkar in early 1980s, a young guy -- I think he was from Switzerland -- he walked out into the desert at night and was not found again.

World Away:
I once saw a documentary that briefly talked about hippies dying of an O.D. in Kabul.
Some were buried in the American Cemetery.

Ice One:
A few times, I met parents looking for their children.
Also Interpol came to show pictures on the beaches in Goa.

Sleeping Forest:
In the mid 1980s, there were a number of foreigners

murdered in the Malana area.

I always remember, back in those days, flyers posted in guesthouses, with a photo and description of a missing traveler.

It was always quite sobering to see.

I heard stories, years ago, about it being related to the hashish trade.

Who knows? But it's deeply disturbing.

I remember hearing about drowning in Kovalam [a beach along southwest Kerala state] years ago, from those unfamiliar with being in big surf.

Also a number of people were poisoned by the local mussels, which they had collected.

But not prepared properly.

All Mucousless:
I was in Kovalam beach in the early 1980s, and came across two people laying dead on beach.

I found out they were two Indian Airline pilots.

The strange thing was, nobody was doing anything.

In fact, keeping away.

Sleeping Forest:
Does anyone remember the notorious [redacted] Guesthouse on Khao San Road in Bangkok?

There was a constant stream of dead junkies coming out of there in the mid-1980s.

Live Anything:
The wife of a friend brutally passed away in Goa, a couple of years ago.

She knew India and the area well, was a no drugs, no alcohol, long-time traveler.

She was last seen at a bus stop.

Then disappeared.

Her body was found, severely damaged.

Still very unclear and disturbing what happened.

Think Somehow:
They think she was somehow poisoned.
Really weird story.

The Pudding:
I remember meeting a mother, looking for her daughter.
There were some who died from overdoses.
Were they buried or cremated in India?
Imagine their families.

Enjoy Early:
So many dead.
Most got cremated.
Some undoubtedly in places where no one knew them.

Just East:
Good point. Despite the idealism then -- and the nostalgia now -- there are amongst all the good memories, quite a high number of deaths, rapes, stonings, hepatitis, malaria.
 I consider myself lucky, having only had a couple of Delhi bellies, and arriving back in England with simply an easily sorted case of worms.

Late Talk:
I remember a few who died.
 A German guy used to stay at the steps in Mohan Singh Place [shopping mall] in Delhi.
 He died in the park, in the middle of Connaught Place.
 Also a couple of French guys, and a Portuguese.
 They were all cremated immediately, and I'm not sure the embassies were notified.

Shimmering Joy:
Further down from Mohan Singh -- horrible building -- turn left just before Hanuman Mandir [a park dedicated to

Hinduism's monkey-headed Hanuman].
The small park was home to many junkies in the early 1970s.
Hanuman Mandir Park tragedies.
Shooting in plain sight.
I did sleep there during June 1972, weakened and broke, yet in good spirits, coming from Vrindavan [a northern Hindu temple dedicated to Krishna and his lover, the goddess Radha] in the hyper-hot season.
But I felt hyper-holy after my stay in Vrindavan.

Late Talk:
Yes, it was a hard scene in Delhi in the 1970s and 1980s.

Shimmering Joy:
Well, in those days, I considered junkies as polluters of the freak movement, so much that I felt removed from any sympathy I would otherwise feel for them.
I guess this was the prevailing attitude for most of us.
Sad for them, of course.

Hard Flipped:
Many got lost.

Cave Wonders:
Many wanted to get lost.

Shack Taffy:
Or they were coming back home [to the West], totally mental from abuse of over drug use, and gurus planting weird beliefs into one's brain.
I've known that one in our family.

Spiritual Sister:
I remember seeing lots of strung out junkies in Delhi in 1972.

In Already:
Already in 1968.

Just Loads:
I saw a few Western junkies in Delhi back in the 1980s.
I never understood what they were doing there.
There were loads in Goa, and that I could understand, but Delhi?
Why?
Did they get stranded there trying to get back home?

Way Overland:
Close to the source.
The further away from the big cities, the harder to get heroin, morphine, and speed.

Just Loads:
It was never hard to get *smack* in Goa.
Plus it was a lot nicer than Delhi.

Move Move:
Yeah, but the strung out people lacked the capacity to organize the journey.
They simply keeled over where they were, too wasted to care about the external world.
There were, as there are, pitfalls of which to beware.

Who Disappeared:
Most junkies were Italian and French.

Initial This:
The French had a bad reputation at that time.
I met a Frenchman on a flight to Bangkok, and we shared a room for a few days.
I came back one afternoon, and he had left a note, saying he really appreciated the fact I trusted him, enjoyed hanging out,

ASIA OVERLAND: FREAKS, SMUGGLERS & APOCALYPTIC TRIBES

and said I shouldn't trust any other French travelers as they were all thieves.

My most vivid memory of him was waking up in the middle of the night to see him slapping a bar girl, as he was banging away.

To block out her annoying screams, I adjusted my ear plugs and went back to sleep.

Other than that, he seemed pretty normal.

Enjoy Early:
Junkies came to India long before hippies did.

Some of the U.S. beat [also known as beatnik] junkies, and a lot of Europeans.

I met people who been in India in 1960, well before I set out. So we followed them.

Skull Press:
The German and Austrian junkies I met, had been coming to Pakistan for several years, for the morphine tablets.

Before the heroin arrived.

Way Overland:
I knew Dave from Manchester -- who died because of a ball of opium in his stomach -- where he had been living on the pavement with a cycle rickshaw *walla* and his family.

Dave used to hustle tourists outside a Hilton, or similar hotel, in Karachi [a southern port in Pakistan].

His dream was to have a room in there one day.

Totally Everyone:
My mom travelled to India to look for me in 1980, because I was in India for two-and-a-half years.

She found me in Goa after three days.

Two friends of mine died in Goa.

One got cremated there, and the other one got transferred back to Germany, to be buried there.

Shopkeeper's Daughter:
The top floor of The Crown Hotel in old Delhi, in 1970 and 1971, was called the French Junk Room -- although there were junkies of various nationalities there.

I unfortunately was stuck at The Crown for a few weeks.

I ended up taking care of the five-month-old baby of a Swedish junkie.

Much Friendlier:
Yes, and if you washed your clothes and hung them on the roof to dry, you had to sit there and guard them.

My Legs:
I had forgotten about having to watch your clothes dry at The Crown.

Outrageously Invited:
Ah, the notorious Crown Hotel.
Still the same in 1973 and 1974.

Shock Body:
I stayed at The Crown in 1974.
There were junkies there.
They wanted me to ship morphine back to the U.K. in my sitar.
I refused.
There were a lot of freaks around who looked like they'd got stuck in Delhi years before, and were deep in addiction.
It was sad to see.
Like the hippie dream, turned to a nightmare.
I managed to get back to the U.K. before my drug use became serious.
I really don't think I'd have survived being a junkie in India.

Cobra Meeting:

I will never forget meeting a fellow American on our overland trip, to India from Istanbul, in 1973.

He was traveling back from India, to go back to the U.S.

He had to look up his girlfriend's father, to inform him his daughter had died on a beach in India, from a cobra bite.

Ran Away:
Some of them just wanted to get lost, I think.

I heard about people who threw away their passport, or changed identity.

Even one guy disguised as a woman.

So many stories.

Heart and Soul:
The passport throw.
And "*baba* becoming".
Heard of those.

Gawking Window:
I'll never forget a French junkie falling out of a window from a hotel I was visiting in Colaba.

His twisted body was lying in the gutter.

I rushed down to him, he looked at me, and died!

Already a crowd of Indians.

I got him covered with a sheet, and called the French Embassy.

They didn't want to know, and he was still there hours later.

Awful way to die -- in a gutter in Bombay, surrounded by gawking Indians.

Skull Press:
Horrible.
Wonder what they eventually did with him?
And if his family found out what happened?

Gawking Window:

His friend eventually turned up.

I left the problem with him, so I guess his family got to know.

Sitars There:
Mayflower checked out in Bombay, with Steve Shapiro.
O.D.'d.
Sad.

Slinging Woman:
I heard she [Mayflower] died in Bombay with Steve.

Candy Kilometers:
I knew the sweetest man, named German Michael, who on his first time trying heroin, overdosed and died around 1973 in India.

He was cremated in Varanasi.

And the whole thing was photographed by his friend who came from Germany to see it.

Heart and Soul:
Anyone met a French James around 1972 or 1973 in Afghanistan, and most probably Kabul?

For a while, and some crazy reason, I thought I had lost the last three photographs I had of him, my dad.

I just found them back a few days ago, when going through the picture's trunk.

Patrice, also known as James, hitch-hiked from Mulhouse -- east of France -- until Kabul.

His final destination was India, but he never made it, because he got stuck on opiates in Afghanistan and had to be repatriated to France, for health reasons.

I have not really known him.

I would have loved him to tell me about his road trip to Asia.

James never recovered from opiates.

My mother left him for this reason mainly, and he passed

away of an O.D. in September 1985.

I miss him a lot.

He grew up few years in the 1960s with a violent stepdad, in a region of France that was quite devastated in many ways by World War Two.

His aspirations were wider than his reality.

Best Victims:
Some of the best men and women were victims of drugs, and never made it out of this cycle.

Heart and Soul:
Very true.
James was a very sensitive person.

Best Victims:
I have many friends who where very talented, and special human beings.

Sadly all passed away through drug abuse.

Enjoy Early:
Some of the best, the most gifted, the smartest, became junkies.

And many died even younger than your dad.

Don't ever let anyone tell you otherwise.

Candy Kilometers:
Let us not forget Billy Batman, who died from an accidental gunshot wound, and is buried in Kabul.

My friend Flex said about Billy:

"I helped to lay Billy to rest in that grave. It was the winter of 1971 and 1972. He was my mentor. Taught me how to make pure hashish. I still practice my lessons."

All Mucousless:
My dear friend, Ron Ryan, died near border of Nepal and

India, from an overdose of barbiturates.

He stayed in India too long.

He had a Swedish girlfriend who had committed suicide from jumping from a rooftop in Varanasi.

Especially Still:

I remember hearing about some people from France who were sick, and down and out, and contacted the embassy who refused to help -- and their family also.

I got ripped off all my money, but my dear mother, through the embassy, helped me.

Candy Kilometers:

Many people were so poor out East.

I was one of them when I arrived in Kabul, but a friend first gave me 10 dollars.

And then, when he was leaving three weeks later, he gave me 100 dollars.

And from that day to this, 48 years, I have never been poor.

I actually retired from a U.S. federal job 12 years ago.

Sleeping Forest:

The trail was littered with lost souls.

I remember them near Aabpara Market in Islamabad.

In Paharganj.

In Srinagar.

In Kathmandu.

Different times then.

Smack was the be all, and end all, of so many people's lives on the road.

Near to Die:

In Parvati Valley [above Manali] was killed a couple.

He was Spain, and she was English.

And killed also one French girl, called Sigrid.

I see so many junkies all over India, near to die.

1978 to 1983.

Perk Seeing:
Many went missing in Himachal [state] in the 1990s.
Camping in the mountains.
A local gang was caught, that had been doing it, when they missed a German and he managed to escape them.
His friend got shot.
He was not the first.
The stolen gear was for sale in Manali market.

Shopkeeper's Daughter:
Yes, in the 1980s also.
Some were involved in heroin trade.
Some had stolen from temples.
Others were never seen again.
We lived near the forest above Manali.
Locals always told us, better not to be in the forests after dark, because of bad people.
Very sad.

Lobster Knife:
We met [French serial killer Charles Sobhraj] in Bombay [at a restaurant].
And his girlfriend [French-Canadian Marie Leclerc].
We had lobster thermidor.
Acid Nicholas was at the next table.
And, at another, Bombay Brian was being punched by Jimmy the Knife.
Quite a night.
I was naive.

Cool Fire:
There were a lot of bastards hanging around at that time.
He [Sobhraj] was maybe the worst.

Sleeping Horses:

He's a psychopath.

He knows nothing about why young people travelled and saw the world.

I hope to read that he was taken into a field, and set on fire, and burned to a crisp.

That's what he did to his victims.

He would drug them, steal their money and passports, and then burn them to death in a field.

I'd pay to see him executed.

Arrowhead Typewriter:

He killed a friend of mine in Thailand, Teresa Knowlton, in October 1975.

She was on her way to do a one-month Kopan Monastery in Nepal, and become a [Buddhist] nun.

I'd met her at previous courses there in 1973 and 1974, and she was the driver for the lamas and me, at a meditation course -- at Lake Arrowhead, near Los Angeles -- in July 1975.

I was running the publishing at Kopan, and had given her a typewriter to bring to the monastery.

So when Charles and his little Indian prisoner attendant sauntered into our compound [in New Delhi's Tihar Jail], and he started chatting with us, I said to him:

"Where's my typewriter?"

He looked puzzled, so I explained.

Then he said:

"Oh, she was a prostitute and a drug smuggler, we're better off without her" -- or words to that effect.

I told him that, in fact, she was a sincere *dharma* practitioner [of Hindu and Buddhist doctrine], on her way to get ordained.

So he changed the subject, and asked if I played chess.

So he pulls out his board.

And we had a game.

He was the most aggressive player I'd seen, smashing the pieces down every time he made a move.

He probably would've beaten me, but I like to think that I let him win.

Safer that way.

Anyway, I thought he was an arrogant, lying prick, but didn't know all that much more about him at that time.

He told me personally, that these people -- the ones he killed, although he never admitted that -- were drug addicts and prostitutes, and that he was doing the world a favor by getting rid of them.

That was his bullshit rationale.

And of course, they weren't.

I was only in for a few days -- at that time -- and didn't see him again.

Much Friendlier:

I have always been interested, as I knew people who met him.

One woman had to move out of her hotel in Bangkok, in the middle of the night, to escape from him and his Indian assistant [Ajay Chowdhury].

I was around Kathmandu when the two people were murdered there [a woman traveling from California and her Canadian boyfriend].

And I knew a guy who was in jail with him, and talked to him, in Delhi for months.

He was not part of our scene, but he slithered through it.

Existed Shocked:

We were in Bangkok that year [1975], and never even knew that this kind of scene existed.

Instead, I was rather shocked to see that old friends I knew, from my travels, were smoking that white powder [heroin] and getting strung out.

We quickly got out of there, and went to Laos, and then Bali, instead.

On the Border:

I lost a friend to them [Sobhraj and Sobhraj's French-Canadian girlfriend Marie Leclerc] in Kathmandu.

A girl from Newfoundland [a province in Canada].

I met her on a bus from Athens to Istanbul, a few months earlier.

I jumped off in Turkey, and ran into her and her friend again in Kathmandu.

I went trekking.

When I returned [to Kathmandu], I heard she was missing, but nobody thought anything of it.

Sleeping Horses:

If I ran into him [Sobhraj] in Southeast Asia, he probably would have done me in.

Free drugs would have lured me into his trap.

Obviously Immediately:

I met Sobhraj briefly, in the coffee shop of a hotel on Sukhumvit Road in Bangkok, with a German tourist couple I knew -- slightly about six months or so before the first murders [in nearby Pattaya beach] became news.

I remember him well, despite the meeting being less than 20 minutes.

I disliked him immediately, and the antipathy was clearly mutual.

He didn't welcome my presence during a conversation about what to do and see in Thailand, and I left as soon as I decently could.

My impression of him remains quite vivid.

My meeting with Sobhraj was in the coffee shop of the Chaowalit Hotel in December 1975, where I'd met George and Renate -- the young German couple, about my age, good English, not hippies exactly, but certainly New Age types and doing Asia on the cheap.

We had struck up a passing acquaintance, and they'd told me

a little about themselves and their plans, even mentioning this guy who'd been helpful, who'd said something about passports.

All sounded good.

After breakfast, the three of us were sitting together, and they mentioned this guy would be showing up.

In due course, Sobhraj appeared.

He was fine with them, but I didn't like the look of him at all and he knew it.

I remember him very well and the subject of our discussion, along with my reaction to him.

They were interested in Thailand beyond Bangkok, so liked hearing from me about Sukhothai, Khao Yai and Hua Hin versus Pattaya, etcetera.

Sobhraj was not keen on any of this.

He was keen on gemstones, shopping and the usual sights, temples, and definitely Pattaya.

Obviously he didn't want anything too far from Bangkok.

It was also clear to me that he had some business involvement in mind, concerning stones.

He was au fait with their interests, enough to fit in with whatever they wanted, desiring to be their friend as well as guide.

Despite the fact I disliked him on sight, he was plausible, and they appeared to get on.

He struck the right kind of note with them.

So when I read [about two travelers' bodies found near Pattaya] -- not much later, in March 1976 -- I was concerned and relieved to find out that my two Germans had not been involved.

Given my work and interests, both in London and in Asia, I was not unfamiliar with some of the more dubious types -- some borderline psychopaths -- that swim these waters, and that was the vibe I was getting.

I didn't see them again, but at least I knew they hadn't met a sinister fate, though they must have got a nasty shock when they read about these killings at some later date.

Christmas Dinner:

I didn't meet the despicable murderer, but I was in Kathmandu having Christmas dinner when the American vice consul was called away to see the bodies of two victims.

Also, I knew several of his [druggie smuggler pals, from Denmark and Holland, who shared digs [cells] with him in Delhi's Tihar jail.

A monster.

Beautiful Show:

I met him in Tihar Jail, 1979.

I got into Tihar the exact day I had finished reading *Serpentine* [about Sobhraj murdering travelers in Thailand, Nepal and India during the 1970s].

So when I went in, I asked the inmates where he was, and got to sleep, and I woke up with him next to me.

I told him I had just finished the book.

And he asked what I thought of the book.

So I told him, I understood why he had this life after being treated like shit in France, where he could not have citizenship or passport.

He was the boss in Tihar at that time.

He brought me into the jail director's office, and put his feet on the desk to show me that he was the boss.

I was there [in Tihar] only three days, for some hashish.

When he knew I was going out [being released], he asked me to bring a letter to the Canadian ambassador.

And I did. I brought his letter to the doorman of the embassy.

I got out of jail same day as Marie-Andre Leclerc.

At that time, I was also with a beautiful French-Canadian.

Into Discovered:

I read the book *Serpentine*, and discovered I was in Kathmandu at the same time he was.

Luckily never ran into him.

Learn Fun:
Every year when I'm traveling in India and Nepal, I tell young travelers his story -- which of course they've never heard.
Everyone needs to learn, that even though the hippie trail is fun, one must be careful and wary of danger.
It's a crazy sad story, but I'm glad more people will learn that not everyone on the trail is your friend.

Enjoy Early:
He profited from the trail, but he was not one of us.
On the contrary.

Big Bottles:
I met him in Tihar, where he hit on a friend of mine.
In fact, he tried with every foreign girl.
He could get them all they wanted, and even managed to get private time together.
Even Kiran Bedi [Tihar Jail's first female warden] fell for his charm and fame.
A total sleeky slimy asshole, but apparently irresistible to some confused women.
He is just a sleazy dirtbag, and should have been buried long time ago.
Dirty little ratbag.

Hot Streams:
He approached us in aglow.
I felt a menacing energy from him.
Lucky -- my understanding of him was -- that he resented the ease and money that the traveling gypsies from the West were able to float on through life with, without much of a care.

Grew Easy:
I think his motivation for killing was earning easy money,

with easy crimes -- and hippies were maybe more naive than others -- with no guilt, because he is mad.

His frustration might come from the fact that he grew up with racism.

Struggle Roots:
I agree -- except the naive part.
I think they [Sobhraj's victims] were people in need.
Not naive.
I think he simply exploited this vulnerability of theirs, and dragged them to his web.

Grew Easy:
You are probably right.
With naive, I meant that most of us were not suspicious.
We were thinking, by spreading good vibes, we would only get positive reactions.
Of course we learned fast, because on the trail [across Asia], we all met all sorts of hippies.
I was wondering if I would have fallen in this guy's web, if I had the occasion of meeting him.
I was 18 for my first time on the hippie trail.

Cool Fire:
If the twat was just murdering and robbing Asian tourists, nobody would have bothered a toss.
He would just have faded into obscurity.
He wasn't glamorous or sophisticated, he was just another opportunistic skanky bastard.

Women Amazing:
I never get it why people try to understand the so-called motives of a cunning psychopath.
It's a waste of time.
They are so good at manipulating people.
They have an understanding of psychology, and tell people

what they long to hear.

Everything they say has a kernel of truth. That's what's so confusing.

Even poor, and possibly very badly dressed, we were still treated as if we were special by most local people.

And some freaks went too far, in trying to work that magic.

I was ashamed to see freaks begging from locals, or pretending to be sadhus, but our motives for leaving our countries were many, and complicated.

Unusual Vibe:

I met that monster [Sobhraj] in Delhi.

He was sitting down at my table in The Malhotra [Hotel] in Paharganj.

It was lunch time, and he started a conversation.

I remember, because he said that he was part-Vietnamese, and part-Indian.

I told him that this was a unusual mix, and asked him how it felt.

He gave me a look, and said he did not feel Indian at all.

Then he talked about the precious stone business, and how I could make a lot of money by selling them in Europe.

I told him that I bought my own stones to make jewelry.

He asked me to come to his room and he would show me some precious stones that may interest me.

I said that I never go to anyone's hotel room, and no one comes to mine.

After that, he wrapped up pretty quickly and left.

Also he did not look that good. Small and skinny.

Actually this experience was not really traumatizing, because I had no idea who he was.

Just another strange guy.

Not that charming either. And rather straight looking.

I never thought twice about.

It is dangerous for a woman to travel in India alone.

I was certainly protected by my lifestyle, and common sense -

- maybe more.

He sounded rather vehement about not feeling Indian at all, maybe my remark touched a sore point.

He also had very black eyes, unreadable.

But he was not charming, or special really. And I strongly dislike guys who propose scam precious stone deals, and invite me to their room.

Maybe he did not turn the charm on because I mentioned, pretty early in the conversation, that I had already spent all my money.

I did not feel any evil, or scary vibe either.

Easy Pickingss:
The hippie sect was easy pickings for guys like Sobhraj in the 1970s.

Very unfortunate and sad.

Into Discovered:
It [Sobhraj's murders] has nothing to do with our overland experiences, in my opinion, any more than In Cold Blood by Truman Capote -- book and movie -- has anything to do with Kansas.

Sobhraj also drugged and killed regular tourists as well.

Really Resist:
I met him in Tihar Jail in 1980, because I was arrested there myself.

He was a damn charismatic man.

Luckily, I was too young, and could resist his charms.

I was really afraid of him.

Not in prison, but after I was released.

On the Border:
During those years, we were a small group traveling that route.

Everyone knew him in Goa.

Everyone seems to have known someone affected by him.

When he got out [of Tihar Jail] and was sent back to Paris, he advertised he would accept dinner reservations and conversation, for a price.

He was booked up for months.

I met his ex-wife in Barcelona.

She told me who she was -- after cooking up and serving dinner.

She was working with a Pakistani director, scouting locations for a film about them [her, Sobhraj, and their young daughter].

Late Talk:

I don't think Charles Sobhraj was thinking about the people he murdered, other than a means to get money, and he probably also enjoyed killing them.

Just a perfect genuine piece of shit.

Nicest Friend:

The Canadian he killed in Kathmandu, Larry Carriere, was a good friend of mine.

He was the nicest guy you could ever meet.

I was very happy when he [Sobhraj] re-entered Nepal on a fake passport and was captured, charged, and imprisoned for life.

In India, he had an easy time in jail, running the prison black market.

Hopefully, he is rotting in a hell hole in Nepal.

Personal Hush:

I had several personal connections.

The first was the Turk.

I first met Vitali "Ved" Hakim at the Hotel Malaysia, in Bangkok, in the spring of 1974.

Ved was a handsome guy from Ankara [the capital of Turkey] and quite a character, despite being extremely strung-out on drugs.

I was a bit wary of him, but agreed to travel with him to Chiang Mai, where we later hired a driver to take us out to the opium fields.

The journey was totally insane, with our madman driver blowing a tire, and spinning out, then later getting lost and stuck in mud just near the Burmese border.

Ved, running low on his loaded-up joints, completely flipped out as the rains came pouring down.

We eventually got back to Chiang Mai, having somehow failed to find any opium -- despite being dead center in the Golden Triangle where, if you threw a stone in any direction, you'd probably hit a poppy plant.

Little did we know that we could've walked 10 minutes outside Chiang Mai, and been knee-deep in poppies.

That night Ved, nodding out in his room, managed to drop his heroin-laced cigarette into the folds of his mattress and nearly burned the whole place down.

Next morning, the manager found the smoking mattress, and was ready to kill him.

That was it for Ved.

He missed the air-conditioned rooms of Bangkok, not to mention the room service, and got on the first bus back to civilization.

He thought I was crazy when I told him that I planned on heading further north, to Laos, which was on the verge of being taken over by the communist Pathet Lao [in 1975, after the defeated U.S. military retreated from Laos, Cambodia and Vietnam].

I wound up spending a month in Luang Prabang and Vientiane [main cities in northern Laos], then left just days before the country was overrun.

When I returned to Bangkok, I inquired about Ved at the Hotel Malaysia, and was told by the angry desk clerk that he'd recently disappeared without paying his bill, having left all his stuff in the hotel room.

I thought that was a bit strange, even for Ved.

It wasn't until much later that we learned that Ved's body had been found near Pattaya.

He was the second victim of Charles Sobhraj.

As for the two murders in Kathmandu, I remember well the day [redacted] came to my house, his eyes blazing more than usual.

A police captain had just visited him, and told him about two bodies of Westerners found near the airport, burned and disfigured.

It was all very hush-hush, and hadn't been reported in the newspapers, because the government thought it would be bad for tourism.

[redacted] was known as one of the longest-term Western residents of Kathmandu, and very much in the know.

It wasn't until much later that we learned about Sobhraj.

Enjoy Early:

Apparently I knew him in Bombay, because he also hung out at Dipti's.

But I have no memory of him.

Anyway, I was too poor to kill.

His victims had to have at least 100 dollars.

He called himself a businessman, in some interview.

At least two of his victims were friends, or relatives of friends, of mine.

Naveen Sharma:

There was a Belgian guy who was associated with Sobhraj.

He brought travelers to him in Delhi.

His name is John, from Belgium.

He escaped from Charles, and married a Goa woman.

He was a witness in Sobhraj's case.

He used to come my shop [Lotus Exporters, on Baga beach], sit there, and start selling *dope* to my customers.

Then I told him,

"Do not do this at my place, and do not come to my shop."

Then Sobhraj broke out of the prison and came to Goa.

One morning, I am at my shop. One police in charge of Delhi police, and the other man from Delhi in civilian clothes, came to my store.

The Goa police chief asked me to talk.

He had a photo of Sobhraj and Ajay Chowdhury, and had showed it to John.

He said,

"He [Ajay in the photograph] looks like Naveen."

He got confused.

He thought I am Ajay.

Then he came with cops to my shop.

I was last night at a party. So tired. No sleep. I did not understand what was happening.

Suddenly, two cops flashed their pistols, so I do not try to escape.

Then I, and the police commissioner, sat on the back seat of a car.

I did not say anything.

Then he asked about me.

Then he asked me, "Where is Sobhraj?"

I said, "I do not know."

He said to me, "We have tough guys [brutal police interrogators] in Delhi."

I said, "I have nothing to do with him."

The next day they flew me to Delhi.

He asked me, "What you think about Sobhraj?"

I said, "You and society made him criminal. He was not born criminal. I read *Serpentine*. When he was in Saigon and Paris, he did not get love from family and society. So he turned criminal."

When we landed in Delhi, they put me in a more security part of jail, where more hardcore convicted criminals were.

My neighbor was Indira Gandhi's killer Satwant Singh [Indira Gandhi's Sikh bodyguard who, along with another Sikh bodyguard, assassinated her at home in New Delhi in 1984].

Most of the guys in prison thought I was a killer.

I told them, "It is not true."
But I got privileges, I got massage, *dope*, and food.
My dad was a lawyer.
Then it was big fight in court.
When those crimes [by Sobhraj] were happening in Thailand [in 1975 and 1976], I was in Agra University [in India].
My dad told the judge to get my proof [of my identity] from the university.
After five days, my father got me out.
I was freed.
I was lucky my dad was a lawyer.
The next day, Bombay police got Sobhraj in the restaurant, where tourists go to use the telephone.
The O'Coqueiro restaurant [in Mapusa, Goa].
I still have all the clippings of newspapers, of that time.
[displays yellowing newspapers including a Hindustan Times story headlined, "A Case of Mistaken Identity?" and two stories in The Express headlined, "Sobhraj, David Hall, Nabbed in Goa Bar. Thrilling Drama by Bombay Cops" and "Many Heads Likely to Roll in Tihar"]
During five days in prison, I learned prison life.

Nostrils Frozen:
Yes, I remember the day you were taken, and your girlfriend -- I have forgotten her name -- told me what had happened.
She was really upset, and wandering about with her pet crow in the basket.

Naveen Sharma:
Her name was Regina.
I think in the beginning it was strange, but in prison I had it good.
Got smoke [hashish] and good food.
I was put very secure prison cell.
The death gallows was in front of my cell.
Big terrorists were also my neighbor.

It is great to tell my kids the story.

In jail, mafioso and bank robbers became my friend.

Petty criminals gave me massage.

A funny story is the [redacted] of police, became a friend.

When he came to Goa, we smoked together, and made a party.

He excused me.

I forgave him.

I will tell you how he [Sobhraj] broke out of the prison.

When he was in prison in 1986, he came in contact with David Hall -- an English guy -- who was in Tihar due to some drug-related case.

He came out [Hall was released] from Tihar.

One day, he came back, in a car, with cake and ice cream.

It was drugged.

So all these guys from security [in Tihar Jail] ate and fell asleep.

Then Sobhraj sat in the car, and escaped.

In my opinion, Sobhraj is devil.

He killed many young travelers, just for money.

The Gray Zone:

Sobhraj? Who can possibly comprehend the mind of a psychopath?

I was not in Asia in the mid-1970s -- I was still in school -- but came in the late 1980s.

And how wild, colorful, and strange it was.

And even the underbelly, in which Sobhraj operated, held some sort of dark allure.

I guess he was, and is, very intelligent on a certain level, and utterly ruthless and cunning, as psychopaths are.

But the gray zone he operated in [among foreign travelers in Asia], made it easy for him.

Any other place, he would have been stopped much earlier, I am sure.

Women Amazing:
That's right, it was -- and still is -- so easy to kill someone in India.

Cobra Door:
Sobhraj was staying next door to me at Cobra Vaddo, Baga [just before he was arrested nearby in the O'Coqueiro restaurant].
He was caught by the same man [Senior Police Inspector Madhukar Zende] who had previously caught him [in 1972].

Clean Squat:
In the O'Coqueiro, today -- in the restaurant were he was captured -- there is a statue of the famous Bikini Killer [Sobhraj's nickname from Thailand's media, because his first female victims were found near Pattaya beach wearing a bikini].

Learn Fun:
Hundreds of travelers still disappear on the hippie trail, every year.
It is difficult to trace anyone.
Travelers are flaunting expensive devices.
And lots of desperate people are in need of easy cash.

Who Disappeared:
Who knows how many disappeared without being found?
Or unreported missing?

Some Stretchered:
God, I've got some stories.
A dead junkie being stretchered out of The Malaysia [a Bangkok hotel], in front of a queue of backpackers waiting to check in.

9 • SOUTHEAST ASIA

Secret Nervous:
We got raided by the police at 7 a.m in Mandalay [in central Burma].
Searching for drugs.
And all the suspicious items they could find was my friend's contact lens stuff.

Man Faced:
Being a longhaired and barefoot man, I faced several times this problem traveling.

Under the Galata Bridge:
I just watched *A Prayer Before Dawn*, about an English boxer in a Thai prison.
Took me back to my six years in prison in Bangkok.
Really brought back memories.
It was so realistic, I remembered my time there 1976 to 1982.
So real, that my stomach is in a knot.
Sleeping next to each other on the floor.
Squat down toilet in the back of the cell.
Wearing leg irons, like I did most of the time when I got busted inside for drugs.
Showering out of a water trough, with a plastic bowl.
All too real.
Even the *katoys* -- lady boys -- were right on.

Enjoy Early:

Didn't you make good money inside [Bangkok's prison]? Or am I mistaken?

Under the Galata Bridge:
I sold drugs inside.
Angelique, who came to visit me, made a deal with [redacted].
Her and [redacted] would go up to Chiang Mai [a northern city], and buy some ounces [of heroin], and bring it back to [redacted], to bring into me.
They made money.
I was the dealer in the Foreign Section, my whole six years.
But it was never for the money -- just my habit and food.
Conditions were horrible, but it was easier to get pure heroin than food, which is all I cared about in those days.
Spent the time on the nod.

Eat Rural:
I don't suppose you bumped into my late husband Rimbaud Rural, who was also incarcerated at the Bangkok Hilton [the prison's nickname] circa 1978 and 1979, before they moved him to Chiang Mai?
He was set up by a prostitute who sold him a gram of heroin.
Did three years.

Under the Galata Bridge:
I knew a Rimbaud Rural for sure, if he was in the Foreign Section.
We used [heroin] together.

Eat Rural:
Wow, small world!
He was French-Canadian, so definitely had an accent.
And yes, although obviously he was a user before he got there, it was in jail that he started using needles -- shared ones -- which resulted in his getting hepatitis.

Apparently it was the prison guards who sold it.
[she displays a photo of three smiling young people]
He is the one in the middle
I took this shot on our wedding day.

After returning from Thailand, he then eloped with Green Blossom -- seen on the right here, formerly my best friend -- whereupon her partner on the left killed himself.

Under the Galata Bridge:
I knew him very well, he was one crazy motherfucker.
We were in the same room.

There were 10 different cells in the Foreign Section -- each with 10 or 15 Westerners.

We got high together all the time, and I do remember his last name.

Very small world.

Half the guards sold it to us, and the other half tried to bust us, and extort money from us.

[he displays a photograph of a young longhaired, bearded man wearing sunglasses, standing in what appears to be a yard of Bangkok's main prison, with cylindrical whitewashed guard towers and two foreign men in the background]

That was me, in the Thai prison Foreign Section.
Is he still alive?

I am, only because I got clean, and into recovery in 1982 when I got out.

Eat Rural:
No, he died in the mid-1990s in Montreal, still doing the hard stuff with Green Blossom.

Crack and *smack*.

The doctors apparently couldn't believe he had lasted as long as he did.

Green Blossom came to visit me in England en route to scatter his ashes in Jamaica, which I thought was weird because Rimbaud Rural had never been there.

Not just his ashes, but also his dog's, who had died two years prior and been kept in a freezer!

In what way did he come over as a crazy motherfucker when you shared a cell?

Under the Galata Bridge:
I remember him as violent.
He got into fights.
He was the first French-Canadian I ever knew, and I remember him as a little wild.
May he rest in paradise.

Eat Rural:
He was indeed rather violent, one of many reasons that I left him a few months after our marriage -- which was specifically so that I could remain in Canada and apply for citizenship.
We'd been living together for a couple of years prior to that.
He was wild too.
Sincerely hope he wasn't violent towards you too.

Under the Galata Bridge:
No, I was his [heroin] connection, so we got along pretty good.

On the Border:
I was in the Police Hospital, under arrest, during martial law in Bangkok when the military overthrew the government.
Stopped my escape plans, as there was as curfew every evening after dark.

Sleeping Horses:
In 1978, I was in Patong beach, Phuket [a tourist-friendly island in Thailand] for three months.
The [Thai] kids sold two-inch lengths of plastic soda straws, filled with China White Number Four heroin, for one dollar.
Everyone had heroin there.

I loved the stuff.

No needles.

I snorted match-head sized amounts, or smoked it in *bongs*.

It was a great three months.

My neighbor, a German guy, always had a couple of ounces in a bowl, on a table next to his bed, with a *bong* there, and told me to come use his stuff any time, in case I ran out of my own.

Oh yeah, it was fantastic.

Everyone was doing heroin there, at Patong beach.

And many were sewing it into the linings of their clothes, to take back home.

Plus, kids used to come around [Patong beach in 1978] and sell packs of Marlboro cigarettes, that were emptied out and filled with Thai Stick [a strong marijuana].

They couldn't get all 20 back into the packs, but they could get 18 in there, and they sold the packs for one dollar.

The only time, in three months, in Patong beach that I saw police, is when an Italian couple got naked on their beach towel.

I think 10 police cars showed up for that.

I'm still alive and kicking, living in Southeast Asia.

I had enough brain cells left -- after tons of acid too in the 1960s and 1970s, and *shrooms* too, up until the 1990s -- to have a pretty good career as a headhunter, working out of my homes in Marin county and Napa, California, for almost 30 years.

But, after all that travel, and especially loving Southeast Asia, I knew I had to retire here.

I guess I was lucky to end up with a semblance of good health.

Groovy Bamboo:

I don't have many photos of when I lived in Thailand, but this is one of them [displays a photograph].

It was taken around 1973, in Pattaya beach.

Even though it looks like I was about 12, I was 19 and probably rolling a *joint*.

Because that's what you did in Thailand in 1973.

I had on my favorite bell-bottom jeans, and my red platform heels that I called my Groovy As -- short for Groovy Ass Shoes.

Seriously.

Thai Years:
When I first came to the U.S. some 45 years ago, when my friends learned that I was [Thai] from Thailand, they would approach me and asked me to get them some Thai Stick.

I didn't know what they were.

I thought they wanted a Thai boy.

Penis equals stick.

Sure Doses:
Yeah, the Thai Sticks were the *bomb*.

So were the old-style opium pipes that a couple Chinese parlors had for customers.

The good old days.

So fine.

Especially Pure:
The [Thai Stick] originals were pure bud, tied -- to a 15-centimeter bamboo sliver -- with cannabis stalk fiber, nothing more.

Trishaw drivers [bicycle-powered, three-wheeled taxis] in the provinces, sold them wrapped in newspaper, for 10 baht [less than one dollar] per stick.

In Bangkok, the street price was 25 baht a stick.

This was the late 1970s when Nakhon Phanom, Sakon Nakhon, and Khon Kaen [provinces and cities] were major trade centers.

Thai Stick had pretty much disappeared by the mid-1980s, as Thailand developed economically, and most locals lost interest in *ganja* farming -- especially with the [American] G.I. market long gone.

Best Ages:
The best by a country mile.
Someone gave me a *brick* [a kilo] when I first settled in *Bangers* [Bangkok].
It was so good, it took me ages to smoke it.

Wood Chopstick:
There were lots of copy Thai Stick in the U.S., back in the 1970s.
Mostly cheap Mexican, tied with fishing line, to a wood chopstick.

Old Culture:
Marijuana has always been a part of Isaan [northeast Thailand] culture.
Old folks used, and still use it, in their *tom yum* soup.

Fighting Smoke:
Too bad much of that knowledge went up in smoke, when the trade was effectively eradicated under the guise of fighting communism.

Knock Back:
I remember buying a few Thai Sticks in Australia when I was a teenager, back on the late 1970s.
The sticks were tiny, quite thin, about as thin or thinner than a cigarette, and tied on a very thin stick, not much thicker than a matchstick, and only about 10 centimeters long.
I heard the dealers would separate compressed bricks of it, and cut the sticks in half, or even thirds, and then wrap in aluminum foil, and sell for 25 dollars each, street price.
Very expensive, compared to other pot, but really good.
Amazing actually.
Australia already had some great pot, but this was about as good as it ever got.
Worth every dollar.

I would use it like hash.

I only had to mix a few crumbs with a tobacco cigarette, or a *joint* of cannabis leaf, and POW!

Would knock my socks off.

Houseboat Beautiful:

The absolutely best psychedelic trip, with colors and sounds, was after eating a Magic Mushroom omelette in Kuta [a beach on Indonesia's Bali island].

Garden Experience:

I made a point of complimenting the chef after the first omelette experience, and he tossed on several more the next time I ate there.

The famous Garden Restaurant in 1979.

Village Ants:

Ants ate my L.S.D. in a village in Bali.

Nothing Shacks:

Once I had three grams of *charas*, and six grams of *ganja*, at my house in Bali.

I got an unwanted visit that morning, and spent two years in the local jail.

Sleeping Horses:

It was so much more loose in the early 1970s.

We smoked hashish every day on the porch outside our rooms in the *losmen* [traditional house] in Kuta.

Another example of how loose it was in the 1970s -- in Sumatra [a large Indonesian island], my roommate went to the prison in Medan [city], where two Aussie [Australian] guys were behind bars, for dealing weed.

But the guards let them deal out of their cells.

They had kilos in their cell.

My roommate brought back, to Lake Toba, a half pound he

bought from them.
1975.

Nothing Shacks:
I left France in 1971 when I was 17.
My story was in the mid-1980s. They already had hardened the rules, and informants were paid.
It was not funny to be locked up with real criminals, thieves and murderers.
But now I have mates for life too -- people that you may know.
They are still on the road, but some died.
And I did things -- positive -- that I wouldn't had time to do, outside.
I tried to make it as positive as possible.
This is how I try to remember it.
But I know that it wasn't, really.

Fond Morning:
These days, here in Cambodia, it's very common to see Western travelers completely broke, living on the streets, and begging from the Cambodian people.
I used to disregard them as either junkies, or people who sold off their passports and things, to drink or party.
But actually, it's very easy to find oneself in their situation.
Some of them get robbed, staying in backpacker hostels.
Or drop, or lose, their passports and credit cards.
And once you are in this situation, life becomes very difficult.
The embassies no longer offer much help.
No emergency money or assistance.
Very difficult to get new credit cards sent to these countries.
And unless you can contact good friends or family to help you, your life can quickly become a nightmare.

Clean Squat:
It happened to me in 1981, Goa.

Good lesson of life, even if unavoidable.
And just for one month.
I had to beg in Colaba for a while.
I was just broke, after a court affair.
Not robbed or broke because of junkism.

Hard Flipped:
I got robbed in 1973, in Merauli [on New Delhi's outskirts].
Sleeping in a [archeological] ruin.
In cold February.
My last little bag with everything -- and I slept on it -- was gone.
Six weeks surviving in the streets.

Sleeping Horses:
Pony and I lived in Sihanoukville, Cambodia, right next to [redacted] beach.
We were there for two years, and left in late 2018, due to it becoming a piece of shit with all the Chinese [construction] development ruining it.
There was a bar called [redacted].
They had a room inside, which opened every night at 7 p.m., and a [redacted] guy would show you a menu of every drug imaginable.
And you would order what you wanted right then and there, and purchase it.
Heroin, coke, MDMA, ice, speed, acid, and more I can't remember.
I witnessed friends coming out of that room with 20 hits of MDMA or acid, the main favorites there.
But I always abstained, having had my hard drug years behind me.
At that point, it was only booze and weed.
The really big nights were when the weekly raves would happen.
Almost all young travelers, and many young residents of the

area, went to them.

The [redacted] guy would sell tons of stuff to the people who would be going.

It began at midnight, and went to 10 a.m. the next day.

Too late for an old codger like me.

It was a hoot walking up and down the beach the next day, and seeing some of the hundreds of attendees just totally wiped out, sleeping it off.

Many had come from India down to Southeast Asia.

There were more young travelers then, than there were when I was traveling in the early 1970s.

Morphed Nun:

I had a green nun shoot me up a heroic dose of morphine, while in the grips of a cerebral malarial delirium, in a Thai-Cambodian border town.

Acute panic morphed into vegetable serenity, in a matter of seconds.

Tubes:

I once snorted China White, thinking it was cocaine, and I woke up on a life support machine, in a Cambodian hospital -- with a tube in my hand, in my penis, and a ventilator, and tied to the bed.

The people that gave me the stuff had rushed me to the hospital, to save my life.

When the bill came, it was 3,000 dollars for one night.

So I called the British Consulate, and he said:

"Just pay them and be gone."

Turns out the hospital was working with the guy who gave me the stuff, and cut them in, for bringing me to them.

He also put the bag of heroin into my bag, and he said if I died, he needed it to look like I had been doing heroin on my own.

I didn't stop itching for a week.

I had never done heroin before.

I can't even remember what it felt like.
I passed out within seconds.

Taste Alive:
You are lucky to be alive.
Normally, one would taste a bit before snorting, no?

Tubes:
I did taste it, and it was very funky tasting.
Bitter.
But still made my mouth go numb, so I thought it was just garbage-level trash some Cambodian guy got handed in a bar.
I had no idea it was pure heroin.
I was very lucky to survive it.

Hottest Sources:
From my Cambodian sources, most heroin sold in Cambodia is the DD Double Dragon variety out of Burma, and over 95 percent pure.
A highly addictive substance, with lifelong neurological damage.
But yes, I have heard many people find it replaces the hottest bar girl.

Sleeping Horses:
I got lucky.
On New Year's Eve 2016, in Phnom Penh [Cambodia's capital], I walked into a bar on 110 Street and the girl -- sitting at the end -- and I, smiled at each other.
I sat down next to her, and she eventually spent the night with me.
The next morning, I asked her if she'd like to travel with me for a few weeks.
She said yes, and packed a small suitcase in her dreadful room she shared with four other girls.
We got a bus down to Kampot [beach] and stayed a week,

and then bussed to Otres beach and stayed there for two weeks.

On the way back to Phnom Penh, I asked her if she'd like to live together, and again she said yes.

So we got an apartment across the street from the National Museum.

After three weeks there, we moved to Otres beach.

It was so much better at that great beach, and we lived there for two years, while doing some traveling in Thailand and a couple of months in Nepal.

After those two years in Cambodia, we built a home in Southeast Asia, where she grew up, and we have been living here ever since the end of 2018.

Begged Lucrative:
I went twice to Saigon in 1965, once in May, and again in October and November.

It was terrible.

One could hear the bombs, but the city was still safe.

Millions of [American] G.I.s.

Of course, I am exaggerating by saying millions.

Refugees camped on the sidewalks.

I went by a French transport ship each time, the Messangerie Maritime.

It is a four-hour trip up the Mekong from the open South China Sea, to the city of Saigon.

In May, the riverbank was covered in some of the densest jungle, right up to the water's edge.

In November, the same trip up the river, the banks were bare, it was like the moon.

Not a tree.

Not a vine.

Nothing.

The entire jungle had been defoliated by Agent Orange [a U.S. herbicide].

It was so sad.

It Cared:

I dodged the draft, so didn't have to go the war in Vietnam, way back then.

But now it's one of the places I'd love to live in.

Much Friendlier:

I was in Vientiane [capital of Laos] in 1974, and stayed a little out of the center of town.

I went to the famous night club, which seemed to have an assortment of freaks, C.I.A., Air America types, mixed with mafia guys in fancy silk suits.

I don't suppose any of them were involved in the opium or heroin trade?

I moved on to Vang Vieng [a riverside town], by funky bus, sitting on a bag of rice in the doorway.

That was as far as the bus went.

Too dangerous to go further.

I stayed a night in a [Buddhist] monastery with monks, who were trying to peek through the window when I changed my clothes, after swimming in the river.

Next day or so, I got a ride on a cargo plane to Luang Prabang [a northern city], where I stayed for a few weeks, exploring the town, visiting the cave temple, and waterfall.

You could only go up the river to the cave temple on a boat tour, organized by an American, who was a former spotter pilot for the illegal bombing of Laos.

He was known as Larry the C.I.A. Agent, as his tour office was a branch of one in Saigon, that was known to be a C.I.A. front.

Normally, Larry did not guide the tour but sent his Vietnamese assistant.

Since there were five or six of us, all Americans, he decided to go.

This was an interesting group, as there was a woman who had lived in Taiwan who was a fluent scholar of Chinese, a stringer reporter, a guy who was traveling with his wife before he returned to the States to clerk at the Supreme Court, and me -- maybe one more.

All were university educated.

When Larry started pointing out areas and villages he had helped bomb, he soon found out he had a boat full of left-wing student radicals, who hated the war in Vietnam.

We peppered him with questions about how many bombs were dropped, and why, how many Vietnamese or Pathet Lao were killed, how many innocent villages were destroyed, and why, why, why?

Larry was lucky we didn't throw him out of the boat.

I loved Luang Prabang and stayed weeks.

Smoked a little O in a den, which often had a few of the local cops doing the same.

Finally flew to Houei Xai [a border town on the Mekong River], and crossed back to Thailand, heading south to eventually Singapore.

I returned to Laos in 2000, and still loved it.

Shopkeeper's Daughter:
Not exactly, maybe in January [1975], I met some Americans who said they were caught by Pathet Lao [communist Lao rebels] when trying to go somewhere else outside the city [Vientiane], by hitching a ride on some old truck.

They were held for a few days, and got out of it by insisting they were Canadian.

They had left their passports in Vientiane.

Fortress Hovel:
In the Hotel Lido's ramshackle lobby in Vientiane, February 1975, a New York woman looking like a 20-something Janis Joplin flirtatiously said to an elderly Lao woman -- who silently grinned with a mouthful of crooked teeth:

"Aw, come on, don't just smile. Confess, honey. Confess! This is the Golden Triangle, isn't it? You guys are famous!

"Please be swell, and show a young lady where the opium

dens are. Something close by. Something I can walk to.

"I just got here from India."

Exasperated, Janis Joplin turned to us and said:

"Shit, India -- everybody in India told me, 'Go to Laos, go to Laos, that's where the opium is, opium is legal in Laos'."

Stretching out her two fleshy arms in a patch of sunlight -- brightening her face in the Lido's grimy courtyard -- she beamed:

"And here I am, goddamnit. Vientiane! Laos! Opium!"

Giggling seized her.

She loosened under its influence.

"This old Lao lady has got to understand 'Vientiane' and 'opium'.

"Those two words should be enough to let her know what I'm talking about."

Exhausted, she sat on an upside down metal pail.

"Fucking took me long enough. I went from Calcutta to Rangoon, from Rangoon to Bangkok, and took the bus from Bangkok all the way to Nong Khai, and had to cross the Mekong.

"Took over a week getting here from Calcutta.

"You can't imagine how I just kept thinking, how a dark, quiet room is waiting for me in Vientiane, someplace cool where I can just wrap myself around the long stem of an opium pipe, and dream away."

She scratched her scabbed legs.

"I spent two years in India. Do you know what I had to do to get visas to stay two years?

"I'm an American, so they only give three months.

"Well, I had to beg, borrow and steal to stay two years.

"Every time I went for a fucking three-month extension, I had to throw my passport in the Ganges and watch it sink into the gray, mucky water, and then I'd get a new one.

"It always took me two weeks hanging around New Delhi, to re-apply for another passport."

Sleeping Horses:
When I was in Vientiane in 1975, I was told there was a cemetery there just for travelers who died from overdoses of heroin.

I stayed in a place called Saylom Villa in Vientiane.

I found an opium den a half block from the villa.

I was so into going there, three times a day.

I never travelled around Laos, in that one month there.

My wife and I travelled around Laos in 2017 though, mostly northern Laos.

Such a wonderfully beautiful country.

Robes Dance:
Did anyone ever meet Celine -- or Simone -- in Vientiane around 1970?

She ran a den on the second floor of her place. Vietnamese-French.

And she would make your pipe -- hold it with her toes, end to your mouth -- one hand fanning you with a hand fan, and handing you a cup of tea with the other.

Making you a pipe, in the time while you rested.

Pillows?

I've had an Ovaltine can with a folded towel on the top -- that was probably the most interesting.

But a little wooden bench, with a folded towel on the top, always did the trick.

Fortress Hovel:
In Laos, the opium village was a cluster of huts gone mad.

An opium smoker -- The Joker -- his mouth smeared black from greasy food or something, took us into the smoking hut.

Ba Wai Gau village, 1997.

Inside the hut, I heard loud, desperate gnawing on a bone.

It was the noisy sound of each staccato burst of burning opium -- the smoke inhaled by a villager.

The hut's thatched rooftop pointed into the night sky, sharp as stars' edges.

Each Akha tribesman pulverized what was left of himself by hammering hit after hit, chain-smoking opium, and slanting into the hut-shaped night.

Someone unrolled a pallet-sized, padded mat.

The hut's interior was lit by two beer bottles on fire.

A lean splatter of invisible radio static mixed with heavy breathing.

The Joker became an opium pipe master in front of a blackened, thick glass cone's fire intensifier, which made a kerosene lamp's single flame, underneath, burn severe.

Night collapsed.

Fires flickered on the hills.

A feverish air pushed through the hut while the shriveled inhabitants dreamed.

One Akha tribesman near the door, wanly waved at another Akha, who silently reclined on a low bamboo bed.

Fists of oily, black chunks appeared and disappeared.

A hand-held scale balanced the clayish drug against blob-shaped metal weights engraved with curled inscriptions.

Buyers sniffed and pressed the bitter, sticky mounds.

Amid the slurred rhythms, The Joker passed the pipe.

Houseboat Beautiful:

I was in Vientiane for two weeks, very happy and content, with my chocolate milk and croissants, after visits to the opium dens.

They say Vientiane was The City of 100 Red Doors -- and each one was an opium den.

The first time [using opium] was actually in Sausalito [in northern California], in 1974.

Shoved it up my ass.

Chasing the Dragon is smoking tar [raw opium] on foil, which I only did when I lost all my veins -- and my connections in San Francisco for China White [heroin] -- so I had to use that shitty Mexican tar they ironically call Shiva.

Acutely Shady:
I travelled in Southeast Asia for a year in 1972 and 1973, and became acutely aware of the war as I came into Laos.

In Luang Prabang, the Pathet Lao bombed the airport while I was there.

And there were a lot of Americans in Vientiane -- some quite shady, as if they had deserted.

By chance, I came back into Thailand with an American traveler.

In Udon Thani [a city in northern Thailand], he said he could get us into the [U.S.] military base for a look.

He had the right paperwork, so we got in and had a Coke and stuff.

It was all quite surreal.

Hot Streams:
I used to travel often between Penang [a northwest Malaysian island] and Laos, hitching rides on the endless stream of lorries going up to Udon, fueling the war in Vietnam.

Little did we know as we lay back in the open trucks, blowing the best Thai Sticks, that we were probably lying on napalm and bomb supplies.

What a great and sad time, trying to get to Luang Prabang, and being turned back by the soldiers.

Seeing all of the frightened faces of the refugees fleeing, with just a straw mat, and a water carrier.

Oh this world.

Persian Indian:
I went for a buddy holiday to Thailand in 2009 -- very strange memories.

On one hand, a giant bordello.

On the other, a traditional [Buddhist] religious culture, very similar to my own [in India].

Familiar Sanskrit words are used as shop or metro station

names, very correctly.

Shimmering Joy:
Interesting first encounter.
The added bonus about learning a tonal language is the extreme fine tuning involved, which sharpens your ear-to-brain system, to a high degree.
Can you remember which Sanskrit terms you spotted?

Persian Indian:
Kusum Beauty Parlor.
Kusum refers to a beautiful red flower, or a blossom -- used perfectly appropriately.
Asok metro station.
Mahavidhyala for university.
Even the way they move their palms over a *puja thali* [religious offering], is exactly the same.
They look different, eat different, sound different, but their souls are the same as ours.

Shimmering Joy:
"Giant bordello" would be a confirmation bias symptom.
Perhaps reaffirmed in case you landed on Sukhumvit Road [Bangkok's tourist trench].
Just imagine you getting into Siam [Thailand] without all the sex rap planted in your brain beforehand, and no automatic ushering to these particular areas.
Would you have seen the whole country as a giant bordello?

Persian Indian:
Fair enough.
That's the main reason Indians would go there, before they [Thailand] reinvented themselves as a family destination -- like Vegas.

Dead Water:

My father was born in Malaya in 1919.

His father [arrived there] on a £10 colonial ticket just years before, leaving Lancashire [a city in northwest England] after losing nine siblings, and parents, to flu -- but graced by a maternal uncle who'd earlier presided as Bishop of Rangoon [Burma].

As a child, I conquered my grandfather's writing chest's three layers of secret compartments.

Innermost, were a row of ivory canisters, with a dark resinous base.

Years later, I recalled this, and knew it as being opium.

Sleeping Horses:
I only did the heroin and opium in the 1970s in Southeast Asia.

That was the hardest [drugs] of them all, although I enjoyed them as much as the psychedelics.

My first O den was on Chulia Street in Penang in 1974.

It really wasn't a den, I was just walking by a fat Chinese guy who asked me, as I passed by, if I'd like to smoke some opium.

I said, "Sure!"

And he unlocked a padlock on a tiny shack, just big enough for two people.

He had the porcelain head stools, and I laid across from him, while he prepared the pipes.

And he told me he was a retired insurance salesman, whose territory was Australia, so he spoke perfect English.

Fast forward to my next trip there that year and, in Georgetown, I asked a money changer if he knew where I could buy some balls of opium.

He said he could get me 50, the smallest amount he would sell, the next day.

Until then, he invited me to sit down in an outdoor cafe with him.

And I did.

And he proceeded to use a really long spoon that looked like a coke spoon, but even longer, to hollow out the center of a cigarette.

Then he took a vial of white powder, and gently poured it into the opening, filling the inside of the hole in the cigarette.

He had ordered a sweet coffee with cream, and then stuck his finger into the coffee, and rubbed the coffee all over the cigarette.

He then lit it, and we passed it back and forth, taking hits, while it burned very slowly.

We smoked two heroin cigarettes, and I was feeling a little nauseous but felt great, at the same time.

Is that possible?

Anyway, I went back upstairs to my hotel room, and sat on my bed in this same position for about an hour, before moving at all.

My girlfriend took a picture [he displays a photograph].

I used to bring my own music, knowing it was not easy to find in foreign lands.

I had a few favorite cassettes.

Dark Side of the Moon [by Pink Floyd] which I played all day while tripping on mushrooms with a Balinese guy and his Aussie girlfriend, sitting on a bench at the edge of the [volcanic] crater at Mount Agung in Bali, in 1974.

I had a custom tape I had made in Singapore in 1974 -- Blind Faith's *Can't Find My Way Home*.

Only that song.

On both sides of the cassette -- which I listened to endlessly, usually after smoking opium in Penang, and in Vientiane at my room in Saylom Villa, cuddling a beautiful Chinese lady I met there, who was actually from Berkeley.

Sleeping Cubby:

I found an alley in Penang with a cubby hole, and some fat man in the shadow.

It was in 1976, or around then.

It was a Mister Chang or somebody, with a small den.

He was there, like a sleeping fixture.

Shock Body:
It all ends in tears.
Well, it did for me.
I didn't know the meaning of restraint, when it came to drugs.

Forget Not:
Stuff like this [opium], turned beautiful young beings rapidly into dirty rags.

Robes Dance:
In the 1960s, you couldn't get Number Four [heroin] in Hong Kong, but rather only Pink Rocks -- Number Three -- but they did the trick.
You used tin foil from a Pink Panther Candy bar, folded it in half, and put a rock at the top -- heating the foil with a lighter, and using a rolled up whatever -- following it down the foil and inhaling.
Hence, "chasing the dragon" as the rock slid down the foil.
The name of getting loaded on *junk* morphed "chasing the dragon" to mean most anything about getting high from *junk*.

Begged Lucrative:
I chased the same dragon in Singapore 1965, before it got cleaned up [by police].
I enjoyed the soft pink cloud.

Sleeping Horses:
My favorite purchase though, was in 1978 in Hong Kong.
I got 100 *Mandys* [Mandrex] from a pharmacy that was just about to close for the night.
I walked in while the pharmacist was looking at his watch, and asked if he had them.
He asked me if I had a prescription, and I said no.

He hesitated and then asked:
"How many do you want?"
I said "100" -- and he blew my mind and actually sold me 100.

Under the Galata Bridge:
You can still buy Ambien and codeine from the pharmacy in Tsim Sha Tsui [a Kowloon area's neighborhood], in Hong Kong, without prescription.

Clothes Rip:
Funny story about Singapore.
I drove a Chevy van out to Afghanistan, and filled it up [with hashish].
Then drove it down to Cochin [a southwest Indian port] and shipped it to Adelaide [an Australian port].
While it was on route, two older women [in Australia] got their truck *popped* [inspected], coming from India.
Word was, Customs [in Australia] was ripping all rigs apart.
So, abort!
Abort!
I flew to Singapore as my ship docked there, and took my truck off, while waiting for another ship to take it to northern Europe.
I drove to the Y.M.C.A. [a Young Men's Christian Association's hostel], and stayed there for awhile.
When driving back into the port [in Singapore] with the van, there was a billboard showing a junkie with a needle, and various drugs.
It showed him hanging by the neck on the gallows.
It said:
"Transporting drugs, punishable by life in prison or death."
I thought, that's pretty harsh, and drove in.
The things we would do for a little smoke, back in the day.
Speaking on behalf of myself, I'd like to say, what an idiot.
We believed in the freedom to intake into our bodies, the

substances we choose.

Chants Creator:
One is entitled to their own cognitive liberty.

Clean Squat:
There are four different species of papaverum somniferous [opium].
The white one is used to make morphine and heroin.
[displays a photograph]
These others are decorative, with very little latex.

Hard Flipped:
You can make a strong tea, and get a little high, with super long cooking.
Crush the whole poppy, and boil half-an-hour.
It works with all species.
It's like in Chefchaouen, Morocco, when I saw the face of the poor local boy, addicted to what we call *rachacha* in France.
I didn't fancy to try it.
Opium has to be purified, at a minimum to become laudanum.
It's better take pure white heroin, very addictive too, but not harmful for the body.

Robes Dance:
The best way to find a den was grab a rickshaw driver, pantomime smoking a pipe, give him some rupees, kip, dollars, whatever -- and he'd pedal like shit.
'And we all made out just fine.

Initial This:
My introduction to opium was in the hills of northern Thailand, 1983.
I can confirm that over 20 pipes is ill advised.
Not only was I unable to piss, I wasn't sure what I was trying

to do.

A long night of floating above my spot on the floor followed.

Realized Woman:
We were in Chiang Rai [a northern Thailand town], when I walked into a room and saw my husband, lying on a bed with a Thai woman.

And then I realized, they were sharing a pipe.

Fortress Hovel:
An Akha tribe's village headman, in northern Thailand 1975, sang his own simple song like a nursery rhyme, when he smoked.

Glazed, he droned:
"Hello my friend, opium / Do you love me? / I love you. / I love only you on the world. / Only you / On the world.

"You laugh for me? / You laugh little bit for me? / If you don't laugh, I don't love you. / Opium? / You love me? / I love you.

"You laugh one more time? / You laugh? / You laugh now?"

Then he inhaled a mammoth lungful.

As he sucked the smoke, the burning opium spit loud demonic laughter, echoing around his hilltop hut.

The tribesman, curled and drugged, watched his grinning dreams roll in the dirt in front of him, mumbling exotic poetry through their unseen mouths.

After a few more pipes, he talked to himself behind cupped hands.

Sometimes squeaking.

Sometimes arguing.

Then he rested like a powerful creature under tons of murky sea.

A nearby smoker coughed.

The Akha drank a cup of tea.

He sang again:

"You can keep the airplane / I don't want the airplane. / You can keep the money / I don't want money too. / I don't want anything in the world.

"If I want the world / I smoke opium. / Opium takes everything to me. / When I need woman / Opium can take woman to me too. / When I'm smoking."

He stopped, unable to sing any more because his tongue melted into red sludge.

He staggered into the dirt floor.

His brain became an escaped beast.

Eventually, dawn crashed through the hut.

Another day began, unraveling in dreams.

The *Bom Shankars* Clan:
I made it a point to experience every O den in Asia.
But I knew better, not to make it a daily habit.
Therefore, I was never hooked on the shit.
I really loved the ritual, and the relaxing mood it put me into.
Kind of an Oriental romance.

Hot Streams:
Yes, the ritual.
The silence.
The unspoken words said through the eyes.
The seduction of the Orient, but the necessity of understanding restraint.

Strange Mountains:
Skating on thin ice.
It was fun, and then something else came along, hopefully.

10 • MEDIEVAL WORLDS COLLIDE

My Love:
Me and my love at that time, Aruna, made our way back from India [to Europe] by local buses and trains in 1980.

A real fancy trip.

We got to Athens without a penny left.

But we needed a ticket to go by ship to Brindisi [an Italian port on the Adriatic Sea].

So we walked into a travel agency run by some youngsters, in attempt to trade my Native American jacket for tickets.

But the [shop's] guys were quite skeptical about that.

But then a girl who was working there fixed her gaze on the only thing my girlfriend had allowed herself, a beautiful Rajasthani long skirt.

And I was saying, "Oh no, please not that."

So Aruna asked, "Will you give us two tickets for it?"

"Yes," the girl replied.

So we crossed over.

Especially Still:
Many of us were ordinary working class kids, traveling with very low budget.

Indian people thought we were very rich, because we were from Europe and from the Western world, but how wrong they were.

Most of us were poor students, and very young.

We did not wear rags because we wanted to pretend to be poor.

We were poor.
Not all of us, but most.
I am talking about the early travelers, around the 1960s and 1970s.

On the Border:
Most of those hippies travelled for a few months, played the role, and went home.
Got jobs, and became their parents.
The freaks and travelers were more committed to the road.
A lot of them are still on it.

Silk Soldier:
I wasn't a hippie, I was a soldier who just happened to travel the trail and Silk Road a few times.

Stationed Work:
I had a work friend who was stationed with U.S. Army in Pakistan during Vietnam War.
On his R & R, he would travel off the beaten path into northern Pakistan.

Impressive Earth:
All my friends and lovers from that time of the hippie trail, are lost or passed away.
You are the only ones I can share my experiences with.

Early Picture:
Same here.
You mention India, and people look at you like you're crazy.

Late Talk:
Yes, we were probably all marked by India for life.

Gift Alive:
Anyone one here know Kentucky Mike?

I'm looking for him to return a gift he gave me.
I can't locate him.
Afghanistan and India, 1970 to 1974.
I don't know if he still alive.

Candy Kilometers:
I knew him, but have no idea where to start looking for him.
Maybe some Hog Farm person might know.
I knew him in Asia, and back here in California, but he moved on and who knows where.

Became Bolinas:
I last saw him in Bolinas [a northern California coastal town] around 1978.
I liked him, and have long wondered what became of him.

Under the Galata Bridge:
I knew him in Goa, back in the day.
Just another one of the really cool characters I met in our scene.

Lobster Knife:
Yeah, I liked him.
Last time I saw was in Bolinas, early 1970s, along with Nerval Electric.
We had a crazy few months.

Pure Tribe: [displays a photograph captioned: "Tom the Bom, Steve Shore & Kentucky Mike in Afghanistan."]:
I met Tom for the last time in 1989, in the Florida Keys, where I was at the time.
He was pretty paranoid.
In 1995, I had a message from his brother, telling me that Tom died.
Well, he is now in a better place waiting for old friends to join the party.

Rest in peace.

Under the Galata Bridge:
I saw him [Tom the Bom] in New York in the 1990s, maybe 1993 or 1994.
Went to his apartment.
He was completely paranoid, kept turning the TV up so high, so nobody could hear us.
I couldn't take it.
In his own words, he told me he was so ugly he couldn't get laid in a whorehouse with a fist full of hundred dollar bills.
A shame, I knew him as a powerful and beautiful man.
Thank god I got clean before I lost my mind like him.

Talked Clean:
Yeah, that is what I heard, he had gotten back on the *horse* [heroin], and was riding it.
That was sad, because I knew how long he'd been clean.
He'd fallen off his *horse* -- after several years clean in Europe -- in 1968 in Micaucan [a town in Mexico], and talked a friend into giving him some, and when he took it, Katherine went ballistic and threatened to leave.
He never touched it again, right up into the late 1970s.
Sad. He was an exceptional outlaw in the better times.

Strong Culture:
I was out for adventure, and culture.
After my initial travels, I was interested in meditation, and made a strong connection with Indo-Tibetan Buddhism.

Amalgam Tenets:
From my extensive travels, I absorbed assorted tenets from all the cultures where I spent time.
This includes influences from Islam, Sikhism, Hinduism and Buddhism.
This amalgam serves me well

I do not think of myself as religious, but I do have faith.

Influence Strong:
I took refuge with a Tibetan lama in 1992, and it has still a strong influence in my life.

Vibe First:
I became agnostic.

Romance:
I think one of the big things about spending a lot of time in Asia is, you see how religion and culture are part of daily life and, in general, it's a great thing.
In Bali, it is probably most apparent.

Shopkeeper's Daughter:
I had no religion when I went, and still don't follow any religion.
I can enjoy, and be interested in, their religions as an outsider, but don't feel any inclination to join in, or try to feel part of it.

Individuals Hierarchal:
Organized belief structures, including communism, have a tendency -- despite the possibly good initial intentions -- to develop into hierarchal structures that serve to keep the top of the pile, historically men, in power by repressing others.
I include consumerism and capitalism in this list, as that has replaced older beliefs -- in richer populations.
You can't investigate any belief structure without coming across persecution within it, or wars, and persecution to those seen as unbelievers.
I understand that fear is a great driver towards any belief, but individuals can experience meaning without adhering to any belief.

Into Discovered:
I went on an adventure to new places, and was only interested in learning more about people and religions I didn't know anything about.

I came home changed by my experiences, but nothing to do with any religion.

Spiritual Sister:
For my sister and I, it became a spiritual journey when we were in India in 1972.

An audience with the Dalai Lama and a 10-day Vipassana [Buddhist] meditation course with Goenka [Satya Narayan Goenka, an Indian teacher of Vipassana].

I guess I was looking for something beyond my religion of upbringing.

Totally Challenging:
Most Hindu women are treated pretty bad, and I had to go there to see that.

Million Million:
It is different [today], but during the early Vedic time [of ancient Hinduism] -- around 3000 B.C. -- it was a peaceful civilization, where everybody drank psilocybin during the sacrifices, very often, and during full moon, and harvest.

That helped them to love women.

After the monotheists' invasion, people changed.

Retreat First:
I wish they had continued to drink psilocybin together.

Struggle Roots:
Conquerors [monotheistic Muslims and Christians] had nothing to do with [destroying] women's rights in India.

On the contrary, they contributed to the development of women's rights by either introducing new civic advancements --

female rulers, and interfaith marriages -- or by abolishing malpractices.

For example, Arabs and Turks [abolished] infant burial.

And the English prohibited *sati* [Hindu widows committing suicide by jumping into their husbands' burning funeral pyres].

Mystical Tantric:

I know several Indian women personally, and their lives are filled with struggle, danger, abuse, mistreatment and discrimination.

Indian culture today is dominated by regressive, chauvinistic, sexist, misogynistic men of all ages.

Violence and abuse are part of daily life for millions of Indian women.

Enjoy Early:

Hundreds of millions, unfortunately.

And in villages they [widows] traditionally had to live in a hut, on the edge.

And if they were young, they had no protection from the men.

In old Hindu thinking, the wife was to blame, if the husband died before her.

Weird Worshipping:

I visited *Bhagwan Sri* Rajneesh's *ashram* in Poona in 1979 -- later known as Osho.

It was indeed an interesting and weird experience.

I could never understand why so many people chose to walk around in the same clothes, worshipping the same.

The sect turned out to become totally mad when they moved to Oregon in the U.S.

Into Discovered:

Makes you wonder if humans have some kind of loose screw in their heads, to be able to lose their minds like that.

Really disturbing.

Even now, they [Rajneesh and Osho] are still selling his brilliance.

Reminds me of the movie *Being There*, where everyone thinks Chance the Gardener has the brilliant answer to everything, when he says almost nothing.

Under the Galata Bridge:

Unfortunately I was not yet on a spiritual journey. I went there for the cheap drugs, and freedom from police persecution.

It was only after the drugs took me to the gates of hell, that I was able to get clean and start my spiritual journey.

Not big on religion, I was brought up Jewish.

But everything was in Hebrew, and I gave it up after I got the money [gifts] at 13 [years old] for my *bar mitzvah*.

I went with a friend to his Catholic church, but bowing down on my knee was not for me.

When I started traveling, I got to Istanbul, and they claimed there is only one god and Mohammed is his prophet.

Pretty much like the Jews, who claimed they had the only god.

I got to India, and there was dozens of gods.

I liked the idea of Buddha in Kathmandu and Manali, but ended up in a Thai prison where the Buddhist prison guards were evil.

I found my higher power in the rooms of recovery, and I believe completely this power shows up anytime two or more addicts get together, to help each other stay clean.

My god and yours may not be the same, but I'm sure they are friends.

Street Shocked:

I did have some help from the holy books of India, but the *I Ching* transformed my entire life.

And Herman Hesse [a German author].

One night, someone told me the storyline of his brilliant

book, *The Journey to the East.*
Next morning, in February 1978, I bought a one-way ticket to India.

Who Disappeared:
I saw many wasted people in my travels, including the man in the mirror.

I Shamanic:
I follow shamanic practice.
India was, and is, part of that journey.

Very People:
I travelled through all the world's religions, and met many living gurus and masters, and their teachings.
Yoga masters, such as Swami Gitananda and others.
Babaji of Herakhan, Ammaji, Sai Baba, the Dalai Lama, Dina Rees, and Sheik Nazim have been my teachers.
I had great interest in all the old mythologies of this world, and have lectured on mythology and philosophy.
I was a hardcore esotericist for a very long time.
The last few years, however, I have been involved in refugee aid and climate protection policy, and I'm very down to earth now.

World Away:
I was not on a spiritual journey.
I was after adventure, and getting away from a job I did not like.
I did read a book on world religions before I left, and was glad I did.

Initial This:
I was on a journey to discover everything -- other cultures and religions.
I arrived in 1982 with a strong interest in all things Tibetan.

My first destination was Ladakh [India's northwest state, bordering Tibet].
Buddhism became my spiritual practice of choice.
Nepal and India became my fascinations.

Cave Wonders:
Thank goodness I kept cults and fads at arm's length on my travels.
I did smoke copious *chillums*, deciding whether or not if I was a *sadhu* though.

Just Loads:
I just took shit loads of drugs.
Bom Shankar.

Solemn and Respectful:
We did go for hash and god.
My friends call me a HinJew.

My Legs:
I didn't convert to a different religion, but I added to my knowledge and beliefs.

Deal Better:
One of the main goals of my first trip to India was to see Ramesh Balsekar [a teacher of Advaita Hinduism which focuses on the oneness of Brahma] in Bombay.
He was the real deal, and sitting with him every day, for 10 weeks, changed my life for the better.
I wouldn't say it was a change of religion though.

Root 12:
I went to visit him too, in his apartment, after a 10-day Vipassana retreat.
Advaita is interesting, but my root guru is Prem Rawat, who I went to meet in 1970 when he was 12.

Nothing Formal:
I watched Hinduism in action while I was in India and Nepal for nine months, in 2017.
I came back to the United States.
I deep dived into the difference between atheism and agnosticism.
I gave up Christianity in 2018.
I found out, on that journey, how Buddhist I am.
Nothing formal.
Just continue to live my life.

Existed Shocked:
I'm a pantheist.
I went for the hash.

Clean Squat:
Thanks for your honesty.
Same motivation for me.
Cheap drugs.
Escape winter, and factory, and mainstream.
India is perfect to demystify the religion hoaxes, duplicate *babas*, or the guru nirvana business.
Most are just mainstream hoaxes, only a few have divine spirit.
And they're not on the tourist trail, and not in the nirvana or yoga or the guru business.
Some hippies also believe in aliens, Indigo Children [New Age supernatural children], astrology, numerology, and more.
They have faith in their feelings.
I'm maybe too Cartesian.
Descartes and Voltaire are more my cup of tea.

Fortress Hovel:
I started out in 1972 with a deep belief in surrealism, and soon added animism.

The best of both worlds.

Million Million:
I had the supreme experience on my first acid trip in 1970.
Now I consider myself Vedic.

Skull Press:
I think I went to get away from my mother.

Clean Squat [laughing]:
Mother India took the place.

Sitars There:
My friend Virginia became a Buddhist nun.

Own Yogic:
After five months walking through India, I ended up in an *ashram* near Payannur in Kerala.
I stayed there nine years, studying Adveta Vedenta.
The *ashram's* name was Nataraja Guru Island Home.
A few hippies went there.

Reed Times:
If anything, it reinforced my atheist inclination -- the madness of religion being on full display everywhere.
I did attend a Krishnamurti lecture in Bombay in 1979, and had many friends who were *sanyassins* of the *Bhagwan* [Rajneesh] in Poona, but it never occurred to me to join this or any other sect or religion.

Dead Water:
At barely 17, I sought out mescaline in 1969, quickly followed by L.S.D..
I was on the path to reconcile my education with the real world.
I was then a scientist, if you can classify that as a belief.

I went on to study physics at university, by which time, the concept of Big Bang theory became predominant.

And with that, came comparisons with ancient religious scriptures from many cultures.

Dropping out in 1971, I read much on Tao and Buddha.

After misadventures, I travelled overland to India.

Spirituality was certainly a key, but not religion.

I met with the Dalai Lama, who told me that belief in reincarnation was not important, that it was a cultural belief only.

I did sit with Goenka, but fell ill with pneumonia in the monsoon.

I sat with Krishnamurti, and fell at the feet of Anandamayi Ma.

I am still a scientist by heart and nature.

Belief and religion are not for me.

Only a desire to understand.

Women Amazing:
With all that God talk, let's not forget that until recently -- in the West and, until today, in the East -- there was no choice whatsoever about being religious.

You were killed in many exotic ways, drawn and quartered -- literally pulled apart -- beheaded, and thrown into a river to see if you would float, etcetera.

So don't be fooled about temples and churches acting all nice now.

It's because they lost the power to force people to come for services.

And even though they feel like murdering just as before, they are not allowed to do that anymore.

Late Talk:
How Indianized were you all when you returned home?

I couldn't sit normally on a toilet, but would squat on top of it with one foot on each side of the rim.

Cubicles Appear [laughing]:
When my employer started to use a lot of Indian contractors, footprints mysteriously started to appear on the toilet seats at work.

All my colleagues were initially bemused.

But I knew exactly the reason, and it bought back memories of my own time traveling through India.

When I explained to them, and then went on to describe Goa's pig toilets, everyone was shocked.

The majority of the U.K. population haven't travelled anywhere, let alone India decades ago.

A few weeks later, signs went up on the toilet doors, explaining how Western toilets should be used, which again would give me fond memories of my time India.

By the way, the Indian method is apparently much better for your back, so I've been told, and has come in useful, once or twice, for me whilst I've been out hiking in the U.K.

Fortunately it's lot easier to maintain balance perusing a smartphone than a newspaper.

I was in China this time last year, down south.

I walked into a public *loo* -- four cubicles, of the three-walls-only type.

No front door.

All occupied, each occupant at 90 degrees to the opening.

All squatting down, in a perfectly aligned foursome, all perusing their phones.

Surreal sight first time.

Second nature, after a short time.

Romance:
Also much healthier.
Sitting on the throne plays havoc with the intestines.

Outrageously Invited:
There is an amusing bit in Salman Rushdie's *Satanic Verses*,

where the protagonist's mother gives him a stern warning about falling into unsanitary Western toilet practices, deeming the use of toilet paper, rather than water, a nasty habit.

Wash Wipe:
An Indian one said to me, if you got shit on your face, would you just wipe it off with a bit of toilet paper?
Or would you wash it off with water?
It's simple.

Hard Boot:
It took me two years to stop climbing on top of toilets when I came back.
Don't laugh!

Years Climb:
I still climb.
Thirty years now.

Retreat First:
Guilty!
As a matter of fact, had I the means, I would have a squat toilet installed in my apartment.
It is more sanitary, plus gives you the perfect position for a healthy back and legs each time you need to go.

Nearly Spaced:
I taught my son to squat on the *loo* to *poo*.
He's 19 now, and still does it, which is good for his bowel health I'm sure.
But I often find muddy footprints on the seat.

The Gray Zone:
Western toilets were one of the more difficult things for me to get used to again, when I returned to Europe after 28 years in Asia.

At the time, whenever I was faced with a Western toilet bowl, I used to climb on it as well.

Problem though, is that with my weight now, I fear that I am going to destroy them.

What I really cannot get used to is dry toilet paper.

Feels like rough sand paper.

In Thailand, where I lived 23 years, we had these wonderful hoses next to the toilet.

Here [in Germany], I only use wet wipes instead.

Life's challenges.

Jug Number:
Use water.
Nature's number one cleaner.
I keep a jug in the bathroom.

On the Border:
They say you know you've been in Asia too long, when the footprints on the toilet seat are your own.

Enjoy Early:
I was India-based for 45 years, as a Hindi-speaking woman.
Now I'm back in Germany.
Not a bad country to live in, but it will never be the home India is.

Priest Happened:
I feel like I'm home when I arrive in India.
It's much tougher, and alienating, coming back to the West.

Red Entering:
Five six-month visits to India, altered me permanently.
My way of seeing, my capacity for acceptance, the blossoming of humility, and the endless gratitude, have never left me.

Survival Uprisings:
The best university on earth.

Sanitized Culture:
I get much more culture shock coming back to U.K.
It's sanitized, boring, impersonal, and in a way more materialistic.

Women Amazing:
Some of us never came home.
By the time we did, there was no home left.
The away had become the home.

Shopkeeper's Daughter:
Me too, arriving back in India feels more like home.
Now we also have a real home there, in Himachal.

Barked and Howled:
On returning, that dilemma about wastage is so common.
I worked as secretary for the Gandhi Ashram, an orphanage kids' home, in Bodhgaya, India.
Mind you, they had a 12-year-old there that had been raised by dogs.
She actually walked on all fours, and barked and howled.

Clean Squat:
I slept for many years on a Tibetan carpet.
Not very romantic.

Shimmering Joy:
That is the original function of a knotted carpet.
It never was intended to be tread on, by high heel shoes, nor table and chair legs.

Sanitized Culture:
Yeah, the Tibetans use it for sleeping.

Shimmering Joy:
The Iranian nomads who started the craft, as well.

Abdul Abdul:
Once when I was visiting my friend Mohammad Issa Afghani, in Swat [a province in northern Pakistan], I needed to go to the toilet.
He took me to an empty area, behind the restaurant he was working in.
"Afghan toilet," he said, pointing.
I walked several yards, when he called me back and handed me several clumps of hard mud.
"Afghan toilet paper," he said.

Abdul Abdul:
I realized, in Herat, that for the price of a roll of toilet paper, I could have three more nights in a hotel.
Plus realizing water is cleaner than rubbing it in with paper.

Slamming Years:
When I came back home after seven years in India, I went to visit my mother.
I had to go to the toilet, but did not lock the door.
My mother came in. "What are you doing?"
After slamming the door shut, I had to explain why I was squatting on top of the toilet.

Touch All:
I teach yoga, so nobody finds it weird.
My students learn to squat, and the healthy aspects of squat-shitting.
They learn to relax, and head wiggle, and drink *chai*.
What else can I ask for?

Affirmative Waggling:

I kept waggling my head as an affirmative response, for ages.

Fortress Hovel:
I still say, *acha* [good, O.K.]

Nearly Spaced:
All the time!
With an appropriate head wobble.

Totally Challenging:
I still say *acha* and *cholo* [go].
And Asia turned me into using water after the toilet forever.
I stopped squatting on toilet a while back.
Fifty-nine years of travel, all over the globe, changes your perspective.

Big Bottles:
My body language is Indian.
Nobody in Europe understands.

Weird Worshipping:
I ended up working in India for 20 years or more, after my initial trip to India.
And I still wiggle my head when talking on the phone with an Indian.

Beard's Shadow:
After my first trip overland to the East, I also quit with my toilet paper addiction.
Never needed anymore.

Sleeping Horses:
I've always been able to walk away from substances.
I did heroin all day, every day, for three months in Phuket in 1978.
When my visa ran out, I had no problem not doing it

anymore.

Same with smoking opium, 10 pipes, three times a day, in Vientiane for a month.

When I left I was fine.

I had been drinking four to five shots of hard liquor a night, for decades, and then quit in February 2020.

No problem.

I also quit weed, and I know weed isn't bad, but I never could smoke weed without having some alcohol in me first.

Otherwise I'd get really paranoid.

So not drinking meant I can't smoke --since I quit the booze.

I don't even like how I feel on the opioids that I do now.

I use them more as a substitute for Imodium [also known as loperamide] with diarrhea.

Ever since my wife hung herself in 2017, I've had diarrhea.

And the opiates help relieve it.

And I don't like how Imodium makes me feel at all.

Dark Talk:
India cured me of a few things, and trying to be Indian was one of them.

Romantic notions about the hippie, drug-taking lifestyle, was another.

What it didn't cure me of was the itch to travel.

Gooey Time:
If India does not rub you, in general, you are not there.
It can really rub you like sandpaper, on an open cut.

Unkempt Rocking:
I preferred smoking *chillums* instead of *joints*, for a long time afterwards.

Spliffs:
I'm still smoking *chillums*.
Spliffs [marijuana cigarettes] only for *ganja*.

Crazy Soap:

Among other things, I used to wash clothes Indian style -- on the bathroom floor, with an Indian soap for washing clothes.

My dad probably thought I was quite crazy.

Late Talk:

Yes, I did that in the beginning after I came back.

I'm quite happy using a machine now.

Crazy Soap:

Yes me too.

But I did enjoy washing clothes on the rocks in the lake of Pokhara, and other places.

Like a kind of meditation.

Peanuts All Rough:

My mother got upset when I ate with my fingers.

Lost all manners, she said.

Chocolate Looks:

For me, arriving in London after Asia, culture shock was Led Zeppelin.

I grew to like them, but was too much all at once.

The Gray Zone:

I have met, and known, some [travelers] who turned to religion, and became *sadhus*, or monks.

I met my [Thai] wife, and turned to photojournalism and writing, and ended up living in Asia for altogether 28 years.

The culture shock [returning to Germany] was beyond belief.

What amplified it even more, was that we lived for the first year in a shelter for homeless families, before we got our own apartment after a year.

Our family language was Thai, so it was really difficult for us.

My son had to learn German.

My wife, fortunately, was many times in Europe for holidays, but even with that it was initially very difficult for her.

Fortunately, since we moved, we were very lucky, and life is now good for us again.

My son went to a normal Thai private school [in Bangkok], until we moved [to Germany] when he was 11.

The only German language school in Bangkok would have cost something like 8,000 dollars per semester, which we of course didn't have.

We lived in a normal Thai neighborhood, so we didn't manage to raise him bilingual -- though from hearing many languages since he was small, he got a language talent, and taught himself to speak English.

In Germany, we have a free school system, and all the help for him he needs, to catch up.

He loves it here, and for him the transition was easiest.

Under the Galata Bridge:

I was kicked out of school at 17, because my hair was too long.

My dad, an ex-Marine, told me I'm not only kicked out of school, I'm kicked out of the house.

I jumped in my 1955 Chevy Nomad, and headed to the Sunset Strip [a main street in Hollywood], where I had been spending the weekend dropping acid and watching some of the best bands of the 1960s.

I moved in with a friend and a couple ladies, right down the street from The Whiskey [The Whiskey A Go-Go nightclub on Sunset Boulevard].

Drugs and freaks became my new family.

Trouble with the police.

And prison.

I jumped my parole in 1969, and headed to Europe.

I escaped from another prison -- the old jail on top of the hill of the old city in Ibiza -- and met Angelique, a great forger -- because I needed [fake identification] papers to get out of Spain.

After that, she got pregnant, and said we had to go to India, where she had already been.

She said if I was going to be an addict, she would take me someplace where I would never be without drugs, and I wouldn't go to jail for them.

We had the baby in Goa, and spent most of the next 12 years in the Far East.

I came back to the States in 1982, when I got out of prison in Bangkok.

I came to Florida, where my parents had moved from Los Angeles with my son, while I was locked up.

I got clean [ended drug addiction] and found recovery, and my new business here, so I've been in Miami ever since, but travelled a lot.

Still clean after all this time.

I haven't seen Angelique in years.

She came here 20 years ago for the birth of our grandson.

She fought with our son's family, and stopped all communication.

She was living in London on the *dole* [government welfare].

I made amends years ago, for any pain I caused her in my active addiction.

She was a great Bonnie to my Clyde, back in the day, but I've lived an honest spiritual life for many decades now.

I wish her nothing but health, wealth and happiness, but don't need her craziness in my life.

Did Why Do:
Why did they put you in jail?
Did you steal, or do drugs?

Under the Galata Bridge:
Drugs.
I wasn't a thief, just a dealer.
I managed to get locked up also in almost every country I went.

England, Ibiza, Spain, Kabul, Delhi, Germany, a police station in Turkey, and finally the big bitch [a six-year sentence] in Thailand.

I used to just consider it an occupational hazard.

I've barely had a parking ticket since 1982, when I got clean and in recovery.

I do go into jails and prisons, to tell my story, and carry the message that an addict, any addict, can get clean and find a new way to live.

Dancing Nowadays:
You know all the ins and outs of prisons around the world.
I am glad you're doing fine now.
Enjoy your freedom and stay safe.

Same I:
I was in the same [Ibiza] prison.

Under the Galata Bridge:
You must have been really bad.
There were no women in that dungeon, when I was there.
It was on top of the hill, underground.
We would walk around a circle path at night with the Spanish [inmates], chanting:

Franco morta amnestia [death to Franco, amnesty -- Spain's dictator until his death in 1975].

After I got out, and came back years later, there was a letter from the U.S. Embassy saying I was sentenced, in absentia, to five years.

But Franco finally died, and they destroyed all the paperwork.

I would have done the whole five years in the circle chanting, *Franco morto*, and finally gotten out -- and have him die.

Thank God I met Angelique and -- with some forgery -- she got me out of Spain.

Fabulously Fun:

Back in 1969 and 1970 New York City, I was a runaway from an intensely, miserably, scarily dysfunctional family.

As a kid of 15 years old, I needed to get away from the violence and perversion of my biological mother.

During those two years in New York City, I identified with being a hippie.

I tried a number of drugs.

Loved the half a dozen acid trips I took.

Went to countless rock concerts.

Went to many antiwar rallies from the age of 13, to the Human Be-Ins in Central Park, and was part of the [Andy] Warhol scene, on the periphery.

Those were my two hippie years.

Never again did any recreational drugs, except a few puffs of hash many years later.

By the end of age 16, I had a chance to leave New York City and go to live in London, where I stayed the next four years, working as a live-in housekeeper, companion, and girlfriend of a writer nine years older than I -- who told me he'd give me a safe place to stay and food, if I lived with him as a companion.

So I did.

It was a refuge from the storm.

London was so much more conservative than New York City.

Isolating.

It had none of the friendliness of New York City, none of the vitality or sense of liberty.

It wasn't a place to be a hippie, so I just quietly blended in. I did odd jobs for money.

During the summer though, I hitched with my younger brother all over Europe and Morocco, sleeping on the beach in Elba [an Italian island], singing Beatles songs with Italian kids there, and swimming naked at night.

Not really hippie, but free-spirited.

Those years that I went to school in London were such a

welcome relief.

Quiet.

Drama free.

However, I struggled with depression, loneliness, and became an alcoholic for two years.

When I turned 21, I went to live in Rome, a city I loved and had visited during summer holidays.

Then in Greece, on the tiny island of Paxos, in a small traditional house for 20 dollars a month.

Not hippie style, just simply.

I'd learned to live by then, on very little money.

That summer of 1975, I hitched to India with a 17-year-old English schoolboy.

I had not intended to travel overland at all, just to Istanbul to buy Christmas presents for my emotionally ill mother.

I kept on going until India.

The English schoolboy was a hash addict.

I aggravated him terribly, because I did not like smoking anything.

It, and the people who smoked a lot, repelled me.

On arrival in India, I fell in love with the country.

The colors, the architecture, the culture, the smells, the people, the animals everything.

Boom.

Utterly in love.

It was the last thing I expected.

I lived in India for five months on 70 dollars.

I became a Buddhist, and studied with Tibetan lamas in Dharamsala.

I returned to New York City, gave my mother the presents I'd bought her, helped her into her fourth marriage to a very rich man, and felt I did my duty.

After working and collecting 6,000 dollars, I returned to India, to the mountains, to study Buddhism and meditate for the next six years.

Zero interest in drugs.

But I did live in a tiny log cabin, no plumbing, no electricity, wood stove, chopped my own wood, picked apples in the orchard, hiked a lot in the mountains.

Loved living like that.

That experience was deeply healing.

In 1982, I went to New Delhi to put what I'd learned to the test.

Got a job in the clothing business there, and worked there for an American for four-and-a-half years.

My boss in New Delhi was intensely hash addicted.

I could see the damage it was doing to him. Daily.

He needed therapy, but smoked instead.

He was however marvelously successful at making money, and we were a great working team. He was creative and dynamic. Amazing at sales.

I did the organizing, the structure, maintained and trained a staff, and kept things sane and steady.

At the end of 1985, my boss and I broke up. He moved to Bali.

I returned to New York City, started my own business selling West African art, jewelry and watches, and worked 14 years doing business writing for a [South] Korean jewelry company, and worked as a building supervisor, and as an elder caregiver.

I did a lot of therapy, free meetings, and lots and lots of reading psychology books.

So my life has been unconventional.

But after the age of 16, I never thought of myself as a hippie.

However, I did live in India for 10 years, and most of the Western people I knew in India did identify with what they thought of as a hippie lifestyle -- smoking a lot of hash and *pot* [marijuana], doing hallucinogenics, spending a lot of time in Goa, hanging out with other smokers.

They seemed to know almost nothing about Indian culture, and did not learn to speak Hindi.

I really did not identify with them at all.

I wanted to learn things, put energy into studying,

meditating, learn Hindi, learn Tibetan, the botany and ornithology of India, its history, and philosophies.

The hash and pot thing seemed to be very mentally dulling.

People who think of themselves as hippies seem to be stuck in the past, identifying with their teenaged self.

I love being an adult, getting older, wiser.

I do love my generation, its dreams and drives, and its interests.

But for me, the hippie thing had its time and now is a whole new time, packed full of marvelously interesting things too.

Just Loads:
For me, even in the 1980s, it all felt like one, big, mad adventure after another.

Israel, eastern Turkey, Kabul, Nepal, and the far out craziness of Goa.

I had nothing against two-week trips to Ibiza or Greece, and enjoyed them very much -- still do -- but I wanted something a bit wilder, and that's certainly what I got.

It was fun and crazy, hard at times, and definitely a bit dangerous.

But for me, it was magical, and it filled me with a sense of wonder and curiosity that 30 or 40 years later still burns brightly.

Late Talk:
We were all on different trips, but some of us ended up staying for many years, living like the locals, and speaking enough Hindi to manage.

For many of us, India became home, and coming back to our home countries was a bigger cultural shock than going to India in the first place.

To me, India will always be home, as well as Denmark is now.

Free:

I did the same overland journey.

The quest was to push the limits of freedom -- money or no money -- and the great adventure into the unknown realms of self discovery.

I was part of a caravan overland to India, so lucky to have played a part in that special time of space and time.

Bom Shankar!

Dangerous Special:
Yes, I agree completely.

We were lucky to have been there at that precise moment in time.

Only those who experienced that trip, know how special it was.

The moment is past, and it can never be that way again.

The world is much more dangerous.

Bom Shiva!

On the Border:
Travel will never be the same.

My sorrow for the youth of today who will never experience that.

Abdul Abdul:
Maybe they'll go to Mars -- but instead with some Mazar-i-Sharif Black.

Initial This:
How about a hippie trail reunion in Kathmandu next year?

Combine it with a bus trip to Varanasi, and end up on a beach in Goa to recover.

We could rent or buy an old bus in Kathmandu, stock it with Godfather beer, Kukri whiskey, copious amounts of drugs -- and a mechanic who could prepare Thai and Indian meals.

Sound good to anyone?

Free beer, free opium!

Elephants, snake charmers, dancing girls, magicians!

[someone displays a photograph of monkeys in India]

Sleeping Forest:
Might be cool for a photo, but if you live where there are lots of monkeys, they can be a terrible menace.

Naked and Barefoot:
I have been traveling by motorcycle in rural and forested parts of India, when langurs or macaques have thrown -- from the top of trees -- large pieces of branch, quite accurately at me.
Dangerous at times.
And they menacingly group up across lonely roads, and will not move.
They are quite an animal.
It's a regular occurrence that monkeys snatch young babies and small children.

Nearly Spaced:
I made the silly mistake of picking up a baby monkey I found in a clearing, while walking in a jungle in Sri Lanka.
I thought it had been abandoned, which of course was not true.
Mama monkey jumped down on me from a tree branch and very badly bit my hand.
Her big teeth penetrated the back of my hand, and came out of the palm.
This was in 1980.

Naked and Barefoot:
I was afraid, a few times, of monkeys.
In situations on my motorcycle, and in the middle of nowhere.
But being bitten?
Well maybe you were lucky it didn't escalate.

I have also heard that langur, in particular, injure Indian people quite badly sometimes.

Firewood Street:
Guys, they're great creatures, but also powerful animals.

Which means that you can -- and must -- understand them, before you let them into your life.

I worked with chimps for a while in a zoo situation, and was taught a few things -- such as body language, and a sensitive alertness -- that are essential.

Approached in the right way, monkeys -- also in India -- are just brilliant.

During my 10 plus years in India, I've witnessed a few situations myself.

Also with pye dogs and elephants.

Unfortunately, Indians very often don't know how to handle animals at all, and start to behave scared, or menacingly, as soon as they see one.

Anyway, the trick with basically any animal, is to stay cool.

Showing excitement or anger is usually interpreted as weakness.

Naked and Barefoot:
Your knowledge is interesting for me.

Maybe you could tell me what would be an O.K. thing to do, when coming upon a large group of aggressive monkeys, spread across the road?

I have waited from a distance for up to two hours for them to leave but, in the end, had to ride fast through them -- which was a stupid thing to do -- as one big male nearly pulled me from the bike.

Fortress Hovel:
Monkeys can become even more wild after they evolve.

Late Talk:

I had some bad experiences too.
Got bitten by a rabid dog.
Not so funny, but I still love all the rest of them.

Chilled Stick:
I remember having to carry a big stick on several occasions.
They weren't all chilled dogs.

Million Million:
In Agra, behind the Taj Mahal, there was a small temple where Westerners came, right on the edge of the Yamuna [River].

And there we saw the corpses of the poor, floating in the water.

After a while the current, which was weak in front of the temple, carried the corpses a little further, where the stray dogs came to eat them.

The dogs were very fat and disgusting.

Danced Dream:
I despise them [dogs].
They have murdered so many!
Attack for absolutely no reason!
They eat the people who raise them!

I had to quit going to so many places because of these lazy animals.

I don't like laziness, and their groveling.

There are places now, people cannot leave their homes, because of stray dogs attacking.

Here in the U.S.A., we already have towns where mail cannot be delivered because of mailmen being attacked.

And that is in the U.S.A.

Can you imagine where feral dogs are breeding by the millions?

I could not sleep in Goa because they barked and fought all night.

I used two sets of earplugs.

Two in each ear.

And still could hear them barking.

They sleep all day, and bark and fight and make puppies all night.

Horrid animals.

Repeat Rats:

No mention of the rats yet?

One Calangute house that I stayed in, had rats visit us, every night.

We kept everything clean, and the food tucked away, but they came anyway.

One evening in the middle of the night, I awoke and, in my drowsiness, brushed something off my hip.

My hand felt fur and my ears heard an angry squeak.

This wasn't my first rodeo.

I got my pen light, turned it on, and found the frying pan.

Now that I was armed, I cast the light along where the floor meets the wall, until I found it.

It was scurrying along, until I made a squeaking noise by sucking in through my closed lips.

It froze, expecting an attack from another rat whom it thought was challenging it.

I then kept up the noise, kept the light fixed on it, then slowly walked over, and whacked it with the frying pan.

Pick it up by the tail. Chuck it outside. And go back to sleep.

Repeat whenever another one is heard.

Home Down:

O.K., fellow travel freaks, I have a question.

Many of us returned to our home countries, or new adapted country.

Given the difficult adjustment, how did you cope?

If I didn't fall in love, I still might be on the road.

I left India in 1979, after four years in Asia.

I met my wife in Sri Lanka, Trincomalee.

We travelled, and married in Kathmandu two years later.

When we were getting ready to leave to go to Amsterdam, I told her that we should enjoy the smells and atmosphere of Old Delhi, it will be a long time before we return.

Disenchanted Social:

I got involved with social and political change groups -- people equally disenchanted with U.S. norms.

Washed Circle:

I wandered for the next 35 years.

Mostly on sailboats.

I finally washed up on the side of a mountain in Virginia, 150 miles from where I was born.

Wrote a book, and consider the circle complete.

Into Discovered:

I had a very, very hard time when I got home.

I had a good job waiting for me, which I am glad I took.

But my personal life suffered a lot, because not one person I know could relate to my experience, and how it changed me.

I came to realize that this wasn't an experience I could share.

And I couldn't be angry with the fact that to everyone I knew, this was just some kind of trip somewhere exotic.

I did find people who did something similar, or who also developed an attachment to India and Nepal and adventure travel -- and developed new friendships.

I've been back to South Asia at least seven times -- I've lost count -- since my 1975 overland trip.

I liked my job, which is why I came home, and it wasn't boring.

I always worked and saved, so I could have money to travel.

Travel was my top priority in life.

The road was challenging but exciting.

Now I'm retired and still travel, with more comfort.

Priority Wow:
"Travel was my top priority in life."
Wow.

Dream Toddler:
India -- I am still there in spirit.
I would never have left in 1976, if my toddler hadn't been very sick.
Culture shock was on landing, back in Europe again.
I still haven't recovered.
Never will.
Living in the U.K. when one has a rational mind is fun at first -- I am French born -- loads of fun.
Very trying lately.
But I have always lived my life following *Bakthi* Yoga [involving devotional Hindu prayers] and still do, to be of service.
I have become a healer, and holistic massage practitioner, after years of drugs.
I would never dream of flying to India.
The fun was rambling the trail, where I shed layer upon layer of brainwashing, to reach India and Nepal -- ready, body and soul.

Secret Nervous:
I don't know anyone from my class, or town, who went overland.
By the time I came home from my first time away at 21, my best friend had a baby, and another friend was married.
Everyone I knew was dating, settling down.
I was the one that really didn't fit in.
I continued with my adventures, in between working, for the next nine years.

Way Overland:

Today -- like yesterday -- only a few will travel in this way.
But they are doing it.
I have seen in the 21st century, in India and Laos, today's youth traveling at a 21st century, grass roots level.
Today's version of what we did before.

Beard's Shadow:
Different trails are also available today, if you keep to the hippie style -- with your rucksack ready -- to walk in nature, avoiding big centers as much as possible.

Sleeping Horses:
There are few, if any, spots left like we visited back then.

Slinging Woman:
We contributed to the destruction of those places -- Bali, Kathmandu, Ibiza, and Formentera, etcetera.

Enjoy Early:
Granted, but mostly because we had such fun and interesting lives, that everybody wanted to jump on the bandwagon.

Slinging Woman:
Yes we were pioneers, and put these places on the map.
What followed was inevitable.

Totally Challenging:
I came from a very stable, middle class background.
The hippie movement invited me in.
It started with the music.
Living in Europe.
Wanting to travel.
Tripping.
Living a cheaper easier lifestyle.
I never was attracted to the religious aspect, or even huge parties of hippies.

I loved the ancient temples and palaces.

Especially Still:
I came back, four months pregnant.
No job.
No place to stay.
The father of my child still in Nepal.
We could not afford two tickets.
I had to start from zero.
With a little help from friends -- and being lucky finding a job rather fast, as a hotel receptionist -- I slowly got it together.
I remember how strange it felt to sit on a ordinary water closet [flush toilet], and to use paper again.
And to have to get new clothes.
I had to look straight at my new job.
I pierced my nose in India and, back in Sweden, people were not used to seeing that at the time, 1973.
So people were staring a lot, and asking what I had done with my nose, and so on.
Some people were rather mean. But most of them thought it was nice.
I am mostly a survivor, and live pretty much here and now.
I have been carrying my memories as a treasure, deep in my heart.
It [Asia] taught me a lot about life, and made me a lot more humble and grateful about things.
As much as it was a culture shock to go through all the experiences during my overland trip, and stay in India and Nepal, it was also a bit of a culture shock to come back home.
But I do feel having good friends and family around me, helped a lot.
And being busy, taking care of my first baby.

Early Picture:
I hadn't seen my mom for 13 years, and had been out of the U.S. for 10 years straight.

I got deported from Montreal back to U.S.

I went back to the hometown in New England, and thought, no way.

You learned not to say you were in India.

Just say Europe.

I went to northern California, which was great.

Back to Asia, with a stop in Hawaii to check it out.

Turns out Hawaii was what I was looking for all this time.

Clean beaches, cool small towns, cheap rents, beautiful weather, and you could work.

Guys would meet the planes at the airport, and offer you jobs.

I ended up working to build a hydroponic farm.

Earned 1,000 dollars the first year, and he gave me a truck.

Soon I was earning 1,000 dollars a month.

Maui population is 50,000.

I am still on Maui 40 years later.

Population 165,000.

There's a lot of Asia heads here.

I'm retired now with pension and insurance.

I finally did something right.

Did I mention Hawaiian girls?

Enjoy Early:

Does anyone remember Count Bruno?

"In London, they call me the Afghan Gorilla."

He first came [to India] some-when between 1962 and 1964, with Dutch Desiree.

Or might he have come earlier, alone?

Wonderful man.

Freaked out in Goa -- "I pee the Ganges, and I shit the Milky Way."

He went back to the West, and became a *mahatma* in the guru Maharaji organization.

Very dear friend.

On the Border:
So tell me, how did you reassimilate when you went home? Or did you?

Herbs Opened:
I opened a store to sell Chinese and Indian herbs, plus free advice.

Future Aura:
I spent the first few months eating everything with a spoon, and wanting to pee in the garden.

Arrowhead Typewriter:
He still pees in the garden.

Future Aura:
Yes, but now only when no one is looking.
Before was Indian style.

Juice Time:
I had to squat on the toilet bowl.

Weighed Life:
I still have friends who jokingly say:
"Don't mention India, he'll go on for hours!"

Into Discovered:
Exactly.
It [returning to the West] was the hardest part.
Your entire life has changed, but you'd better be ready for a lot of talk about the kid's soccer game.
"India?"
"Oh, that's interesting, why did you go?"
"Was it dirty?"
"Did you get sick?"
And my favorite, a really ignorant relative said:

"Why didn't you bring back a child from Mother Theresa's Orphanage?"

Oh my God, I didn't like her before, but after that I always avoided her.

Learn Fun:
I opened a bookshop full of books and crafts from India and Nepal, in Woodstock, New York.

Immediately White:
I opened a *henna* and *mehndi* tattoo shop [using dye made from a plant, for temporary tattoos].

Madly Infectious:
I was sent straight to an infectious disease hospital to be tested for parasites, and finally diagnosed with malnutrition.

Not a good idea to read *Professor Arnold Ehret's Mucusless Diet Healing System* whilst in India.

No one could relate to me because of my drastic change in appearance, and I could not relate to anyone either.

Except I found some old friends, who had been heavy drug users, and within three weeks the party was on.

And I fell madly in love with my friend's husband, culminating in a serious motorbike accident, all within a month of being home.

The Heart:
Though it's utterly inadequate as an excuse, you still have to admit that all that hippie shit out East did have a neo-colonial angle.

Just talk to friends that grew up as children of colonials in the 1960s and 1950s.

Many of them saw the parallels.

Of course all present company excepted -- so we don't go off on an endless round of "No I wasn't."

Grew Easy:
You are right.
We were behaving like colonialists sometimes.
Imposing our life style.
Ordering like colonialists.
Now it is called tourism.

Juice Time:
You can't help but think, white privilege.

Carnival Dude:
The posers were easy to spot.
Bottoms of their feet were clean.

Struggle Roots:
Yep.
True ones were baptized with cow dung under their feet in Benares.

Simple Again:
I continued traveling.
Australia, the States and Canada, then back to England for a few years.
I bought a boat, and then lived in the Canary Islands on it.
And had a health food shop back in England again, but I couldn't get on with the life there.
Far too cold.
And hard work.
And I'm now in my 70s.
I live in Spain and travel to Morocco every now and again, when I need to remember how simple life can be.

Nearly Spaced:
Amsterdam was a good landing place, after years in India.
I had a houseboat there, from 1990 onwards.
All of our friends, coming and going from India, passed

through.

It was a great spot to decompress, and start the process of readjustment to the Western world.

Early Picture:
I was getting Red Leb [Lebanese hashish] pressed in burlap, in Amsterdam 1970.

G.I.s [American soldiers] from Germany came to our boat every Friday, and I always had an assortment for them.

Mescaline was popular.

Begged Lucrative:
You were my competitor.
I dealt Moroccan to G.I.s in Frankfurt, 1961 to 1963.
G.I.s were scared of Arabs.
I never had problems dealing with the Arabs, but the U.S. G.I.s were afraid of them, so they paid New York prices from me.

Under the Galata Bridge:
I did well selling to American G.I.s, and hash to the 7th Fleet [sailors in a U.S. Navy fleet] in Barcelona.

I sold a lot of *smack* to G.I.s in Germany.

Then they got a drug amnesty from Vietnam, and were sent to a drug hospital in Furth, outside of Nuremberg.

I was bringing Chinese *smack* from London, and later Delhi *smack* from India.

I was busted in Germany in 1973, and did seven months until my release.

Carrot Jungle:
Bravo for me taking acid, starting at 15 years old.
It opened many paths in my heart and mind.
I went to India with only a couple hundred dollars.
I lived in the jungle, and very simple rooms with Himalayan families, and had the most heartfelt and beautiful adventures in

my life.

I cherish every moment, and learned at an early age that money is not the carrot to follow.

Survival Uprisings:

We became hippies -- they were officially buried in San Francisco in 1968 -- as a reaction to the commercial society our parents created, or lived in.

We went on the road looking for a community and spirit that resonated closer to our feelings.

Talked Clean:

I remember that flood of kids fondly, as they arrived more every day [in Haight Ashbury].

It took all I could do to run kilos of marijuana into San Francisco from Oakland, so friends could sell it to the kids trying to be cool and hip, in our city full of aging beatniks.

By 1966, we were all looking to find a way out, it had got so crazy.

And for many, like me, I had received my [U.S. military] draft notice.

So, off to Europe, with my [clothing] seams filled with acid.

Early Picture:

I was buying a kilo for 68 dollars, and sold it all on Friday nights on Haight.

Then, off to the country for another week with 300 dollars.

Talked Clean:

I was selling them between 55 dollars and 60 dollars in San Francisco.

You may have had some of mine.

I would bring 10 to 15 [kilos] each week, and distribute them from a girlfriend's place in the Avenues, right off Clement.

They all went to Haight, or North Beach [San Francisco's beatnik neighborhood].

Early Picture:

My trail [across Asia] began in 1966, when dad drove me to the highway in Connecticut, and said:

"Don't come back until you get a haircut."

In November 1967, I hitched out of Haight Ashbury, thinking I'll hitch-hike to Tibet.

Got to Vegas, met a chick, and we went out in the desert.

At 3 a.m., she drops me off on the highway.

Here comes the sheriff of Henderson, Nevada.

Busted me for "drifting."

Sentenced me to 60 days, and a haircut.

They cut my hair off, right in the courtroom, like a public lynching.

I washed cop cars mid-winter, spent Christmas and New Year's Eve fighting with [imprisoned] Mexicans.

Finally released, I walk out the door.

Free at last.

Two F.B.I. agents were waiting for me.

Draft evasion.

They chained me to the floor of their car, and drove me all the way to L.A. [Los Angeles].

I was there three days and released, and I'll never know why.

I hitched to New York City, where I had mailed my sister Blotter acid.

Then I sold it, and got on the next plane to Sweden.

The night before I left, we went to an anti-war demonstration, uptown.

As we left, we got jumped by off-duty N.Y.P.D. [New York Police Department officers].

They dragged us into a tenement hallway, and worked us over good.

Then out of the U.S.A. for 10 years straight.

The Sixties were crazy times.

Oh yeah, I was busted with heroin in 1964, but released on a technicality.

Jailed in Palermo, Rotterdam, Copenhagen, and Montreal.

Like Kerouac [American author Jack Kerouac] said in *On the Road*:

"Cops can smell the jail on you."

Unkempt Rocking:

My first memorable visit [to Amsterdam] -- just passing through really -- was in 1967 on my return from Morocco to England.

I spent a few nights crashing on a "sleeping boat" on one of the canals.

In the hold, was a row of bunk beds, all occupied by travelers.

Many older, and a lot more seasoned than I was.

The stories that got told in the evenings about daring escapes from Turkish jails, being chased by armed bandits while horse trekking across the north of Afghanistan, and the huge conical *joints* of strong black hash that were passed around -- the best ones made with eight or more papers.

Some years later -- after making several more travels of my own, and after returning from India -- I lived there for two years, late 1972 to late 1974.

In squats, on houseboats, and with Dutch friends.

Shimmering Joy:

I [stopped smoking cannabis] back in 1972 while in India, in order to try to immerse myself deeper into the real deal -- India in all its real mysteries.

Shunning the freak scene -- which had already begun to jellify into a pretty silly and vain institution -- with its newly found obsession about who's who, and who's the coolest, most beautiful, and dope-knowledgeable *head* around.

Obsessively mono-talking about everything around *charas* and *ganja* -- while boxing up anyone who did not smoke X-number of *chillums* a day, as a dumb straight.

Thus duplicating the very same hierarchical social pattern

they denounced and fled from, in their own lands.

I quit while in Vrindavan [a Hindu holy town dedicated to Lord Krishna, in northern India's Uttar Pradesh state], as a *Vaishnava bhakta* [a devotee worshipping Lord Vishnu's incarnations, which include Rama and Krishna].

The *sadhana* [spiritual practice] was not compatible.

And anyway, I had developed an aversion to the recurring up-and-down mind-state the smoke subjected me to.

Not mentioning the episodes of intensely traumatic headspins, and disorientations, following some big hits of the *chillum*, facilitating my demise [laughs] as a bona fide *charsi*.

That 1971 to 1972 period in India and Nepal, had been the most mind-and-heart opening experience in all of my early Asian wanderings.

Hottest season, roofless, hungry, totally broke, no entry custom stamp.

And certainly a major wake-up shake-up bell ring in my life, as a whole.

Massive, diverse, and lengthy.

Cool Drama:
There is no doubt The Beatles' interest in Maharishi Yogi -- and their subsequent stay at his *ashram* in Rishikesh -- started an interest in meditation and travel to India.

I was not one of them.

I first encountered devotees of the Krishna movement at The Royal Albert Hall [in London] in early 1969.

It was, what you would term, a Happening -- and called The Alchemical Wedding.

To put it bluntly, we had been *tripping balls* [taking L.S.D.] for about a year, as we were the night of The Alchemical Wedding.

After about 10 minutes of *Om*-like silence, to get us in the mood, the Krishnas came out, chanting and dancing.

There were only six of them. Three couples, who had recently arrived in London from San Francisco, to start a [Hare Krishna temple] center, based on the success of the one they had established in Haight Ashbury.

Quite a sight for us, with their robes, shaved heads, and the ladies in saris.

Everyone started chanting with them, and it was a general good vibe.

Then the Hell's Angels came on.

They started chanting and dancing with them.

It turned out the Krishnas knew them from the Haight.

They [the Hell's Angels] were over [visiting London], with The Grateful Dead and various Pranksters [The Merry Pranksters, California's psychedelic jokesters] -- including Ken Kesey [American author and Prankster leader].

The Angels' appearance -- with the Krishnas -- was spontaneous, as became apparent when they started to take their clothes off.

Next thing the power was cut off.

The powers that be, decided to shut the event down and we went home, mind blown, and slightly bemused.

The Angels' possible thoughts of starting a good old San Francisco love-in [public hippie celebration] had been quashed.

Prior to this, my friend Ronnie and myself had lived an itinerant lifestyle for a few months, around the Notting Hill area of London.

Mainly crashing with friends, and sometimes renting a room.

After a carefree few months, me and Ronnie ran out of luck after being chucked out -- or having to leave -- places in a hurry.

We were on the skids.

Ronnie disappeared for a week, and returned with a big beam on his face.

He met the American Krishnas we had seen at The Alchemical Wedding.

And they had invited us to stay with them in the old I.T. [International Times, an underground London newspaper] offices around the corner.

I must admit, I was hesitant.

All very strange indeed but with limited options, I decided to go with it, for a while.

One afternoon, they told me they were going to [The Beatles'] George Harrison's house to jam with Billy Preston.

The only catch was I had to cut my long hair [to match the Hare Krishna devotees' mostly bald style].

That was a bit of a big deal, back then.

Not only that.

They wanted to shave it, and leave a little tuft on top -- a *sikha*.

And me to put on their strange orange robes.

Obviously I went with it, and was quite *chuffed* [pleased].

I had been a fan of The Beatles for years.

I had a great afternoon chanting and dancing [Hare Krishna style] with George, who was a really nice, down to earth, sort of guy.

Shortly after, we where offered some recording time at Abbey Road Studios, where The Beatles where recording their last album.

We cut *The Hare Krishna Mantra*, which became a hit record.

In the meantime, John Lennon let us stay on his estate in Ascot.

The building we had a acquired for a [Hare Krishna] temple in London was being revamped.

So we stayed at Ascot, doing renovation work for him. About 15 of us.

By then, I had been trained as the temple cook. Pure vegetarian.

Swamaji [Kirtanananda Swamaji, a U.S.-born, Hare Krishna guru] came from America, and stayed there for a short time.

I got to cook for him a few times.

The renovation I mentioned became The White Room on the cover of *Imagine* [an album by John Lennon].

When we opened the London temple, I became the cook and *pujari* [a devout Hindu who prepares a temple's *puja* worship ritual].

After a year as a celibate monk -- no drugs, alcohol, or meat -

- I started to tire of the celibate bit and was told I should marry Swirling Lace.

It was an arranged marriage.

But later, she told me she arranged it.

We have been together now 50 years.

Sooner or later, we both became disenchanted with the whole organization.

After a mind-melting weekend with old friends in London, we decided to split.

Shortly after, we left for India.

Not on some sort of spiritual quest, but to see how the nuts and bolts of Hinduism work, in its country of origin.

And of course, with the traveling, having a really good time.

Raising Tougher:
Was Clear Light Windowpanes [L.S.D.] involved?

Cool Drama:
True that, my friend.

Surreal Atmosphere:
I'm old enough to remember when The Beatles came to Rishikesh [in 1968].

I finally went in 2011, and me and three other travelers walked around the overgrown jungly, sacred grounds of the *ashram*.

It was a bit rainy, which gave it even more atmosphere.

It was quite surreal knowing they were there.

Nearly Spaced:
Great to hear about the intersection of the psychedelic London scene -- the beginnings of the Western love story with Eastern [spiritual] practice and wisdom -- with general chaos, fun, and even The Beatles thrown in, for extra spice.

Way Overland:

Great story.

I'm having a go at imagining San Francisco Hell's Angels and Hari Krishnas dancing together in the Albert Hall.

I can see that.

This airplane -- the Angels and the Krishnas came over on [from San Francisco to London] with Ken Kesey as well -- did The Beatles organize that?

Way Overland:

Yes, seems it was The Beatles -- and not the Dead [The Grateful Dead] -- who were behind that charter flight.

Sleeping Horses:

I didn't go traveling because I was rebelling against anything.

I went to just see the world, meet new people, and get high with them.

I didn't go to India, but I did go to Nepal and Southeast Asia, East Africa, and Indonesia, along with a few lengthy stops in Europe.

Every place was great in it's own way.

Cool Fire:

You sound like me.

It was just about the rock and roll.

That was all I was searching for.

Sounds shallow, but who gives a fuck.

Idealistic Joyful:

We sought a different way of living than our parents.

Simple, non-materialistic, and joyful.

That happened for a while, until it turned into something else, not so idealistic.

Peanuts All Rough:

If you are referring to global peace, love and freedom -- it didn't work out.

For individual happiness, it may have.

Much Friendlier:
We were travelers looking to explore a new world, nothing like where we grew up.
We didn't have guide books, only word of mouth recommendations.
A few people were looking for spiritual teachers.
Most were not.
In Nepal, quite a few people stayed because they loved it.

Perk Seeing:
Discovering new places, seeing new cultures, and living life to the fullest.
Good hash was only a perk.

Cool Drama:
First time around, I have never felt so free, with so little.

Hard Flipped:
Yes with nothing, a *chillum* and *lungi*.
I did two long trips like this.

Free:
I did the same overland journey.
The quest was to push the limits of freedom -- money or no money.
The great adventure into the unknown realms of self discovery.
I was part of a caravan overland to India. We may have crossed paths.
So lucky to have played a part in that special time, of space and time.
Bom Shankar!

Ultimately Travel:

In the 2000s I have spent over five years traveling extensively, in all the countries of the trail, between Istanbul and Kathmandu.

I've also been able to travel to all of the countries which were once the Soviet Union.

China is open too.

Travelers these days can be better informed, healthier, and have more money too.

But this is almost irrelevant.

The significance of these experiences are the changes they make within us.

Do you think there is such a thing as a valid, objective comparison between the experiences you had, with the experiences people can have today?

For sure things are different, but that doesn't mean one is better than another.

Ultimately I think it's rather arrogant to imagine that the experiences you had, back in the day, are much better than those which people can have today.

Weird Worshipping:
Of course it was different then.
The population was half or less.
There were hardly any tourists.
No internet
No credit cards
Not so much information.
There was less violence, less people on the road, few cars.
More traditional.
Of course it was different, but people are born when they are born.
It's never too late.
But I feel very lucky to have experienced this particular time.

Black Proof:
We are all the same in space -- traveling circus aristocrats,

models, outlaws, freaks, eccentrics, writers, visionaries, searchers for dark and light sides of the soul.

In diversity, is the beauty.

Generation Incredible:

To have travelled the way we did, before mass tourism, before places like Goa and Bali got spoiled beyond recognition, before Afghanistan got shot to pieces, was incredible.

We were the lucky generation.

Ran Away:

Foreign travel, like psychedelic drugs, expand consciousness.

The material world will, like all matter, decompose.

Travel experiences do not decompose, but live on and flower.

Unkempt Rocking:

I always had very little, and for a while I had none.

Many French people travelled without money.

I admired them, but they could sometimes be a little crazy.

Unpaid Experience:

Crazy and often disrespectful.

I am French-Canadian, and sometimes suffered prejudices from locals who were ripped off by French travelers, who were leaving unpaid bills in hotels and restaurants.

This has contributed to their somewhat bad reputation.

Sorry but that is my experience.

Unkempt Rocking:

I guess I meant I admired their resourcefulness -- though not a fan of stealing, especially from those in whose country you pass through as a guest.

Little Noses:

The poor French guys deserted the army, because they didn't

want to go to war.

Then when the money was gone, they couldn't run to the embassy like everyone else did, to get them home, because they'd have gone straight to jail.

They became junkies.

And junkies steal.

Myself -- not French -- hitch-hiked back to Europe with no money.

Early Picture:

I, American, left Paris in 1968 with 78 dollars I had earned, loading and unloading trucks at Marche aux Puce [a Paris flea market] for five months.

Doubled that in Afghanistan, and stayed in India for six years on a three-month visa.

Dead Water:

I certainly arrived [in India] as a hippie, but returned as an entrepreneur after a while.

Complete with a suit.

And with a naive understanding of trickle-down economics which, I have to say, has totally failed India, as everywhere else on the planet.

I still have a suit.

But it's reserved for funerals of non-hippies.

Life Positive:

For me, becoming a hippie in 1974 was a great and positive turn in life.

I took a lot of L.S.D., and many other drugs. I became a vegetarian -- I am today.

When I was in Ladakh [India's northernmost state, along the Himalayan border with Kashmir and China] -- where the water was frozen -- the daily bath was sacred.

That is my life.

I love to travel, photograph, and be a digital nomad, always

up to date.
I do my rituals daily, for my Hindu gods.
I do meditation.
I listen to Indian music, and the good music of the 1970s.
And life goes on, this crazy life -- that I so much love.

Enjoy Early:
Quite a few Europeans took the trail to India in the very late 1950s and early 1960s -- even some Americans, like some of the beats, who came before our time and left before our time.

A lot of the early ones were junkies, in search of cheap dope and less worries.

Unkempt Rocking:
British and other European kids were hitching to -- and through -- North Africa, and to India, as well as all around Europe and the Middle East, long before we heard anything about the American hippie movement.

Early Picture:
After my first trip to Kathmandu, I was in Morocco in 1969, telling the cooler freaks all about the overland East.

I saw many of them later in Goa and Nepal.

Someone Something:
The incomparable Dzongsar Khyentse Rinpoche [a Tibetan Buddhist lama, born in Bhutan] gave a talk in Delhi titled, *Why Did the Buddha Leave the Palace?*

His opening remark was:
"Are there hippies in India?"
My thought was, he gets us.
I think we left our comfort because the material life did not interest us.

The L.S.D. had made us curious and fearless, and we went over the mountain to see what we could see.

Dreams Know:
We didn't know it was brave at the time.
Just the things we dream of, and the dreams we follow.

On the Border [displays a photograph of Timothy Leary]:
The original Trip Advisor.

Nice Marks:
Still vivid feelings.
Yes, I don't erase it from my cells.
We were emperor of our life.
Be happy.

Way Overland:
Find your own way.
I think that was the essence of it.
It was dream.
But it was happening, and you would wake up in the morning, and it was happening again.
And after many months, you return to your home place, and try to tell the people there.
And they look at you like you have been dreaming.

Paradise Freaks:
Freaks on the road, destination paradise.

Printed in Great Britain
by Amazon